COUNSELL.. . _

A Practical Guide for Employers

About the author

Michael Megranahan completed his first degree in psychology and then worked in personnel for several years before going to Henley Management College to undertake PhD research. The research focused on the psychological effects of redundancy and stress with the emphasis on developing counselling strategies to help individuals cope with change. After working as an occupational psychologist for the Manpower Services Commission in the area of rehabilitation, assessment and counselling with the emotionally and physically disadvantaged, he joined Control Data as a counsellor for the employee assistance programme, the Employee Advisory Resource (EAR). EAR, established in 1981, was the first workplace couselling service of its kind in Britain. It is now a separate and autonomous company based in Uxbridge providing services to many organisations throughout the UK and Europe. Michael Megranahan is the Operations Director for EAR.

In addition, the author is a chartered Occupational Psychologist and an Associate Fellow of the British Psychological Society, a Member of the Institute of Personnel Management and Chairman of the Employee Assistance Professional Association (EAPA). He is a past Chair of the Counselling at Work Division of the British Association for Counselling and is currently the Editor of *Employee Counselling Today*.

COUNSELLING

A Practical Guide for Employers

Michael Megranahan

Institute of Personnel Management

©Institute of Personnel Management, 1989

First published 1989
Reprinted 1990

Phototypeset by Illustrated Arts, Sutton, Surrey and printed in Great Britain by Dotesios Printers Ltd, Trowbridge, Wiltshire.

British Library Cataloguing in Publication Data
Megranahan, Michael
Counselling
1. Personnel management, Counselling
I. Title
658.3'85

ISBN 0-85292-397-X

Contents

Acknowledgements

Throughout the writing and preparation of this book I had the good fortune to be able to draw upon the support and expertise of others working in specialist counselling areas, many of whom have made significant contributions to the book and enabled completion to be achieved.

I should therefore like to thank Tony Bates, Helen Brown (Adult Guidance Unit), Jo Walker (Pre-Retirement Association), Ian Hoare (Insight), Dinah Wheeler, Andy Hunter, Gladeana McMahon, Pam Rickard (Cruse, Guildford), Dr Alison Woodcott, Dr Jane Chapman, Margaret Surrey, Sarah Drabble.

Special thanks must be extended to the staff of EAR who have tolerated my irritability and anxiety that I suppose must accompany the preparation of any book. In particular, I am grateful to Lynn Williams who also had the daunting task of typing (and amending) the draft text.

Introduction

The use of counselling in the workplace is being increasingly acknowledged as a valuable process which benefits the employees, manager and organisation. The individual is seen more and more as an asset, particularly with growing skill shortages in different geographical areas and industrial sectors. Each employee requires initial investment when joining an organisation for recruitment, induction and training, as well as on-going costs resulting from further training and development. Ultimately every organisation is dependent on the quality of the people working within it and the relationships they form there.

Line and personnel managers continually try to motivate employees to increase their contribution to the organisation's objectives. Their ability to do this will rely partly on established methods like salaries, incentive payments, bonuses and other benefits; more importantly it will also depend on good communication, an understanding of the employee's need and expectations, and an environment where there is scope for individual growth and development. Counselling is a positive process which can help to protect the individual within an organisation as well as enhance communication and foster a climate of trust and openness. Without an effective system to achieve this, the most sophisticated policies and procedures will fall into disrepute, with each individual employee left to cope in whatever way he or she can. The repercussions will eventually affect the whole organisation.

The post boy with a hangover who misplaces an urgent document will potentially damage the credibility and reputation of the organisation. The managing director who fails to communicate effectively with her team, due to family and job pressures, will also adversely affect the productive functioning of the organisation. Both are experiencing pressures which affect them as individuals but each situation will have repercussions on other parts of the company. Both are assets which are currently experiencing diminished productivity. Both can be restored to full effectiveness but this will only occur where an organisation recognises the need to protect and help its employees. The provision of counselling, supported by appropriate policies, is one way in which the organisation can begin to ensure that it protects its human resources.

The provision of counselling in the workplace does not mean that employees are molly-coddled nor should it be regarded as a process which is applicable only to people with problems. Counselling is a dynamic process which varies according to the needs of the person and their circumstances.

Many of the pressures that affect employees are potentially emotionally charged they are therefore often left unresolved. Changes in mood, erratic job performance, withdrawal from personal relationships, displays of anger and so on are often accepted or ignored, both by colleagues and managers. This lack of confrontation can quickly become collusion as attempts are made to cover up the outward signs of a problem. People do not feel it is their place to get involved in someone else's problems, they do not know how to approach the person, feel embarrassed, lack the confidence and the skills to interact constructively with the person. The only constructive thing they feel able to do is to prevent the problem surfacing. In the end the situation worsens.

The personnel and line manager offer help, information, guidance and counselling every day. As soon as someone asks for help, counselling may occur. The type of help that is given within this counselling and the quality of the interaction will vary according to the person's understanding of the other party's needs; also the level of awareness by that person of the demands this places on them and their ability (and desire) to fulfil these needs. The most appropriate help and support for the other party can range from listening and giving information at one end of the spectrum to referring the person to a specialised resource, at the other. Counselling may be viewed as a framework within which different helping strategies are appropriate for different people at different times. The ability to identify what is needed, when and why, are integral to the process of counselling.

There may be many different occasions in a person's life when choices need to be made, such as a career choice, whether to leave or stay, or seek promotion vertically or laterally. Whilst the employee's mind is thus preoccupied, he or she may not be wholly committed or attentive to their work role. This can result in accidents, increased absenteeism and employee turnover, poor quality work, decision making and problem-solving and poor employee relations.

A person may want to make changes in the way they have been living or working or in the way they have been responding to people and events around them. Or there may be some underlying, as yet unidentified feelings affecting their general sense of well being, or unresolved feelings concerning a recent or past event, eg being passed over for promotion, or bereavement. Counselling is a process which helps the person work through these types of issues, understand them better, identify feelings and ways of responding (which may have been previously submerged) and see how these are relevant to the problem.

Counselling is therefore a process which enables problems to be identified and clarified and to facilitate the exploration of potential solutions or ways in which the problem can be managed more effectively by drawing on the individual's inner resources.

Therefore, counselling:

- is not thinking or acting for another person, nor is it directing them towards a decision
- is not repeating clichés about what someone else ought to do
- is more than simply being sympathetic towards another person's feelings, talking something over or merely the application of techniques
- does not impose solutions, opinions, values or judgements. It does not minimise, negate or question the worth of what the person wishes to discuss
- is not about criticising or manipulating the person.

Counselling does involve the counsellor in efforts to see things from the other person's position and listening carefully not only to what is said but how it is said.

Counselling is also a mechanism for building self reliance in an individual by assisting them to make decisions and fulfil commitments. Support from the counsellor in helping to see through decisions is another important ingredient. However the support should be given without it becoming a crutch or encouraging dependence.

Counselling skills (as distinct from counselling) are a set of techniques used in a counselling relationship to assist in developing effective communication between two people based on trust,

openness and acceptance. It has been proposed that a number of
key qualities are needed by the counsellor to achieve this relationship,
including empathy, genuineness, respect and a non-judgemental
attitude.

The skills of counselling are essential to the process of counselling.
However counselling is far more than the application of a set of
techniques. It is to do with accepting another person's feelings as
relevant and important to the tangible problem being presented. It
is also to do with understanding human nature and realising that
people are alike in some ways but unique in others. This insight
enables the counsellor to draw out any deeper thoughts and feelings
held by the person, which previously may have been unconsciously
held back and yet be relevant to what is being discussed.

All people using counselling skills need to be aware of how they
are seen by others and to an extent they need to know and understand
themselves. This means being aware of their own needs and
experiences so that they may be adequately attuned to and
realistically perceive other people's needs and experiences. This
concept of personal insight can be illustrated by the Johari Window
(figure 1).

Figure 1
Modified version of the Johari window

A Known to others Known to ourselves	B Known to others Not known to ourselves
Not known to others Known to ourselves	Not known to others Not known to ourselves

Source: Nelson-Jones R. *Theory and practice of counselling psychology*

Each person will have different degrees of access into each window.
This applies equally to the counsellor as it does to the person using
counselling skills. The counsellor should however have had the
opportunity through training and supervision to have explored each
in greater depth.

This exploration may be likened to a mountaineer. A person
trained in the skills of mountain climbing on the foothills of the
South Downs would be ill-equipped to lead an expedition to the
Cairngorms. All people in a counselling role – including the

professional counsellor – need to recognise how far they can progress in a counselling relationship. Following our analogy, whilst a mountaineer may feel confident to go to the Cairngorms, the same mountaineer may recognise that the Alps would be too hazardous without further training or experience, not only to the people following him or her as a guide but also personally, and would therefore pass this job to a more experienced guide. There is a clear responsibility not to attempt anything which falls outside the bounds of experience and knowledge.

The practice of recognising professional limitations takes place all the time. A doctor in general practice possesses a wealth of skills and knowledge but would not attempt open heart surgery. Similarly the manager using counselling skills will gather information from the employee, check the possible causes of the problem, and clarify areas of uncertainty or ambiguity. The manager may, however, recognise that the problem falls outside the bounds of existing experience and use counselling skills to motivate the employee to seek further help and assistance to resolve the problem. A counsellor may similarly need to refer the client to another source 6f help at a certain stage in the counselling relationship.

In Britain innovative and forward looking organisations such as DuPont (UK), General Electric (USA), Prime Computer (UK) and Nuclear Electric, have introduced an employee assistance programme provided by the Employee Advisory Resource (EAR). They have found the following benefits:

- lower employee stress and anxiety
- better work performance
- less time off work to deal with practical problems
- less time spent by managers on employee domestic problems
- less time off sick
- gives positive image to employees and their families of a 'caring employer'
- ability to refer if employee problem is suspected.

An increasing number of organisations are introducing counselling in order to maintain the mental well-being of employees. The benefits extend into all aspects of an organisation's operations, including improved internal communications, external customer contact, safety record and decision making. The benefits are extensive and tangible.

Summary

It is a fallacy to believe that people do not experience problems, and that when that happens it does not interfere with job performance, and that the organisation is powerless to respond constructively.

Overall, counselling is a perspective, a way of approaching things, as well as a set of skills. Provided the people in counselling roles observe the boundaries of their experience, skills, training and confidentiality, the line between counselling skills and counselling is academic. Imperative however to the effective use of counselling and counselling skills in the workplace is the need for the person in this role to be respected, well regarded, trusted and credible.

This book is designed to support and augment the personnel or line manager's existing counselling skills. It does this by addressing a number of specific areas where face to face communication is necessary and through which employees may seek help and assistance from their manager, or conversely where the manager recognises the need to offer help and assistance to an employee. The book is not about counselling skills; these should be acquired through a course of training. Rather it provides guidelines for good practice in specific counselling situations to enable counselling skills to be used to their best effect.

Each chapter alerts the manager to the thoughts, feelings and emotions that the employee is likely to be experiencing in specific situations, as well as the potential reaction of the person who is fulfilling the counselling role. Areas where the organisation can provide practical support, eg new policies, are examined and the need for referral to and support from outside agencies is highlighted where appropriate. A manager should not, for instance, become involved in offering long term counselling to someone suffering from AIDS, but should be expected to provide support. Conversely, the manager should play a full role in talking to an employee about relocation. Involvement by the manager in both situations is vital, but the degree of involvement will vary. Each chapter is designed to be independent, although many of the chapters overlap and should not, where this occurs, be read in isolation. The book is structured around four main areas:

Section 1

This section examines subjects which are likely to arise in the formal work context and where the line or personnel manager would be expected to play a full role. Counselling skills used in these areas should enhance the existing policy process for dealing with for example, discipline, redundancy, performance appraisal etc. Underlying problems may emerge from interviews in these areas which fall outside the workplace, eg a discussion about relocation may reveal marital problems. Some of these potential areas are examined in Section 2.

Section 2

This section examines those areas which are principally non-work but which are known to have a significant impact on the individual and consequently the workplace, eg mental health, marital problems, bereavement. All these areas are likely to require referral to a specialist counselling agency and details are given of professional counselling agencies.

Section 3

For organisations considering the introduction of a counselling service, this section addresses some of the key issues that should be examined. Questions which should be asked of potential service providers are listed, as well as some models of counselling services in the UK.

Section 4

How do you know which is a good counselling skills training course? How do you refer an employee? What about confidentiality? This last section addresses many of the questions that may be prompted by preceding sections.

Further reading

Books

De Board Robert. *Counselling people at work: an introduction for managers.* Aldershot, Gower, 1983. 137pp.
Reprinted in paperback as *Counselling skills,* Aldershot, Wildwood House, 1987. 137pp.
Egan Gerard. *The skilled helper: a systematic approach to effective helping.* 3rd ed. Monterey, Brooks/Cole, 1986. xviii, 480pp.
Kennedy Eugene. *On becoming a counsellor: a basic guide for non professional counsellors.* Dublin, Gill and MacMillan, 1977. x, 336pp.
Murgatroyd Stephen. *Counselling and helping.* Leicester, British Psychological Society *and* London, Methuen, 1985. 165pp.
Nelson-Jones Richard. *Practical counselling skills.* London, Holt, Rinehart and Winston, 1983. ix, 245pp.
Reddy Michael, *The manager's guide to counselling at work.* Leicester, British Psychological Society, 1987. 145pp.
Standing Conference for the Advancement of Counselling. *Counselling at work*: papers prepared by a working party.
Watts A G (*ed*) London, Bedford Square Press, 1977. 92pp.

Articles

Hall J. 'The contribution of counselling to a better working environment'. *Counselling,* No 46, November 1983. pp 21-25.
Hall J *and* Fletcher B. 'Coping with personal problems at work (at Control Data Ltd)'. *Personnel Management,* Vol 16, No 2, February 1984. pp 30-33.
Novarra V. 'Can a manager be a counsellor?' *Personnel Management,* Vol 18, No 6, June 1986. pp 48-50.
Reddy M. 'Counselling in organisations'. *Training Officer,* Vol 21, No 8, August 1985. pp 236-239.

SECTION ONE

This section is concerned with those problems that arise in the work context and where the manager is likely to play a full counselling role.

1 Stress

Introduction

Stress is something each one of us can relate to and has probably experienced. But how accurate are we in our thoughts about it? Do we really admit to ourselves (much less anyone else) that we have experienced – or are experiencing – stress? Would other people understand and be sympathetic or helpful? These and a host of other questions are crucial. Understanding the dynamics of stress and developing the ability to recognise and to help others cope with stress are essential management skills now and for the future.

Stress is in many ways a nebulous concept. It has been examined from many viewpoints, particularly in the last 15 years. In the context of employment, stress has tended to be associated with executive positions in organisations and has therefore assumed the status of an élite malady. Research such as that undertaken by the Labour Research Department in 1988 shows that this assumption is mistaken. Less senior employees may talk about having more 'hassles', leading 'hectic' lives or 'finding their nerves on edge'. Though not particularly eloquent, these 'non-technical' expressions are as revealing as the more complex expressions used by academics and management in providing important early indications of the beginnings of unmanageable stress.

There is a narrow divide between stimulating pressure and debilitating stress. The divide becomes blurred when for instance people begin to worry more and more about problems that need to be solved or over which they have little control. Worry may occur in many circumstances. Frequently it is where a person goes over and over a problem without ever getting closer to an answer. Past events are relived with the constant thought of 'If only I had . . .' These thoughts prevent any chance of moving towards a solution. No analysis takes place, no learning or self insight is possible, – regret or fear take over. The person feels unable to cope and starts to exhibit changes in behaviour that can interfere with normal day-to-day activities and relationships with other people, or lead to one of the stress related illnesses.

Sources of stress

In order to begin to cope effectively with stress, it is essential to recognise and understand its sources. Focusing on the individual and his/her ability to cope is frequently the approach taken but this is rarely sufficient and account must also be taken of the person's environment. In the workplace this may ultimately mean seeking ways of altering any stressful organisational norms, management style and practices.

A number of models showing the sources of stress on an individual have been developed; the most widely used is that of Cooper and Marshall (1975). They identified many areas that may give rise to stress (see figure 2 opposite). Even in relatively stable workplaces, any or all these factors can apply, which only emphasises that *any* changes in the work environment can lead to increased stress.

In addition to the emphasis in the Cooper and Marshall model on work-related stresses, the debilitating affects of stress from the individual's private life need to be considered. The Holmes and Rahe Social Readjustment Rating Scale (SRRS) (see figure 3) helps to illustrate the potential stresses a person may experience arising from changes to their life. The SRRS is a rating scale depicting the relative amount of coping behaviour required for 43 different life events.

Whilst stress is essentially subjective, with each individual able to define personal stresses and pressures based on past experience and apprehensions, there are a range of objective events to which most people will respond. The first items listed by Holmes and Rahe, bereavement and divorce, are good examples of this. Within the 43 items listed a number refer directly to employment experiences. Holmes and Rahe found that events occurring within a 12 month period which totalled over 150 points resulted in a higher incidence of depression, heart attacks and other forms of serious illness. Later chapters in the book consider many of the significant stressful life events identified by Holmes and Rahe.

Figure 2
Sources of work stress

Intrinsic to job
  Too much/too little work
  Poor physical working conditions
  Time pressures, etc

Role in organisation
  Role conflict/ambiguity
  Responsibility for people
  No participation in decision-making, etc

Career development
  Overpromotion
  Underpromotion
  Lack of job security
  Thwarted ambition, etc

Individual
  Personality
    Tolerance for ambiguity
    Ability to cope with change
  Motivation

Relations within organisation
  Poor relations with boss
  Poor relations with colleagues and subordinates
  Difficulties in delegating responsibility, etc

Organisation interface with outside
  Company *vs* family demands
  Company *vs* own interests, etc

Being in the organisation
  Lack of effective consultation
  Restrictions on behaviour
  Office politics, etc

Source: Cooper *and* Marshall. *Stress and pressures within organisations.*

Figure 3
Holmes and Rahe's Social Readjustment Rating Scale

Event		Rating points
1	Death of spouse	100
2	Divorce	73
3	Marital separation	65
4	Prison term	63
5	Death of close family member	63
6	Personal injury or illness	53
7	Marriage	50
8	Fired at work	47
9	Marital reconciliation	45
10	Retirement	45
11	Change in health of family member	44
12	Pregnancy	40
13	Sex difficulties	39
14	Gain of new family member	39
15	Business readjustment	39
16	Change in financial state	38
17	Death of close friend	37
18	Change to different line of work	36
19	Change in number of arguments with spouse	35
20	A large mortgage or loan	30
21	Foreclosure of mortgage or loan	30
22	Change in responsibilities at work	29
23	Son or daughter leaving home	29
24	Trouble with in-laws	29
25	Outstanding personal achievement	28
26	Spouse begins or stops work	26
27	Begin or end school or college	26
28	Change in living conditions	25
29	A change in personal habits	24
30	Trouble with the boss	23
31	Change in work hours or conditions	20
32	Change in residence	20
33	Change in school or college	20
34	Change in recreation	19
35	Change in church activities	19
36	Change in social activities	18
37	A moderate mortgage or loan	17
38	Change in sleeping habits	16
39	Change in number of family get-togethers	15
40	Change in eating habits	15
41	Holiday	13
42	Christmas	12
43	Minor violations of the law	11

Source: Holmes *and* Rahe. *Social Readjustment Rating Scale.*

Bearing in mind the subjective nature of stress, each one of us should be able to scan the list and rate some events as more significant than others. In addition we may want to add to the list events which we would rate highly but which do not appear.

One area identified by Cooper and Marshall as stressful within the workplace is the manager-subordinate relationship, a significant factor in any organisation and one which is often overlooked. The way people are managed will have an effect on their mental, emotional and professional well-being. A 'good' boss can help employees grow and perform at maximum capability, while a 'bad' boss can literally make them ill. The hierarchical nature of most organisations makes this source of stress potentially the most prevailing, but it is also a source that should be both identifiable and amenable to change.

The specific sources of stress that a 'bad' boss may be responsible for are varied. Three examples are considered here: being unpredictable, eroding self esteem, and creating win/lose situations.

Being unpredictable

Even the most change orientated employees like predictability from their managers. By this, they don't mean stagnation or boredom, but the knowledge that a certain action will produce a certain outcome, that good work will merit praise and mistakes will earn a reprimand.

An unpredictable manager can cause employees to spend more time wondering about the boss's mood than they spend at their work. In some offices, there are elaborate employee networks to warn when the manager is coming. Although the situation may seem humorous, the long term health effects of working for an unpredictable boss can be disastrous – ulcers and increased risk of heart disease.

Eroding self esteem

A sense of self esteem is a vital component of a healthy productive employee. Extremely low self esteem has been linked to illness.

Managers may erode staff members' self esteem for a number of reasons, both conscious and unconscious: a desire to force an employee to resign, jealousy or competition, low self esteem on the part of the manager, or personality conflict. Whatever the reason, destroying self esteem takes a number of forms:

- humiliating an employee in front of colleagues
- making unwarranted or unjust criticisms
- denying an employee recognition, promotions or awards
- taking credit for work an employee has done
- ridiculing or disparaging an employee.

Creating win/lose situations

One unfortunate by-product of business mentality is the 'win/lose' concept. If one side 'wins' the other side, by definition, must 'lose'. When a manager wins a round at the expense of employees the employees begin to feel downtrodden and submissive.

Constantly creating win/lose situations can lead to a number of undesirable results:

- the atmosphere becomes distrusting and hostile
- sensitivity and empathy are stifled
- authority conflicts become frequent and bitter
- new ideas and creativity are discouraged
- deadlocks are created and decisions delayed.

The individual's response to stress and its impact on the workplace

The ability to cope with situations will vary from person to person. Coping is a process and not a single event. Before a situation becomes manageable several different emotional and practical stages will need to be addressed, since a change in one area will have subsequent repercussions on another area. New coping abilities will need to be learnt and initiated before progressing further. Coping is therefore an on-going activity which will involve drawing on existing skills and sources of support as well as learning new coping skills.

In attempting to cope with a situation the person may:

– Do nothing and hope it goes away
– Go it alone. Face up to the problem and attempt to deal with it without drawing on the support of others
– Talk to a friend, spouse or work colleague. This may be an effective response to the problem. Just to talk it through and share the problem, receiving advice and suggestions on what to do may broaden the choices available and provide encouragement for action
– Visit the GP, particularly if there are signs of ill-health. Time restrictions for probing the root cause may be limited and if no specific symptoms are found the outcome may be some form of prescription, eg tranquillisers. The symptom is thus treated but not the problem
– Discuss the problem at work, especially if it is affecting work performance. Discussions may be initiated within the area of the company that the person perceives as confidential or non-threatening, protective and impartial, eg trade union, personnel, occupational health or welfare
– Talk to their manager if they feel able to trust and confide in them
– Contact a specialist agency. Where the person has successfully identified the nature of the problem and knows where help can be found, direct contact may be made with a specialist agency, eg Citizen Advice Bureaux, Alcoholics Anonymous
– Seek the help of a professional counsellor, where the counsellor may adopt the premise that the person is the expert on their own problems and can be helped to decide on their own solutions.

Apart from the first two options, all the others involve talking to another person or persons. None is mutually exclusive and a person may talk to several different people from different backgrounds before taking action. The action taken may alleviate or solve the area of concern. However, the old adage 'a problem shared is a problem halved' does not reflect the importance for the outcome of the quality of the interaction. The belief that stress is something which you must cope with in silence for fear of being exposed as someone who cannot do their job effectively is a dangerous falsehood – although still widely believed, especially by those who are unaware of the adverse effects of stress on individual performance and morale. The person to leave is not going to be the person who cannot cope, but rather the skilled and mobile person who will seek out structures and management styles that allow him or her to work to their full potential.

For those who are unable to leave to find new jobs, discontent is expressed through more subtle means. They may be off sick more, produce shoddy work, or spread general lethargy which affects morale. This may prompt corrective action from the company in the form of disciplinary measures, and this in turn confirms to the employees that management misunderstands the root of their problems. A comparable situation is the person who goes to the doctor to discuss a bad back or headache, only to be despatched with a lotion, bed rest and tonic. In both cases only the symptoms and not the causes are treated. No constructive communication takes place, and indeed the climate for such communication is often prohibitive.

Those people who accept and work within a stressful environment or cope well with a variety of work and personal stresses potentially run the greatest risk of experiencing problems at a later stage. Reactions to stress need not occur immediately. The reaction could take place the same evening at home, or next week in a drinking binge, or at any time (and place) in the future. Grief, for instance, may be effectively blocked by someone for a long period, perhaps one of the characteristic traits of the British stiff upper lip, but this can only be achieved temporarily. The suppressed grief may come to the fore at any time in the future, triggered by another (and often seemingly unrelated) event. When such a delayed reaction does take place, the blow to the person's self image is very much greater. Dismay and disbelief are experienced, whilst the stressful period that preceded it is forgotten.

What happens to the person when stress is experienced

People respond to stress in different ways. There is no definitive check list of symptoms. It is possible to identify the more typical reactions that people have when they are experiencing stress and these can provide an early warning before the onset of more serious problems. The following list is divided into three broad areas:

- Physiological signs
- Emotional signs
- Behavioural signs

Physiological signs
- Eyestrain or sore eyes
- Trouble sleeping/insomnia
- Muscle strain or pain in neck, back, arms, shoulders
- Stomach pains or digestive problems
- Nausea or dizziness
- Tightness or pressures in the chest
- Headaches
- Indigestion and diarrhoea
- Impotence or reduced sex drive

Emotional signs
- Depression
- Periods of irritability or anger
- Feelings of failure; inability to cope; irrational dread of future events
- Problems of concentration; daydreaming
- Loss of sense of humour and interest in life
- Believing that one is not liked or cared for
- Feelings of isolation exhibited by withdrawal and problems in communication
- Swings in mood
- Worry about physical health
- Feelings of tiredness

Behavioural signs
- Less care in personal appearance
- Forgetfulness, clumsiness or accidents
- Increasing periods of inactivity whilst at work
- Difficulty or unusual slowness in decision making
- Taking more time off work, eg longer lunches
- Accident proneness including car accidents
- Increased intake in alcohol, or use of other drugs
- Over or under eating
- Declining job performance
- Increased absence.

In addition to the outward manifestation of stress, the person's internal thoughts and emotional processes will be affected. Murgatroyd (1985) put forward a list of internal consequences of stress for a person whose coping ability has diminished. Whilst not every person will have the same experience, the list vividly illustrates the extent to which stress can affect the person's whole being.

1   The way people see themselves:
   – They feel that their self esteem is threatened
   – They lack confidence in themselves
   – They deprecate their own abilities
   – They question their own worth
   – They defend idealised versions of their own behaviour.

2   The way they experience the world:
   – They find reality both complex and overwhelming
   – They see their position in the world as determined by people other than themselves
   – They experience the world as a place in which they have to use tactics like denial, wishful thinking or helplessness in order to survive, even though they can recognise some of the implications of such tactics.

3   The way they experience their own emotional world:
   – Anxiety and feelings of panic predominate
   – They feel helpless and overwhelmed
   – They feel indifferent
   – They cannot accept praise or compliments.

4   The way in which they think:
   – Their thinking is disorganised
   – They feel unable to make decisions or to take responsibility for their actions
   – They lack the ability to 'stand outside their situation' and review their predicament with any objectivity
   – They are resistant to change.

5   Their physical state:
   – They do not attend to their physical needs
   – There is loss of appetite

- Sleep patterns are disturbed
- In extreme cases, some psychosomatic illness may occur – eg headaches, muscular tension
- Prolonged experience of stress can exacerbate existing symptoms – including heart disease and cancer.

Whose job is it to recognise stress?

The view that the typical manager is autocratic, tough-minded and non-supportive of employees is an erroneous one, but one which remains by and large the perception of employees. Managers have long been aware of emotional conflicts in the workplace and have attempted in their own way to lessen the impact of such conflicts.

The approach taken is usually very direct and consists of gathering information, assessing this in relation to the circumstances, and deciding what the employee should do to put the matter right or prevent the problem interfering with work performance. Some employees are likely to respond positively to this approach since they have never been encouraged to think about ways in which they themselves can resolve the problem.

To recognise stress in his staff a manager does not need to be a psychologist or doctor: he/she is ideally placed to observe direct behaviour and be aware of changes in the health, habits and work performance of staff. This emphasises the need for the manager to know his staff well. One significant and straightforward indicator that all is not well is an employee taking excessive time off from work due to sickness. Subtle differences in behaviour may include the person who usually smokes 20 cigarettes a day, increasing to 40 a day; more frequent and longer visits to the toilet, and so on.

The earlier that damaging stress is identified, the easier it is to take steps to reduce it. This may be through the arrangement of more support, personal encouragement or even the temporary reduction in work pressure, a solution which needs to be handled with care to avoid reinforcing any feelings of failure or insecurity. Employees will always find an outlet to voice their stresses. Where the stress arises from the workplace this outlet may be the line or personnel manager, and this should provide useful feedback for the company in examining its practices. The company and management, for its part, should encourage, seek and act on feedback.

Presenting problems

Stress is often (but not exclusively) initially presented as a physiological problem. Such symptoms include pains in the lower back, chest and neck, higher blood pressure, an inability to sleep, upset stomach and general tension or nervousness. Dr J Kearns (1986), BUPA Occupational Health, has observed that unfortunately both doctors and managers tend to medicalise these problems. Managements look at absence figures in terms of quantifiable problems; in reality, however, these are much more subjective for the sufferer. As we have discussed, the subject nature of stress is often overlooked by the manager or personnel department when considering an employee's behaviour.

People tend to present what they believe are appropriate problems for the person they select to talk to. Consequently the nurse or doctor will be asked about physiological problems, the manager about work problems and so on. On occasions this 'appropriateness' may seem illogical or erratic. This can indicate that the person is uncertain who to talk to or that they are seeking an answer that they will find acceptable.

In addition to physiological problems there may be any number of other issues which are being presented as symptoms of a deeper underlying problem. The problem the person chooses to talk about is often one of several with which they are grappling. These may be used as a way of establishing contact with a source of help. The presenting problem in this context also provides an opportunity to the person to gauge the probable response from their selected source of help to the deeper issue.

Alternatively the various indicators described on page 14 may provide a basis for managers sensitively to initiate conversation with the person to establish whether there is cause for concern.

Broaching the presenting problem

The likelihood of an employee opting to discuss with a colleague or manager either work or personal problems is dependent on many factors. These will include the person's personality, eg open or shy, the perceived and actual willingness of the manager to be involved, the skills the manager possesses to encourage discussion, and the environment they are in, eg the risk of being overheard or interrupted.

Many people will be reluctant to talk about personal problems, thoughts and experiences with a person who has authority over them since to do so may be seen to be potentially damaging to their future employment prospects and security because of an implied inability to cope. However, there are several existing channels in an organisation for the employee or manager to initiate constructive contact to discuss ways of managing or solving concerns affecting work performance.

Formal contacts

Both line and personnel managers are provided with built-in contacts with employees by the organisation. These include redundancy counselling, career development and disciplinary interviews, all usually caried out by appointment and in private.

Formal contacts may well provide the opportunity to identify and discuss underlying issues but first the manager needs to be aware of their possible existence behind the presented problem; for example, an expression of frustration with the job during an appraisal interview may result from pressures in the person's domestic life. The manager may then need to use several different helping strategies including counselling skills.

Informal contacts

The informal contact in a work setting may happen on a daily basis or be far more infrequent. Detection of symptoms is often not easy but awareness may develop with time. A few words exchanged in the canteen or corridor may disclose a person's concern. Simply asking people how they are will often reveal events in the person's life that they may want to discuss more fully, facts the manager may find it helpful to be aware of, or elicit a response which suggests that all is not well and which should be followed up later.

Further, the manager who knows their staff well will also know those who will open up and moan about anything and everything; those who will always be 'fine', and those who need encouragement.

Review

It is common for employees at all levels of the company to believe that if they reveal any negative attributes, they will be censured by management or their peers and therefore they devote considerable effort to concealing them. They may also keep problems from the

24   *Counselling*

family and friends or reveal different aspects of the problem to different people. On occasions this may be a way of trying to find the type of help they want, or it may be a symptom of the struggle they are experiencing.

It is when the ability to conceal signs and symptoms becomes difficult to continue, that employees are more likely to seek help or respond to offers of assistance. The problem will emerge ultimately in changes of behaviour, declining job performance etc. Once the employee is ready to respond or seek help the manager and personnel department need to be equipped to react in a clear and constructive way.

If the manager or personnel department are already promoting themselves as contact points for support in these areas, then it is possible to encourage people to seek help at an early stage. Often it is the employee's fear of his or her manager's reaction to their problem, which prevents this action from taking place. I have found that once these types of fears have been discussed and dispelled, the employee has the confidence to go to personnel or their manager and often returns expressing surprise and relief at the positive, immediate and unconditonal support that is offered.

The manager's response

Everyone responds differently to any given situation and even where the personnel manager may be promoting a 'counselling shoulder' for employees, this may be the last place the person will call. People will invariably exhaust their own network of support first, depending on the problem and often the status of the person. Managers, for instance, appear to find it harder to confide in others because of their status and belief that they should be infallible (particularly to their peers).Shop floor workers tend to be more open and prepared to discuss the things that upset them.

Where there is no other focal person for support and consultation, the line or personnel manager may find themselves in situations where they are asked for help or required to instigate some action. Even the best managers may sometimes ignore signs and symptoms which may have adverse consequences later, or try to take on too much without professional help. The type of negative responses that may be adopted by a manager fall into the following categories:

Covering-up

An employee's poor work performance may be covered up. This may occur as a result of the manager's own anxieties of the consequences of confronting the issue. Consequences may include fears of damaging an employee's reputation and future promotion prospects; a belief that it is 'none of my business'; the fear that it may cause a scene; or that it will be an embarrassing subject.

Optimism

If the manager consciously separates the skills and experience which they know the employee possesses from the reliability necessary for the employee to make a positive and practical contribution to the productivity of the department, they may end up with the attitude that 'they do a good job when they are here' with the net result that nothing is done to change the situation.

Ignoring

When the manager believes that to confront the employee may result in the employee leaving – voluntarily or through dismissal – an offer of help may be withheld until it is too late.

Sole responsibility

Here the manager feels responsible for the action and behaviour of all employees. As a consequence they may feel a need to deal with all departmental problems irrespective of their nature and origin. A manager responding in this way may feel that it would be an admission of personal failure to encourage an employee to seek help elsewhere.

Managing stress in organisations – the employer's response

Employers are very reluctant to admit that stress affects either their employees or their total organisation. There are numerous reasons why companies and individuals have not taken any initiatives to deal with stress. These need to be understood before effective steps can begin to be taken to overcome the inertia that exists.

At the organisational level:

Organisational image – the company's management believes that to admit that stress exists would result in bad press and adversely affect relations with customers.

Employee relations impact – open acceptance of stress would be admitting that the working environment and climate was damaging to the employee's well-being. Demands would then be made of the company to alleviate the stresses.

Feelings of impotence – even if stress is openly acknowledged there is often confusion and ignorance about what can be done effectively to reduce it.

At the individual level:

Lack of insight – this also applies to the organisation. Often there is a complete lack of insight to the type and degree of stress that exists. Consequences of stress are blamed on other events or people, eg the state of the economy, the strength of the unions, a lack of co-operation from suppliers, internal departments, colleagues, air conditioning and so on.

Avoiding the issue – many people accumulate a multitude of minor tasks which they deal with ahead of the important tasks. This is deceptive to both the individual and company since both believe that a large volume of work is being achieved. Such superficial activity can only continue for a short time. Eventually crucial areas of work cannot be put off any longer.

Personal credibility – this single powerful area will lead everyone at some time or other to accept or take on activities and responsibilities which it would be more sensible to decline. Most over-work is self-imposed. This may or may not arise from the workplace, eg invitations to join committees, give talks, be the darts team manager etc. Why does this happen?

- There is a fear of being seen as weak by fellow colleagues and friends
- Fear of being seen as unstable or incompetent

- There is the need to uphold the 'image' seen by colleagues, friends and family
- There is a need to act in accord with one's personal self-concept.

Despite the increasing attention attracted by stress in employment in recent years, employers have been slow to respond, at least openly. Some employers, eg police and nurses, have commissioned reports into their occupation in order to ascertain the extent of the problem. Commercial business has adopted a far more low key approach. Changes to the company atmosphere assisted by increased awareness on the part of management are required, but these are difficult to introduce. One approach considered 'safe', since it is moulded easily into the organisational climate as acceptable practice, is the stress management course. Of all the different approaches examined here to reduce stress, it is this course which is given greatest scrutiny since no self respecting training department would be without the resources to schedule such a course.

The stress management course

Stress has in many ways become a safe and convenient hook on which to hang all employees' problems. An equally convenient bait for the hook has become the stress management course. Perhaps trawl would be a better description, with the proliferation of stress management courses.

Stress management courses are often intended as a preventative for stress-related problems rather than as treatment for existing ones. The idea is to teach workers greater control over those aspects of their lives which are subject to stress.

Stress management methods include muscle relaxation, biofeedback, meditation, time management, assertiveness and combinations of these methods. Each technique, in isolation or combination, may be effective for some people some of the time.

Little research has been done to assess the durability of any of these techniques for employees who have participated in courses. What evidence is available suggests that the longer term benefits may be few. Courses that are not supported by other changes in the person's life or which fail to equip the person with the skills to implement changes merely teach more efficient coping strategies and do nothing to reduce or eliminate the sources of stress. Such an approach to stress has been described as an 'inoculation approach' in that it potentially adapts the employee to poor work environments.

Particularly doubtful is the stress management course conducted outside the workplace. Evidence shows that the immediate beneficial effects may have more to do with being away from the workplace (and possibly family), being in a comfortable environment, the intention to 'do something about my stress' and a credible training strategy, all of which conspire to smoke-screen the stresses being experienced and to which they will be returning.

Often among the most beneficial aspects of a stress management course is the information that is pooled by the participants, a feature usually promoted indirectly by the course design. The part of the course intended to help the manager recognise stress in others prompts reflection on their own problems and behaviour which they share with other course participants. They subsequently feel less isolated and more able to talk about their concerns. Where this is carried over to the workplace, many benefits are achieved, although much will depend on the culture of the company.

Stress management courses should involve the wife and family of employees and the course should also be available to all employees of the company. This involvement should help to develop two-way support and understanding processes.

Improved communications

The open exchange of information can alleviate stress in the workplace. Communications within business is an area which has attracted a lot of attention and many different approaches have been developed in an attempt to reduce the delays, distortions and difficulties frequently associated with communicating through formal channels. Even the most effective communication processes within a company will eventually reflect the interpersonal skills and attitudes of the people who are required to support it. This will invariably mean the managers and supervisors.

Line and personnel managers need to be actively involved in the process of seeking, giving and receiving information through both formal and informal channels of communication. The outcome will be a a greater awareness of the mood and feeling of employees which should enable more effective decisions to be made and implemented. These decisions should be based on the fundamental principle of communication, ie that it is a two-way process. Decisions that are based on reliable and accurate information and which incorporate or acknowledge not only any factual content, but also employees' concerns (the emotional content) will demonstrate an interest and willingness to involve people in the decisions that affect them. As a consequence people are more likely to be committed to achieving the agreed outcome.

The problem is that not even the best designed communication structures can work unless people trust them and can see results through using them. Even the most straightforward of issues may seem daunting if the only avenue for discussion is in a group or with a specific person to whom they would rather not talk. Indeed the manager may find group communications daunting. There are so many variables that standardised communication formats probably only work for one way dialogue – from manager to staff.

Counselling skills help contribute to good communications. However, good communications are hard to foster and maintain and there is a crucial need for consistency. Without consistency it is likely that the information will not be believed, management will be viewed with distrust and the company with suspicion and cynicism. The effective and appropriate use of counselling skills by line and personnel managers should enable open communication to prosper at all levels of an organisation.

Where the organisation is able to demonstrate the ability to hear and respond to concerns, accepting that each person in the work group has a contribution to make, then trust and respect will follow. The development of this kind of information flow does not interfere with other formal procedures and policies concerned with communication. Indeed where open dialogue exists and is accepted as the norm, then formal procedures should be enhanced and not be bogged down by mutual suspicions.

Letting employees know the 'big picture' – the organisation's goals and how their department, their job and their specific tasks are important to those goals – enables people to feel in control and more responsible for their actions. If subsequent misunderstandings arise then the manager or personnel department should be prepared (and best placed) to respond to these and to ensure that morale is unaffected. Employees are rarely stupid, but lack of information simply leads them to develop their own interpretations of events using the grapevine system. If the manager has done an effective job building up the requisite level of trust and respect, then his/her employees will consider this the best source of information and disregard the rest.

Overview

Employees who are experiencing stress will find themselves overwhelmed by tension and pressure. This reduces their ability to think clearly and respond constructively to a situation. A manager may respond by trying too hard to give the person the techniques to cope with the pressure. This can lead to a cycle of interaction which involves a 'Why don't you...', 'Yes, but...' pattern. The manager has a degree of insight to actions which may be useful for the employee to reduce the stress. The employee, due to the extent of the pressure, is unable to hear the proposals and has a reason each time for why it would not work.

People who are attempting to avoid making a personal decision, and therefore avoid accepting responsibility for their actions, often go down this route. They would rather attach blame for their circumstances on something or someone else. This has the effect of 'proving' that they cannot do anything to alter their position themselves, ie it is not their responsibility to act.

Very often this cycle of interaction results in an evasive spiral. The options are seen as an either/or choice. Backing away from both options is all too easy if both present a dilemma in their outcome. A counselling interview can widen the range of options that the person has available and will enable tension to be reduced. The real needs of the person will then emerge in such a way that responsibility is accepted. Simple questions within a counselling discussion like the following may be useful:

- What options do you think you have?
- What do you think you should do?
- What have you already considered doing and rejected?
- What were the pros and cons of these options as you saw them?

This will help the person face up to the stress situation and promote some objectivity in their thinking. It will also enable the person to check whether their original thoughts were reliable and to look at how their own actions influence the situation.

The next stage may be to encourage the person to break the situation into manageable parts. This will enable the person to view the situation as a series of small (and achievable) steps that can be taken towards resolving or managing the stress. How can I please my boss and myself? What do I really want? What conditions would make this possible? What prevents me from introducing these conditions?

Stress can prevent a person seeing events objectively and reliably. Emphasise with the person the need to work things through objectively and rationally and check with them how they can begin to organise themselves to meet the demands being placed on them. Prioritising different aspects of the stress situation can be helpful as well as exploring any positive elements that may exist.

It is important to avoid confusing false reassurance with genuine support and encouragement. Over optimism and confidence in the person's ability to cope can lead to the person feeling that they must make quick progress. If these expectations are not fulfilled, the experience of letting the helper, eg manager, down may contribute to the stressful situation.

Encourage the person to take responsibility for their situation and to work with other people to achieve their objectives. The person should also be helped to identify other people who may provide sources of support to the person. Isolation from existing or potential support and a dependence on the manager or helper will not provide a long term basis for managing future stress situations.

Teaching the person how to manage future stress situations should be an integral feature of the help and counselling given. The reasons why the person was unable to cope should be looked at and ways sought in which this can be avoided in the future. Their normal coping responses may have been inadequate or inappropriate for the situation. This part of the helping relationship requires a more active response from the manager.

The following chapters cover specific stressful events and outline practical approaches the manager can take to help the individual cope with their situation more effectively.

References

Cooper C L *and* Marshall J, 'Stress and pressures within organisations'. *Management Decision.* Vol 13, No 5, 1975. pp 292-303.

'The Social Readjustment Rating Scale', Holmes T H *and* Rahe R H. *Journal of Psychosomatic Research.* 11, 1967. pp 213-218.

Kearns Dr J. *Stress and the City.* Paper presented at 'The Management of Health' symposia. BUPA Occupational Health, 1986.

Murgatroyd S. *Counselling and helping.* Leicester, British Psychological Society and London, Methuen, 1985,

Further reading

Books

Arroba T *and* James K. *Pressure at work – a survival guide.* McGraw-Hill, 1987.

Coleman V. *Stress management techniques: managing people for healthy profits.* London, W H Allen, 1988. 124pp.

Cranwell-Ward J. *Managing Stress.* London, Pan, 1987. 165pp.

Goodworth C T. *Taking the strain: managing stress at work.* London, Hutchison, 1986. 132pp.

Marshall J *and* Cooper C L, *(eds). Coping with stress at work: case studies from industry.* London, Gower, 1981., xvi 236pp.

Orlans V *and* Shipley P. *A survey of stress management and prevention facilities in a sample of UK organisations.* London, Birkbeck College, Stress Research and Control Centre, 1983. 42pp.

Articles

Beehr T A *and* Newman J E. 'Job stress, employee health and organisational effectiveness: a facet analysis, model and literature review'. *Personnel Psychology.* Vol 31, No 4, Winter 1978. pp 665-699.

Cooper C L *and* Marshall J. 'The management of stress'. *Personnel Review.* Vol 4, No 4, Autumn 1975. pp 27-31.

Duckworth D. 'Managing without stress'. *Personnel Management.* Vol 18, No 4, April 1986. pp 40-43.

Fletcher B C *and* Payne R L. 'Stress and work, a review and theoretical framework'. Part 1. *Personnel Review.* Vol 9, No 1, Winter 1980. pp 19-29.

Fletcher B C *and* Payne R L. 'Stress and work, a review and theoretical framework. Part 2. *Personnel Review*. Vol 9, No 2, Spring 1980. pp 5-8.

Torrington D P. *and* Cooper C L. 'The management of stress in organisations and the personnel initiative'. *Personnel Review*. Vol 6, No 3, Summer 1977. pp 48-54.

2   Redundancy and Change

Introduction

The importance of employment is emphasised from an early age with the result that it becomes central to a person's identity. Employment, until the early 1970s, was thought to be a relatively stable aspect of a person's life. However the 'job for life' concept has gone and redundancy has become a common feature of all occupational groups.

In 1965 the Redundancy Payments Act (RPA) formalised the approach to implementing redundancy in Britain. It also coined the emotive phrase redundancy (not used outside Britain) which means 'superfluous to needs'. The RPA determined that every employee over the age of 18 years and with more than two years continuous service should receive a pre-calculated financial payment as compensation for loss of employment. Compensation was however secondary to the actual objective of the RPA, to increase labour mobility.

Although some employers continue to pay the statutory minimum, many employers provide enhanced severance terms. These are either additional or better financial payments – the IPM's Redundancy Code suggests that 'an additional payment at the same level as the statutory entitlement is not uncommon' – or a range of additional measures designed to enhance the outgoing employee's chances of finding and adjusting to new employment. Some of the additional provisions are designed to help employees cope with the change that is forced on them by redundancy.

Redundancy and change

Redundancy forces change on an organisation and the people within it, both those staying and those leaving. The reactions of both these groups can be influenced by the organisation and a positive outcome will result in beneficial consequences for the individual as well as the organisation.

Changes in an organisation will often, either by design or by consequence, reflect on such issues as job status, job content, relationships with peers and supervisors, working conditions, payment systems and numerous other aspects of a person's job. The whole organisation tends to be affected by change in any part of it.

Even when managers use their most logical arguments in support of change, they frequently discover that employees are unconvinced of the need for it. The effective use of counselling skills can help but they need to be used in conjunction with practical organisational initiatives. This chapter puts forward certain measures that organisations should consider at a time of change, particularly redundancy, and illustrates why counselling should be used to help employees come to terms with their changing circumstances.

It is not so much the nature of the change as the employee's attitude towards the change which is crucial. People are inclined to listen to their feelings more than the facts, and to use these feelings accordingly to make decisions. Consequently to try to help people come to terms with change on the basis of logical argument is ineffective because the logic will not have a direct effect on feelings.

How do individuals respond to change?

People in organisations, including managers, will generally resist change. Sometimes the biggest barrier to the introduction of change is resistance by managers to take on new methods of management.

Despite this tendency, there is often a counter-balancing desire for new experiences and other associated gains. Change can, in whatever form it takes, be successfully managed. If it is not, however, then problems will emerge in the form of lower morale, poor communications and a decline in confidence in the organisation and its management.

Resistance to change may have some benefits if it causes those motivating the change to clarify more sharply their reasons for wanting it and to define the outcome.

Responsibility for change

Management initiate most changes and therefore the responsibility for achieving change effectively lies with them. It is the employees however who will influence the final outcome since it is they who actually implement the changes. Employee support is therefore essential: in the case of redundancy this particularly means those people who are staying.

Communication with and involvement of employees is essential. Even if a change will affect only one or two in a work group of ten persons, all of them need to know about it in order to feel secure, and maintain group co-operation and an awareness of the new arrangements. Management often fail to realise that activities such as communication, that help get change accepted, are themselves usually disrupted by it. Management therefore needs to make a special effort to maintain such important stabilising social processes in times of change.

Change is all the more damaging in its impact if it is introduced suddenly, is spread over a long period or where despite anticipation it is poorly planned. Managers are often guilty of failing to devote sufficient time to analyse the methods and processes for change and to appreciate the full consequences on the work environment and employee attitudes.

The types of reactions that employees have towards the changes that occur due to redundancy are dependent, in part, on the culture of the company and the way in which the redundancy is announced. In organisations where there is no past history of redundancy it is more likely to result in feelings of shock and disbelief even where the redundancies were anticipated. In organisations where there is either a cyclical employment pattern or where redundancies have already been implemented, perhaps as part of an ongoing reduction process, shock is less evident.

Individual differences

We have already observed that each person will respond differently to different circumstances. Some people will welcome change as an opportunity to achieve new goals, while others will adopt a negative attitude. The following paragraphs illustrate areas of concern that people, particularly employees remaining in a company implementing redundancies, are likely to experience.

Security

There may be fear of job loss and associated income and/or status, as well as altered relationships with people. Increased turnover is very often a feature of organisational change: when new technology is mentioned, for instance, without explanation or full information, employees often assume that their jobs are threatened.

Change in social life

Where change requires the person to work different hours, travel to different sites, move to a different position within the offices or workshop or even relocate then the impact begins to affect social activities.

Relocating employees involves uprooting both the employee and his/her family. New schools need to be found for children, new social networks need to be built up; all take time and are an added stress on the employee. (See chapter 8).

Threat to self image

Changes in a person's job content, however small, may adversely affect the morale of an employee and contribute to insecurity. All employees adopt a sense of ownership of their tasks and responsibilities (including those parts they do not like) to the extent that even small changes are perceived with suspicion: the trolley boy at the local supermarket who collects both trolleys and baskets is likely to see the introduction of someone to collect the baskets as an erosion of his responsibilities; appointment of a deputy to a manager will be viewed as a threat; the chairman who resists all offers and suggestions of help in delegating tasks is feeling similarly insecure. Job content and role is very personal, and actual loss of a job through redundancy can mean that a significant part of the person's identity is lost too. Self confidence is eroded and the person can feel excluded from society.

Familiarity

Familiar work routines provide a less threatening and more comfortable existence. People may say that they feel in a rut, but how many of those people would actually consider changing that rut for something new and unknown?

Fear of the unknown

Fear of the unknown is basic to all resistance to change. Change and uncertainty go together and both contribute to feelings of discomfort. The outcome is a natural desire to prevent uncertainty. Redundancy heightens feelings of uncertainty. For some re-employment may seem remote and unlikely, the loss of structure and activity difficult to adjust to.

Fear of change

The anticipation of the consequences of change in an organisation is frequently more negative in impact than the change itself. Rumour, conjecture and secondhand knowledge of changes elsewhere all combine to generate fear of change and subsequent resistance to it.

Individual differences in response to redundancy

Faced with redundancy people will immediately think about their own pressures, pressures which will be influenced by a number of different variables. For instance, a married woman whose husband is in secure employment, who was not pursuing a career and with few financial worries, may focus on other non-work related activities. Whereas a man in his mid-thirties with a mortgage, wife and two children to support may focus on the financial pressure and consequently re-employment. A number of practical steps can be taken to help employees face their immediate pressures and enable them to consider what they can do and how they should do it. For some people, however, the pressures will seem insurmountable and represent a crisis. Managers should be aware of this possibility and the related symptoms in order to provide additional help.

The types of variables that will influence a person's reactions include:

- age
- sex
- financial commitments
- size of severance payment
- personality
- environment, ie redundancy may occur frequently
- support from family and friends
- length of employment.

Age

This is implicitly associated with other factors, eg responsibility, social networks, status, investment in the job. Younger employees may find themselves isolated if their peers are employed, rejected from home as being 'under their mother's feet'. Older employees may believe that their chances of finding new employment are few: 'too young to retire, too old to get a job or relocate' is a common dilemma. People who are in their mid-30s to late-40s will experience a halt to their career or job progression.

Sex

Many men continue to see themselves as the breadwinner. To lose a job is therefore a blow to the male pride and ego. No other source of recognition and security can be seen. Women who have returned to work may not want to go back to duties in the home, having acquired an identity outside this environment.

Financial commitments

These may be in the form of a large mortgage, school fees, hire purchase arrangements or simply having sufficient income to feed and clothe the family.

Severance payments

It is a common myth that every person being made redundant receives a large cash severance payment. Often the money will only provide for a few weeks or months ahead. If a very large payment is given this may provide the person with the scope to think about investing it in a business venture or to provide a degree of security for the future.

Personality

No two people will respond the same way to redundancy. Some may become quickly resigned to it, others will become angry and bitter, still others see it as a time of opportunity.

Environment

This can be divided into two areas: (a) support from family and friends. If this is good the person will be able to lean on them for help and encouragement. If it is poor and the family reinforces any feelings of self blame then the person will feel isolated and depressed. (b) Some parts of Britain have come to experience redundancy as a way of life. In these areas any stigma associated with unemployment may be lessened. Conversely, where redundancy is not common the person may feel a sense of shame.

Length of employment
This aspect is crucial when determining whether the person qualifies for statutory redundancy payment and how much. It may also have a profound influence on the sense of attachment the person has toward their job.

People with longer periods of employment with the same employer are more likely to experience a greater sense of loss and find it more difficult to adjust to different environments. The feelings of anger or disbelief may be greater and acceptance of their circumstances more difficult to achieve. All these factors need to be considered in counselling. A number of models describing the reactions of people to job loss have been developed and these are discussed next.

The traditional model of individual response to redundancy

A number of different models (see figure 4 opposite) have been developed by researchers and these are typically used by redundancy counsellors as a basis for talking to employees. The models that exist have, however, recently been criticised (not least because they have been accepted as the normal reaction cycle which people are expected to go through). This potentially becomes a self fulfilling philosophy and redundancy counsellors 'fit' the individual's response into the reaction cycle. This has the effect of perpetuating the need for a specialised agency to deal with the anticipated fluctuations of emotions the employee should pass through. On the one hand this devalues the important role that line and personnel managers should play in the process and on the other, hands over the responsibility for the actions of the organisation to a third party.

Redundancy counsellors have a contribution to make and generally provide a service that is well received by employees and employers. However, employers should not lose sight of the fact that they potentially have the skills and experience to provide an equivalent service (particularly the practical aspects) to redundancy employees and that, in addition, regardless of the outside services available they will still be confronted with the emotions of employees

(those both leaving and staying) and should therefore be equipped
to deal with the issues that will be raised.

Figure 4
Reactions to job loss

Hopson and Adams (1976)	Immobilisation minimisation	depression test accept reality	search internal- for isation meaning
Harrison (1976) (Eisenberg and Lazarsfeld (1938)	shock optimism	pessimism	fatalism
Hill (1977)	initial response (trauma, denial)	intermediate phase (depression, accept reality)	settling down to unemployment (adaptation)
Briar (1977)	job loss (shock, optimism)	joblessness as a way of life (self blame, depression)	inertia

Source: Hayes and Nutman. *Understanding the unemployed.*

Practical issues for redundancy implementation

The organisation should be able to implement redundancies and
facilitate change in a way that can reduce the degree of any
resentment and bitterness that may be experienced by employees
when announcements are made. This involves effective
communication in order to keep people informed of what is
happening.

The first indication that redundancies are in the offing will arrive
via the company grapevine. Rumours spread quickly, not only in
one location but across geographical locations. Often they will gather
pace and exaggeration along the way. Many businesses restrict the
flow of information in an effort to avert problems of this type or use
it as an excuse to avoid telling their employees what is happening.

Such attempts to keep information away from employees are
misguided. If information is withheld, the grapevine assumes the
role of company communicator. A channel which will at best be

misleading is at worst malicious and damaging. Redundancy counselling as a separate activity should not begin as the employee is about to leave, but should, as said earlier, be an ongoing process of communication with additional aspects introduced when terminations become necessary.

Companies often put forward the following reasons for keeping redundancy quiet:

The company *may:*

- potentially lose customers
- experience a fall in market share
- have a decline in morale
- cause key people to leave.

This needs to be balanced against the impact on employees when information is withheld.

The company *does* experience:

- a decline in morale
- a loss of key employees
- a lethargy in management
- an increase in anxiety and insecurity with employee's thoughts concentrating on:

- who will it be?
- how much will we be paid?
- when will we know?
- how will it be decided?
- do I plan for the future?
- and so on...

The reactions of employees when the grapevine is allowed to thrive makes a manager's job all the more difficult. Employees want answers to questions. Managers often only know as much as their staff and are therefore not able to answer them. Resentment will grow and this can adversely influence the perception of any positive measures that are introduced if redundancy is implemented.

Other factors which should be considered in order to facilitate the implementation process and foster trust and understanding in the workplace include:

- Redundancy notification – how will the initial announcement be made and when, eg by individual interviews, or at group meetings.
- Where a number of line managers are informing individual employees of redundancy it would be helpful to bring these managers together to enable them to discuss their own anxieties, fears, and expectations of needing to notify people of redundancy.
- The person giving the news to the employee should be a senior manager or chief executive supported by the personnel manager. This has the effect of showing the employee that the company cares about the way the news is communicated and showing the managers that the 'buck' has not been passed to them.
- The reason for redundancy should be communicated accurately.
- The method of selection needs to be understood and seen to be fair.
- Evidence of alternative solutions, if considered, should be explained with reasons why they were rejected.
- Information concerning the redundancy package should be prepared and clearly understood. The type of package given should be consistent with any existing policy agreement and should be applied consistently to all employees (particularly if no agreement exists). With emotions running high employees are quick to feel that the company is 'ripping them off' if inconsistencies are perceived or packages are misunderstood.
- Effective communication should also be accompanied by an acknowledgement of the emotions that will exist at a time of change, particularly redundancy. Facts alone are insufficient for employees. An opportunity to express and talk about the anxieties and uncertainties that exist is important, even where it is known that no additional practical measures can be introduced.

Guidelines for the redundancy interview

The manager who is informing the person of redundancy should be aware of the following guidelines and be supported by the organisation in efforts to achieve them:

The manager should not:

- attempt to use humour to establish rapport. Losing one's job is not amusing. In instances where humour is used it is for the interviewer's benefit and not the individual's

– make assumptions for the other person. Statements like 'You'll be alright, there are lots of other jobs around', illustrate a total lack of understanding of the person's circumstances. The issue is job loss not potential re-employment. It also assumes that re-employment will overcome all problems

– try and get the interview over quickly. This will reinforce feelings of rejection. Allow sufficient time for the news to be given and reactions to surface. Let the individual decide when to leave the office

– immediately give the person all the details about the redundancy package. If the person responds with shock they are more likely to mishear or misunderstand what they are being told. Limit the information to a few important items, eg date of leaving.

The manager should:

– acknowledge the person's feelings
– have full details of the redundancy package ready and available for people who want it. Be prepared to reiterate points later
– leave the opportunity for further discussions open
– give the date of the last working day as this will enable the person to start making plans
– be direct
– be consistent between people
– explain the circumstances surrounding the dismissal and why their job is no longer viable.

Redundancy counselling measures

Although there are examples of employers who have been prepared to help employees when a redundancy has occurred as far back as 1958, in recent years more organisations have turned to redundancy counselling in an effort to dismiss employees smoothly and humanely. The type of help comprises a range of measures, which may include some or all of the following:

– advice on state benefits
– help with writing CVs etc

– career guidance
– retraining
– new employment initiatives
– counselling
– enhanced severance terms
– financial advice and budgeting
– job search advice
– self employment help
– interviewing skills training.

An indication of the extent of the use of these types of provisions in Britain can be gauged from a 1984 survey of 100 companies representing a cross section of businesses which asked the extent to which companies went beyond the statutory minimum requirements when implementing redundancies. The response shows (figure 5) that the emphasis remains on financial compensation but that increasingly other measures are being used.

Figure 5
Company redundancy provision

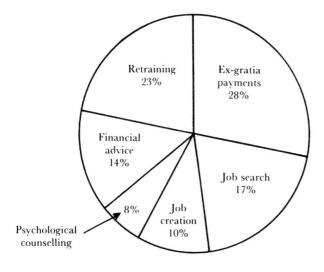

Source: Megranahan MS. *'Counselling at Work'*

The survey also confirmed that anything other than financial compensation tended to be regarded as redundancy counselling. When specifically asked about the counselling given, employers said that they saw the objectives of counselling in the following way:

- giving information
- reassurance
- clarify thinking
- release of emotional tension, eg anger
- reduce anxiety
- coping with change
- communication.

Job search (which included CV writing, interview presentation skills, etc) was considered to be a separate activity.

In an IPM survey, (see Burrows G, 1985) which focused on the redundancy counselling carried out by consultancies, four stages were identified and used as a basis for investigating the consultant's emphasis in the redundancy counselling process. The four stages were termed:

1 crisis counselling
2 careers advice/coaching
3 coaching
4 job finding.

There are clear boundaries between these different stages although different people may need greater help with some areas than others and it is unlikely that people will move through a neat progression from crisis to job finding. The crisis may, for instance, come much later when the person realises the problems associated with achieving resettlement. In some cases, eg senior management, this particular issue is catered for by the consultancy who support an individual until resettlement is achieved.

Various helping strategies are involved in redundancy counselling which range from advice and information to counselling. Managers may be involved in any of these areas and specialist agencies should be equipped to deal with all of them.

The distinction between the different areas is shown below:

Financial planning
Pension questions } information giving
Statutory benefits

CV compilation
Application forms } teaching and guidance

Interview training
Job search activities } coaching

Domestic crises
Personal stress } counselling
Anxiety

The different areas are likely to overlap and clearly one can affect another. For instance, sound financial advice may alleviate domestic problems and anxiety. There may be a need for the manager to refer the employee to specialist resources, particularly at the counselling end of the spectrum. Care should be taken when referring employees to specialist resources. As far as possible the resource should be researched by the company in order to ascertain the methods used, calibre of staff, evaluation criteria and so on. Burrows (1985) provides a good basis from which to select redundancy counselling or outplacement specialists.

Summary

A great deal has been written and publicised about the thoughts and emotions of people who have been made redundant. Typically they will be angry, bitter and resentful. No effort is made to emphasise that they are still the same people: the only difference is that they have been given a date from which they will cease to be employed by the company. Emotions will certainly appear, not only in those who ares leaving but also in those who are staying and losing friends and colleagues, in those who have been told they have to stay but would rather have left, in managers who will need to inform the employees of the redundancy, in personnel departments who are required to implement the administrative aspects and who are expected by employees to answer a range of questions from state benefits to pension arrangements and also cope with varying degrees of emotions. Redundancy is an event which affects the whole company and for which the company is responsible.

Change, for whatever reason, can with forethought and planning be achieved with the knowledge and confidence that the company can alleviate pressure on all employees and enable an effective transition to take place that can enhance the company's prospects.

In the chapter on stress we discussed the adverse affects of too much or prolonged stress. Gradual change is more likely to be accepted than excessive and rapid change. Employees need time, training and support to adjust to new situations.

Further reading

Redundancy

Bretherton Michael *and* Dunn Christopher. *Making redundancy work for you.* Enterprise Counselling Publications Limited in association with Professional and Executive Recruitment and Institute of Personnel Management, 1984.

Burrows Giles. *Redundancy counselling for managers.* London, IPM, 1985.

Chell E. 'Redundancy and unemployment: the role of the personnel manager'. *Personnel Review*, Vol 14, No 2, 1985. pp24–31.

Consumers' Association. *Dismissal, redundancy and job hunting.* London, Consumers' Association, 1976 (Amended 1980). 140pp.

Cooper C L *and* Hartley J. '*Redundancy:* a psychological problem?' *Personnel Review* Vol 5, No 3, Summer 1976. pp 44–48.

Institute of Manpower Studies. *Redundancy provisions survey.* Falmer, Brighton, IMS, 1981 (Manpower commentary 13) Part 1: Commentary, Part 2: Statistical tables.

Institute of Personnel Management *The IPM redundancy code.* London, IPM, 1984. 8pp.

Organisation development and change

Confederation of British Industry. *Managing change: the organization of work.* London, CBI, 1985. 99pp.

Goodridge Mark, Fear Elaine *and* Rigglesford David. *Managing change: the human resources issues.* Cambridge, Employment Realations Resource Centre, 1985. vi, 70pp.

Leigh Andrew. *Effective change: 20 ways to make it happen.* London, Institute of Personnel Management, 1988.

MacKay 1. 'Making changes at work: a checklist'. *Training and Development.* (UK) Vol 5, No 1. May 1986. pp 34–35.
Marlow Hugh. *Managing change – key questions and working papers.* London, Institute of Personnel Management, 1975. 68pp.
Thorn Jeremy. *Managing change.* London, Industrial Society, 1986. 20pp (Notes for managers).

3 Career Counselling

Introduction

Most of us will, at one time or another, have reflected on our job and on occasion may have felt like giving it up and doing something different. Often this is just the result of a bad day at work, and we recognise these feelings as such. For a number of people, however, feelings of dissatisfaction with their occupation are very real and not transitory. This can have a significant effect on their attitude towards their work and their life in general.

Although managers may feel it appropriate and part of their role to give advice and information to employees about careers in their particular field, they probably would not feel equipped, nor see it as their role, to help any employee who was considering completely new directions. In discussing mid-career change, this chapter is not intended to be a 'potted guide' on becoming a careers counsellor. That would not be appropriate or realistic. What this chapter does aim to do is to provide those in a management or supervisory position with some basic guidelines to help in an effective way employees who appear to be considering changes.

Why the manager?

Managers are well placed to help employees start to reflect on their present occupation. The manager should have a good understanding of the demands and nature of a person's particular job and also of the employee in their work role. This knowledge provides the basis for the manager to be able to help an employee look constructively at where their strengths and abilities lie. Others who could provide this help within the organisation include senior colleagues with a similar specialism, personnel, trades union officials or the training officer.

The changing pattern of work

The days of leaving school, learning a skill, and spending the next 40 or more years within that particular occupation – possibly with the same employer – are obviously gone. We are encouraged to be flexible, to expect change, to see our skills as 'transferable' from one occupation to another. Technological advances force change upon us, and our working situations. People also tend to expect a higher degree of job satisfaction than in the past. Despite continuing high unemployment in some areas there are more choices available, particularly for younger people. Further and higher education is more widely available and people of all ages are being encouraged to take up and continue education throughout life, with organisations like the Open University (who have a range of management courses), the Open College and the development of distance learning from colleges such as Henley Management College.

The impetus to look for new directions and opportunity in careers may be caused by external influences, for example new technology or the threat of impending redundancy, or may develop from a personal feeling of needing to be more fulfilled and satisfied with one's working life. Other reasons may be due to changes in health; the desire to return to work after starting a family; the felt need to change from a stressful occupation, eg from fire service or nursing.

Career choice – the theories

How do people decide on their careers? In answer to this question many people would say: 'By chance; I just happened to get a job and it started from there'. Circumstances and 'chance' may play a part, but it is likely that some element of selection came into it. To decide whether a particular kind of work is right for us we consciously, or subconsciously, make judgements about whether we find it interesting, whether we feel we have the abilities and personal qualities demanded by the job, and whether it fits with the particular criteria that are important to us as individuals – the opportunity to travel, to work independently, to help people, good prospects.

Awareness of what we as individuals find interesting and satisfying, and awareness of where our strengths and aptitudes lie, gradually evolve over time, from childhood onwards. Accordingly, career choice has been recognised as being a developmental process. Unfortunately, external factors force us to make particular decisions at certain times of our life – school leaving being the most obvious. The start of our working life really tests whether the ideas we had about ourselves were correct, and every particular working situation will help us to learn something more about ourselves, eg that we prefer to work on our own rather than in a team, we cope well with particular problems but not with others. As we mature, perceptions, attitudes and values may change, and as a consequence the kind of job that suits us best will also change.

Career change or career development?

The changes we all experience as we mature may lead us to look for new challenges or roles within the chosen occupation. This aspect of change, described as career development, is a positive and progressive process. In many organisations there will be well developed staff review procedures in which the manager may be involved. Some employees, however, may not see their needs and ambitions being met within their current company, and may be looking for a change of employer while remaining in the same occupation as their next step. Others may feel their needs can only be fulfilled by a change of occupation, and it is these employees who are likely to feel more confused and uncertain as to what to do.

Why should the manager help?

Dissatisfied employees are likely to be less productive, and to give less to their job. It may mean a lot to someone to know that their manager is concerned and willing to listen, and this may lead to a more positive attitude towards their work. Similarly, there may be small changes that could be effected within the organisation that could remove frustrations, or make use of unused talents and abilities. Alternatively, if someone is very misplaced, then it is better for them to be referred to organisations that can help them to move on, releasing this discussion to someone who should be objective and neutral in their approach to the situation.

Where employees feel restless in their job the manager should also be aware of the following problems that may arise if nothing is done:

1 Restless employees can become very disruptive in the organisation and begin to affect other people. What starts as a small problem can quickly grow out of all proportion.
2 The fact that someone is restless may be a positive feature. It may be that the person is under-utilised or under-employed. Skills and development potential are being wasted by restricting the person to a job or role where they are bored.
3 If the problem is addressed openly, the manager can create an atmosphere of mutual respect and understanding.

How can the manager help?

1 By recognising the signs that all does not seem well with the employee.
2 By providing an opportunity for the employee to start to talk it through with the manager.
3 By providing the employee with information as to where to go for further help and advice, if appropriate.

Recognising the signs

Thinking about a change of career is often triggered off by negative feelings towards one's current occupation. People feeling dissatisfied with their job may show it by losing motivation, being disinterested in their work, or perhaps looking stressed and worried. If they don't see solutions to their problem and feel trapped, they might display feelings of bitterness, resentment and general frustration. Obviously every individual reacts differently and some employees may purposely hide any feelings of dissatisfaction since they believe it may jeopardise their own position at work.

Talking it through with an employee

As mentioned in the introduction, the manager is not a careers adviser. However, he or she is well placed to provide an opportunity for that employee to start to reflect perhaps more constructively on their current feelings, and start to identify where their strengths and abilities lie. One way in which these aspects can be monitored is through a performance appraisal scheme (see chapter 6).

People considering change need to go through the following process:

Stage 1	Stage 2	Stage 3	Stage 4
Look at your present situation	Identify the changes desired	Identify and consider the options open to you	Take action

Stage 1: Personal stocktaking

In considering changes for the future, it is necessary to look at our experience, and to see what we have learnt from it about ourselves – in terms of interests, abilities, motivations – and what we have to offer. This is what is meant by personal stocktaking. Addressing the question 'Where am I now?' is a fundamental stage, without which further decision making is difficult.

In practical terms the manager can help by assisting the employee to explore and clarify his or her feelings about their job. Is it that they are feeling bored, frustrated, undervalued, pressurised? What does that person mean by the terms they use to describe these feelings? Employees may also experience guilt about feeling dissatisfied, and feel they ought to be thankful to have a job at all.

Having put these feelings into words, the person may be able to identify more clearly what exactly is causing those feelings.

The reasons could include:
- the job has changed substantially (perhaps as a result of new technology) and they find it less satisfactory
- they find younger people 'overtaking' them, and find this hard to accept
- they have begun to find certain working conditions more difficult to cope with, eg physical demands of the job
- they have developed personally, and find the work no longer a challenge
- their motivations, or feelings about what is important to them in work, have changed, eg the status, money no longer attracts,

a feeling of wanting to do something more 'worthwhile' – what do they mean by that?
- they find particular people difficult to work with
- lack of positive feedback (eg recognition, encouragement, appreciation) from managers, clients or customers may make employees feel undervalued
- illness may necessitate a change
- changes in personal life – death of a parent, divorce, children leaving home
- they foresee redundancy in the future
- they want to try and develop an interest or career idea they've always had 'before it's too late'.
- a 'mid-life crisis' which is fuelling a feeling of restlessness
- the job never fulfilled their expectations
- they took the job for particular reasons at the time, unrelated to whether the job would be interesting to them, and circumstances now allow them to look at more suitable alternatives.

Getting people to pinpoint more precisely where their dissatisfactions lie can help them identify more easily what they would look for in a job.

Looking at the positive side

If someone is finding one particular aspect of their job difficult, this could colour their outlook and cause them to lose confidence in their ability to cope with the job as a whole. The manager can encourage the employee to spend a little time looking at any positive aspects of their work by helping employees to:

- identify any aspects of their job in which they do find some satisfaction
- identify any particular abilities and skills they might have
- identify the positive personal qualities they bring to their jobs, eg methodical, good at coping with difficult customers, conscientious and so on.

To help identify positive aspects, the manager could ask the employee to reflect on any previous jobs they have done, and on activities they may have done outside work, and talk about anything that brought them enjoyment and satisfaction in those situations.

Stage 2: Identify the changes desired

Having helped the employee thoroughly explore their feelings about their current occupation (and perhaps having discussed other jobs and activities they have found rewarding), this may naturally lead the manager on to enable the employee to identify which *particular* aspects of their job they wish to change. It will often relate to the part of their current job that frustrates them most of all.

The changes desired could range from wanting the opportunity to use specific skills that are not used in their current work, or the opportunity to work with the public in a more direct way, or the opportunity to 'see a job through', to take more managerial and decision-making responsibilities.

With some employees, the manager may well be able to help the employee to identify such factors fairly specifically. With other employees, they may find it difficult to help the employee to articulate anything more precise than 'I want a job that's more interesting – but I don't know what'. This employee will need more time, and perhaps help by more objective assessment techniques (tests etc) to help them get further forward in their thinking, and at this point it would be appropriate for the manager to refer the employee to the more specialist help provided by careers guidance agencies, which are described at the end of this chapter.

Stage 3: Identify and consider the options open

Having identified the changes desired, the first set of options that the manager can help the employee to consider are as follows:

a) *Can the changes desired be effected within that particular company or organisation?* For example, providing the employee with further training or moving them to a different section or department with different responsibilities may help. The manager could have a key role in enabling such changes to be brought about.

b) *Can the need be fulfilled by taking up new activities outside of the employee's working day?* They could join courses or clubs or take up voluntary activities for example. If this seems to be the case, the manager should refer the employee to the other agencies listed at the end of the chapter, which will provide the employee with comprehensive up-to-date information about what opportunities exist locally.

c) *Could the change be effected by moving to a similar job, but with a different organisation?* Managers themselves may have some knowledge and experience they can bring to the discussion of this option.

d) *Can the need only be met by considering a complete change of occupation?* If, on discussion with the employee, this seems to be the option that might best provide a solution, again the manager should at this point refer the employee to an organisation which can provide specialist help to identify what particular career options might be appropriate for that employee.

Step 4: Take action

The manager will only have a direct role at this stage of the process if the changes desired can be effected within the organisation (option (a) above) which the manager can help initiate. Taking action relating to options (b), (c) and (d) may be more effectively achieved with professional helping agencies who have the specific knowledge and expertise to help the employee further. However, the manager can continue to provide the employee with support and encouragement, by keeping in touch with how their ideas and plans are developing.

Confidentiality

To be effective, discussions with an employee need to be carried out in an atmosphere of trust and confidentiality. Any employee will be very reluctant to talk openly to a manager unless certain that particular information, worries, admissions of failure or negative feelings towards their job will not be used against them elsewhere at a later date. The issue of confidentiality should be defined with the employee at the beginning of an interview (see chapter 24).

Other sources of advice and information

Referring to other agencies

It is preferable for the manager to provide the information to the employee, and encourage them to make contact. It is a misplacement of confidentiality for managers to pass on names and information about their employees to outside agencies, unless they have the permission of that employee to do so. If the manager feels the

employee may not have the confidence to make the initial contact,
the manager could ask the employee for permission to pass on his
or her name to an agency, and ask the agency to make contact direct
with the employee.

Educational guidance services for adults

This is a network of services where the public can get information,
advice and counselling to help them get into education and training.
The service is free of charge. A directory listing these services
nationally is available from Richard Edwards, NAEGS Secretary,
at Waltham Forest Education Shop, Chestnuts House, 398 Hoe
Street, Walthamstow, London E17 9AA, at a cost of 50p. Alternatively,
your public library should have information about any local
educational guidance service.

Careers service

Part of the local education authority, the main function of the careers
service is to help young people, but many offer a guidance service
to adults. They provide information about careers, education and
training opportunities, and most careers services offer individual
careers guidance discussions to adults. The address of your local
Careers Office can be found under the Education Department of the
County Council, in the telephone directory, or you may see publicity
in your local library.

Private vocational guidance services

These offer careers advice to any member of the public on a fee
paying basis. Their services are often advertised in the press, or you
could look in your local Yellow Pages/Thompsons Directory, to find
any local agencies. The British Association for Counselling (BAC)
and its Counselling at Work Division (CAWD) also have directories
of people working in this area.

Libraries

Public libraries are a good source of information about a range of
learning opportunities in your locality, such as those organised by
adult education services, community groups, and other
organisations.

Colleges/polytechnics/universities

Local education institutions will obviously provide leaflets about the range of courses they offer, and such publicity will often have a named contact or telephone number for further information. In some instances, for example if you are a recent student, you may be able to make use of the resources of the college's own careers service.

Jobcentres

Jobcentres advertise any government funded retraining opportunities currently available and will be able to provide information about these. For job-seekers (whether employed or unemployed) jobcentres are obviously a good place to start looking to gain a feel of the local employment market. PER (the Professional and Executive Register) is available to help those seeking managerial, professional, supervisory or technical posts.

Professional bodies and institutes

Professional bodies often publish careers information about their particular field of work. It may be worth getting in touch with the professional body of any occupation that is being considered for information and advice. Reference libraries will probably be able to help you find the address of the national headquarters, who then will be able to put you in touch with any local contacts.

Further reading

Books

Collins Roger R and Hunt John W(eds). *Managers in mid-career crisis.* Sydney, Wellington Lane Press, 1983.
Golzen Godfrey and Plumbley Peter. *Changing your job after 35.* London, A Daily Telegraph Guide, 1984.
Hopson Barry and Scally Mike. *Build your own rainbow: A workbook for career and life management.* Lifeskills Associates, 1984.

Local Government Training Board. *Changing Direction.* A personal and career planning kit, 1986.

Morphy Leslie. *Career change.* CRAC (Careers Research and Advisory Centre) publication, 1987.

Pates A. *and* Good M. *Second chances.* The guide to adult education and training opportunities published by COIC (Careers and Occupational Information Centre), 1987.

Watts A G, Super D E *and* Kidd J M *(eds). Career development in Britain.* CRAC publication, 1981.

Article

Super D E. 'A theory of vocational development'. *American Psychologist.* Vol 8, 1953.

4   The Career Break for Women

Introduction

Although attitudes towards women's employment issues have been well-aired since the inception of the Equal Opportunities Commission and the Employment Protection Act, the problems of combining family commitments and work are as real today as they ever were. There tends to be two schools of thought on 'women issues'; those on the one hand who accept the existence of equal opportunities legislation and argue that women should be treated no differently than men at the workplace. On the other hand there are those who believe in the 'holistic' approach towards employment and personal problems. They argue that women with children in particular cannot departmentalise their lives into 'domestic' and 'job', that there is likely to be an overlap between the two and that a woman's perception of her work will be influenced by her domestic and family environment.

Although this is not the place to enter into a theoretical debate, there are two points which are generally accepted: firstly, working women themselves are usually the first to admit that as soon as children appear, the boundaries between work and home become less clearly divided. Secondly, many women's career expectations and ambitions change dramatically after childbirth. Indeed, time taken off for child-rearing often proves to be a major obstacle to job advancement in the long term. Alternatively, an increasing number of women are waiting until they are older (mid to late 30s) before starting a family. They will have often established a career by this stage. Counselling for women at work can help them clarify the above conflicts and other allied problems.

There are two major points in a woman's working life when she will need to think about and plan for her requirements: a) before stopping work to have a child; b) when returning after a period at home for child-rearing. Both stages require an element of planning and decision making, which only effectively takes place after some self analysis, particularly with regard to life style and ambition.

Stopping work due to pregnancy

The attention that individual women give to this event, in terms of
how it will impinge on their work situation, varies. The first baby
can be a time of considerable excitement and trepidation. It is often
difficult to predict accurately what will be involved. A woman who
already has children will probably have an expectation based on
experience. The role of the counselling interview should be to discover
how much thought the woman has given to how pregnancy will
affect her current and future employment. The areas that need to
be considered include the following:

- maternity rights and entitlements according to the law
- practicalities – when is she stopping work and for how long?
- options for the future. Does she want to return to work and
  what are the choices available to her within her particular
  company or organisation?

This last point is crucial. In Britain 90 per cent of women return to
work after child-rearing, and at a faster rate than in any other
European country. The keynote is choices and the provision of
information so that the woman can make considered decisions about
the sort of lifestyle that she wants and the role of work within this
lifestyle.

In terms of the approach of the manager, care should be taken
within the form of questioning that is adopted. Because the paths
that women can take vary, there is no 'right' or 'wrong' way to
regard employment. The non-career woman should not be made to
feel any less important than the woman who wants to map out a
future at work.

The manager should try to avoid posing tactless, loaded questions
such as: 'I suppose that as you're on a junior clerical grade you
won't be thinking about how to continue your career after the baby
arrives, will you?' Or 'I suppose you've decided to stay at home
until your child is five, and there's no point in our discussing career
structures for when you return, is there?'

The questions asked should contain no element of prejudice or
judgemental assumption in them. The point of the counselling
interview is to help the women consider the options by providing
adequate and accurate information on the rights and opportunities
that exist.

The number of choices available to her can be increased if she understands the rules: for example, the length of time that she needs to have been with an employer in order to qualify for maternity benefit, etc. Many women will want to plan their pregnancies, and in these situations, the information provided by the manager can be invaluable.

Employers sometimes criticise female staff for 'changing their minds' about their intention to return to work. This often happens because of unforeseen circumstances, eg the baby proves to be more demanding or time-consuming than the woman had anticipated. A counselling interview can help the woman feel she has not let herself or the company down. She may be confused and unsure about stopping work completely. There is also a possibility of a conflict with her husband/partner if the woman wants to continue working and he is resistant to this. Financial hardship may also be a practical issue. The woman may need to continue working despite wanting to do otherwise. Indeed, there could be all sorts of pressures on the pregnant woman behind the scenes. The pregnancy may not be planned; she may be experiencing conflict with family, friends, work colleagues and others if she is intending to have a baby without support from the father. She may be a divorcee, unmarried or her husband may be redundant or unemployed. These days many women become the breadwinner out of necessity, not choice.

If she already has one or more children, she should be accustomed to juggling work and domestic responsibilities. But the arrival of another child will force the issue of priorities for her time and commitments. She may be in danger of overstretching herself, or have to reassess the support she is getting and that she needs if she is to continue with work.

The ability of each individual to handle pressure and the psychological stress that can accompany decision-making varies. Some people agonise over their lives, others take life's ups and downs with greater equanimity. Lack of concentration may emerge as a problem. Popular myth about pregnancy points not only to food fads but also to a more ebullient emotional state which, so it is said, is caused by hormonal changes. But the manager should not take such symptoms as a foregone conclusion. If problems emerge, the manager should show tolerance and understanding but at the same time should avoid patronising the member of staff.

It has been common in the past for men to adopt a patronising attitude towards pregnant women, being virtuous and superior as well as polite and fatherly. Such a tone is usually well intended but can be offensive. Pregnancy is not an illness, rather a temporary state of being, so the woman does not need to be mollycoddled or treated like a sick patient but as an equal.

It is common for people to formulate moral judgements from their own experience, but a good manager will have a more global perspective. A male manager may have a wife who is a full-time mother without a paid career but this should not cloud his judgement about other paths that are open to women. The female manager who does not have children may be unfamiliar with the pressures and dilemmas that need to be addressed. Women managers who have had children may adopt an authoritarian position and lecture the employee as to how she should feel, behave and cope.

In other words, prejudices for or against different lifestyles should not be formed on the basis of one's own experience. Or if they have already been formulated, they should not be manifested towards staff. The process of being aware of one's assumptions and examining preconceived views is an important part of counselling another person. The manager who can do this is likely to have a more positive attitude towards staff relations.

Returning to work after a break

The problems for a woman returning to work after a break will vary according to the length of time she has been away from the job and to the sort of work that she used to do and is returning to. Over the last ten years changes have been rapid in many industries due to new technology, unemployment and variations in supply and demand. To take an obvious example – copy typists are less in demand, nowadays than word processor operators. Most women are aware of employment changes and may well be frightened of facing the consequences of change. There will be other areas of concern:

1   Their lack of confidence will be compounded by a long period at home. Usually, the longer the period away from paid work the worse the confidence problem.
2   They may also lack support from their partners for their efforts to return to work and may be expected to cope with the housework and children as well as their job. This is only a problem for the manager if work performance is affected. Avoid the impression

that questions about home life are 'prying' by making some constructive yet impersonal suggestions. For instance, the manager could point the member of staff towards a book like *Women Working It Out* (see Further reading) that gives practical advice on childcare and other ways of alleviating the burden.

3   They may have little knowledge of the job market or of training and educational opportunities. The manager can help by providing information and guidance in these areas. Extra training or a course to give further qualifications is one way of reducing the likelihood of the woman missing out in career terms because of an absence for childcaring.

4   It is likely that they will undervalue their skills and the experience that they possess and may feel guilty at apparently abandoning their traditional female role, although they will probably at the same time enjoy the re-discovery of an identity separate from the home. The ultimate dilemma for any working mother comes when her children fall sick during work time. If this happens, the manager should not be too harsh. Indeed, companies who employ large numbers of working mothers, for example in electronics production, usually say that absenteeism rates for women are no worse than for men.

In short, the aim of counselling for women returning to work should be to ease the transition from home base to work, build confidence and thereafter show a sensitivity towards the sometimes stressful 'double' existence that a working mother faces. Constructive feedback at the workplace is important: when the member of staff does well – tell them so!

The manager can also help by ascertaining what areas of work practice, if any, are new to the person since she has left to have children. The manager should then be able to outline ways in which the woman could tackle these problems. Some companies offer formal induction to help with updating, others offer 'refresher schemes'. In some cases the professional associations covering individual trades offer refresher courses, eg pharmacy. Indeed, this last example is a good one, as one company, Boots, also introduced a 'retainer scheme' for pharmacists whereby female staff could return to work by easing back in gradually on a part-time basis. But the scheme has not had a big take-up because many pharmacists prefer to work on a 'locum' basis in private pharmacies with a daily rate which is higher than the wage through the 'retainer scheme'.

The more the woman 'keeps her hand in', the less likely it is that she will have to return to work at a lower level, but nevertheless many women have to return to work to a job at a lesser grade than the one they had previously, due to fierce competition in the job market (37 per cent of women returners take work in an occupational category below that of their last job). Once the woman has settled into a routine and got used to being back at work again, she may feel under-stretched or exploited. She may also feel uneasy about having to take orders from people much younger than herself, and about the competition in the labour market from younger women. Counselling can help a person to value her own positive attributes, and to understand, or at least assess, the way forward and plan accordingly so that she can achieve career advancement if she wants it.

It may be that the company has a job share policy which will enable two staff to share a post without loss of employment benefits or career status. In some cases female employees may want to take the initiative in suggesting an individual job share package by finding their own partners and proposing a 'modus operandi'. Job share schemes, flexitime and workplace nurseries are all a great help to women with children and are something that a manager should know about and discuss with the individual if circumstances permit. At least three of the major clearing banks have formal retainer schemes for female staff. Job share is now well established within many forward thinking local authorities and within several departments of the civil service. Mobil Oil is amongst one of many organisations which have established women's networks to identify practical solutions to the problems faced by women at work. They now have a 'maternity advice pack' for staff. A report published by the former Training Commission (MSC) lists the various initiatives that employers have taken and concludes that if companies are to make the best use of their investment in women's labour, their employment policies should make provision for the probability that most women will have chilren at some time during their working life.

So, in helping overcome the career break, probably more than anything else the existence of another person for discussion in a dispassionate way is the biggest bonus for a woman returning to work. Encouragement, sensitivity and an understanding of the pressures on today's woman, and on her family, are essential qualities in helping to provide reassurance, build her confidence and give her a point of reference that she would not otherwise have.

Further reading

Chapman J. *Women working it out.* Careers and Occupational Information Centre, A paperback guide for women who are either wanting to return to work, widen their horizons or change direction. Available from COIC, MSC, Moorfoot, Sheffield S1 4PQ

Truman Carole. *Overcoming the career break – a positive approach.* Report published by The Training Agency (formerly MSC), Moorfoot, Sheffield S1 4PQ.

The Working Mother's Handbook – a guide for parents in choosing and finding child care (see below).

Employer's Guide to Child Care – covers the same areas as above from an employer's perspective (see below).

Both available from The Working Mother's Association, WMA, 22 Webbs Road, London SW11 6RU. WMA is a registered charity self help organisation providing information about childcare for working parents, employers and other organisations. Through the national network of self help groups it also provides support and advice on a local level to working mothers.

Resources

Association of Accounting Technicians, 154 Clerkenwell Road, London EC1. Tel: 071–837 8600. Information on training in accountancy.

Business and Technician Education Council (BTEC) (Publications), Central House, Upper Woburn Place, London, WC1H OHH. Tel: 071–388 3288. Specific job-related courses in business, leisure, design and other areas.

Careers Research and Advisory Service (CRAC), 2nd floor, Sheraton House, Castle Park, Cambridge CB3 OAX. Tel: 0223 460277. Runs courses entitled 'Managing the Career Break'.

Distance Learning Centre, 90 London Road, London SE1. Tel: 071–928 8989.

Distance Learning Centre, South Bank Polytechnic, Manor House, 58 Clapham Common North Side, London SW4 9R2. Tel: 071–228 2015. Home study tuition for nurses.

The English National Board for Nursing, Midwifery and Health Visiting – Careers and Advisory Centre, 170 Tottenham Court Road, London W1P OHA. Tel: 071–388 3131. Contact them if you want to return to nursing.

The Industrial Society, Pepperell Unit, Robert Hyde House, 48 Bryanston Square, London W1H 7LN. Tel: 071–262 2401. Runs one-day courses aimed at making career choices, returning to work and confidence building.

Maternity Matters, 5 Culverden Road, Balham, London SW12 9LR. Tel: 081–673 1457. Counselling, information and support for pregnant women and new mothers to help them overcome the problems of taking a career break.

Careers for Women, 4th Floor, 2 Valentine Place, London SE1 8QH. Tel: 071–401 2280. Helpful advice centre. Occasional training days, counselling service and postal information service.

National Extension College, 18 Brooklands Avenue, Cambridge CB2 2HN. Tel: 0223 316644. A wide range of correspondence courses.

The Open Business School, PO Box 76, Milton Keynes MK7 6AA. Tel: 0908 653772. Part of the Open University. Runs home-tuition courses in various business subjects.

The Open College, Freepost, PO Box 35, Abingdon OX14 3BR. Tel: 0235 555 444. A new venture which runs like the Open University but offers less academic courses. Geared to practical subjects and careers.

The Open University, Watton Hall, Milton Keynes, MK7 6AA. Tel: 0908 274066.

The Training Agency (formerly Manpower Services Commission), Moorfoot, Sheffield S1 4PQ. Runs courses for women returners within the employment training programme. Contact local training offices for details.

The Women's Computer Centre, Wesley House, 4 Wild Court, London WC2B 5AU. Tel: 071–430 0112. Short courses for total beginners.

Women Returners Network, Hatfield Polytechnic, PO Box 109, College Lane, Hatfield, Herts AL10 9AB. Tel: 07072 79490. Provides a network of advisors aiming to promote education and training for women. Contact them for a full list of regional networks.

5 Retirement

Introduction

Helping employees to prepare for retirement from paid employment must be one of the most topical challenges personnel managers currently face. People are retiring from their jobs at a rate of over ten thousand a week. A small but growing proportion of these represent early retirements, a trend which is accentuating the overall growth in retirement expected in an ageing population structure such as in the UK. By 1995 the Henley Centre for Forecasting predicts that one in five people will retire at age 50.

The transition out of a paid employment role into a more self-directed lifestyle raises many different thoughts and feelings in those affected. It is believed that people with certain attitudes, for instance acceptance or optimism, towards this major life change do better at adjusting than others. The foundations for a successful older age are laid earlier in life, and reaction to retirement often corresponds to a person's reactions to earlier events and phases in life when major transition was required (eg from school to work, parenthood).

Preparation for retirement is one way of giving an opportunity for taking stock of the situation, and starting a process facilitated by the use of counselling skills, of working through feelings and difficulties that arise. The process should not be seen as a vehicle for getting people to adopt 'appropriate' attitudes, or else pre-retirement preparation might (rightly) be suspected of being a coercive activity in the interest of producing a workforce that 'goes quietly'.

What should managers do?

Making the case for pre-retirement

The manager who wishes to introduce pre-retirement planning into his or her organisation needs first to engage the support of senior colleagues, possibly up to Board level. The company climate may already be right for this sort of development, or alternatively some ground preparation may be necessary. Either way the manager needs to make a good case for the use of company resources for such purposes, and to be clear about aims, objectives and expected outcomes.

The general thrust of such a case, in whatever way it applies to particular companies' circumstances, is that employees who are rendered more confident about their future are likely to fulfil their work roles in a more effective way. Some managers put it more negatively: anxious employees with unexplored worries on their minds might be more likely to have accidents, go sick, give bad customer service etc. Viewed positively, pre-retirement preparation, like any form of training, should give people greater understanding and ability which in turn aids their decision making ability and performance.

Another major justification for company involvement in pre-retirement preparation is that it reflects well on the employer and such provision is increasingly expected as part of a good employee benefits package. With greater personal responsibility for decisions about pensions, related forms of preparation for retirement are also likely to be higher on employees' agendas. The company which is concerned for its community involvement image, as well as its employee care, will wish to see the sort of pre- and post-retirement activities that enhance its local standing (eg pre-retirement secondments or release for voluntary work or educational pursuits).

Finally, on making the case for pre-retirement provision, appeal can be made not only to the experience of companies who do offer it, but also to the support given to the pre-retirement movement by key agencies in the employment and education fields. The Pre-Retirement Association (PRA), for instance, has as one of its main objectives to convince opinion leaders of the value of retirement preparation. In addition to the 400 or so corporate members of the Association (consisting of employers, unions, institutions and other organisations) support for pre-retirement preparation has also been given by such bodies as the CBI, TUC and the Institute of Training and Development.

What do managers feel about dealing with pre-retirement preparation?

Managers as individuals may resist the idea that pre-retirement preparation is a worthwhile activity for an employer, because of ambivalent feelings about their own long-term future.

Alternatively, personal contact or experience may have alerted them to the value of preparation. They are then able to convince their colleagues, and enlist co-operation. It has even been known for the imminent retirement of a company board member to prove the vital trigger.

Much also depends on the organisation's climate and commitment to its 'human resources'. If the atmosphere is secure (in the sense that people know where they stand), challenging and supportive, and communication is good, there will be less anxiety about the task of introducing retirement preparation. If the situation is less promising, responsibility for pre-retirement provision can be perceived as being the 'short straw' that nobody wants, or even as the task that heralds one's own departure. Once integrated within a successful personnel training or employee benefit policy, however, pre-retirement provision can bring a great sense of achievement to its proponents, whether they be at a relatively junior or senior level.

Managers who are convinced of the value of pre-retirement preparation talk about employees' greater sense of confidence about the future, of their being able to make informed choices, and being less likely to feel resentful or worried. The sometimes-voiced managerial fears that encouraging thought about retirement will create anxieties in people, or make them lose interest in work, are unfounded.

Other attitudinal difficulties some managers may have are to do with their views about older workers. They may feel that no-one over 40 can change or learn. Or they may be concerned that older employees will not take kindly to a younger person taking an organising role in an activity that can be highly personal. They must be assured that older people can and do learn new information, skills and attitudes with the right atmosphere of encouragement and motivation.

In relating personally to older workers who are potential retirees, acceptability can be gained by giving time, attention and respect. A paternalistic attitude which encourages dependence is probably not helpful, but listening, empathising, helping people to find their own solutions, and knowing when particular difficulties require special help are the keys to a successful relationship. If there are more serious difficulties with manager's attitudes, which perhaps border on an 'ageist' approach to older people in the workplace,

then these should be acknowledged. A more sympathetic individual
will need to be identified to develop the pre-retirement work.

Preparation for running a pre-retirement programme

Managers' feelings about dealing with pre-retirement education can
be more systematically explored by training, which can be done in
a variety of ways. A few tailor-made short courses exist for those
who are either new or experienced in the task of organising pre-
retirement programmes. These are run by the National Pre-
Retirement Association (at its Field Study Centre in Manchester),
and occasionally by some of the locally based pre-retirement
associations (list available from PRA), or the Industrial Society. A
few large companies also have in-house tutor/organiser training for
other staff who have pre-retirement responsibilities.

If a manager is unable to participate in a particular course, he or
she should try to organise their own training experience. This could
consist of finding out about, or sitting in on, other pre-retirement
programmes. A number of different settings should be tried, such
as public and private sector employers, colleges of further education,
community groups etc. Ideas for developing one's own programme,
and what could be achieved, could then be clarified by talking with
others already involved. The National PRA and its local associations
in the field also offer such consultation, or help with relevant contacts.
Reading some of the ever-expanding literature on pre-retirement
education is also a useful initial preparation for the manager who
wishes to sort out what is desirable and possible for his or her
organisation. A basic reading list is available from the National PRA
(address at the end of this chapter).

The organisation of a formal course or programme of events is
the most recognised form of pre-retirement support. Such provision
can be anything from a relatively isolated one-day seminar or a
programme running over a number of years. The buying-in of a
pre-retirement preparation service from one of many agencies can
be a substitute for the firm's own provision.

Organisations who wish to offer preparation for retirement should
first discern the needs of their employees (clients, members etc) and
then gauge what particular contribution it would be best to make.
This can be done in a variety of corporate contexts – training,
counselling, employee benefits, welfare etc.

The most exciting employment-centred retirement education is currently coming from firms who plan a multi-purpose strategy for employees starting ten years prior to expected retirement. This is then seen as part of the company's on-going involvement with an employee's development and loses the label 'retirement preparation', which can make the whole exercise more acceptable to both employers and employees. The sort of topics popularly covered in short courses, regular discussion groups, day workshops etc that make up such a long-term programme can then be dealt with in a more helpful and flexible order. For instance, financial planning and health are areas of interest that benefit from an early presentation, so that real changes can be made by people where necessary. Information about state retirement benefits or requirements (eg taxation) can be provided nearer the time for leaving.

With regard to methods used within retirement preparation, as distinct from its content, a variety of approaches is now seen as desirable. Various research projects have criticised contemporary course methodology as being of a largely out-dated and authoritarian lecture style, overloaded with information. One of the reactions to this was to recommend almost exclusively 'interactive' methods for all situations (retrenchment was another). Development since the mid-1980s has led to an evaluation of many different styles of working with older adults, especially the different methods that can be used in a long-term, 'mixed-menu' programme. Lectures can be the most appropriate means to deal with certain retirement education needs, to generate enthusiasm, and to give ideas. On the other hand, sensitive groupwork and counselling can enable people to come to terms with feelings that any amount of additional information will not touch. The key emphasis is on the quality of what is offered. Bad handling of either type of approach (and of course there are many more), or bad planning so that inappropriate methods are used, will not help the participants or the company's image.

The following are some examples of programme planning that have been observed by the PRA over the last five years:

1. Groups of employees meeting regularly over an indefinite period of time, and thereby growing into a 'self-help' activity organising their own programme content.
2. Fixed-term programmes where participation is defined in length but extending over a considerable period of time (say five or ten years).

3. Shorter preparatory events which can be residential or non-residential, can extend full-time for up to a week or part-time over several weeks. These are best where maximum variety and choice of content are offered, even though time is limited.
4. Brief events – the 'short-course' approach to pre-retirement – have come in for criticism, but it is their isolation rather than their brevity which renders them ineffective. A pre-course session and/or post course meeting will extend the usefulness of the limited short course. Best use of such a format is within a long fixed term programme, as one or more of a number of events.

The content of the programme is ideally derived from the participants themselves, who are best placed to judge what they need to know. The tutorial expertise required to elicit and then meet the needs of the group will be high on the manager's list of resources to be obtained. Even with short courses an element of this approach is worth trying for the commitment and interest it generates within the group.

The debate over right content for preparation for retirement has continued since the 1950s. Experience shows that, regardless of whether people's needs are elicited in the way suggested above, or whether a programme is largely pre-planned, there is a consensus about the sort of issues that can be dealt with. The manager will have to decide which combination of these could be most effectively or appropriately tackled by the programme to be planned. Here is a selection of the possibilities:

Time management and new routines
Recreation and leisure
Health, including exercise and diet
Personal relationships
Personal financial resources, including pensions, taxation, investment and money management
Accommodation choice and security
Social and other community services
Educational and personal development
Work, including voluntary activities
Consumer and legal affairs
Ageing and self-image

The retirement process

Today's retirees tend to be younger, healthier and, arguably, in better material circumstances than previous generations. These are very broad generalisations, however, and the individual or family faced with retirement may not fit the 'average' picture, or may indeed feel relatively disadvantaged in relation to their expectations, or to others in retirement. It is nevertheless possible to generalise from research, as follows:

Factors likely to promote satisfactory retirement

Health shows a strong and consistent relationship with adaptation to retirement. Poor health may be a cause of retirement, but is not proven to be an outcome of it.

Income is similarly strongly related to a positive or negative retirement experience, and more directly bound up with the loss of paid work than health.

Positive outlook is important, and contains within it a number of different concepts, eg looking forward to retirement, willingness to retire (or acceptance of it), degree of control over decision to retire, self-confidence about being retired.

Status and occupational and educational differences seem to be less predictive of the type of retirement experience than income and health factors, although they may be related.

Activity is a concept much beloved of pre-retirement educators, and generally believed to be of major importance to a satisfactory retirement. Good health and sufficient money with which to pursue hobbies or interests are probably of greater overall importance.

From this summary, the manager who wishes to engage in providing preparation for retirement can deduce some initial aims. Planning for health and income in retirement are probably top priorities and by their long-term nature need to be considered as early as possible.

Status, occupational and educational backgrounds, whilst being indicative of the general material framework within which retirement takes place, do not require different approaches to pre-retirement preparation. Needless to say, though, the information content of preparation will differ with groups of different material backgrounds.

Social class and gender also have special significance in later life, and ethnicity, though yet to be researched in this context, would add further diversity (see Battersby, 1985).

Positive retirement outlook (as defined above) is something the employer, if not the pre-retirement educator as such, can play a major part in, through its pension and personnel policies.

Peoples' feelings about retirement

Coping with change at any time of life requires a degree of maturity and security that is not necessarily linked to age. Retirees can be encouraged to think back to how they handled times of major change in their lives, in order to give themselves confidence.

For some, the break with a normal or long-term employment-dominated life-style can be a dream, for others a nightmare. An initial 'honeymoon' period may give way to dissatisfaction with the new arrangements; or the trauma and difficulty of the transition may resolve into a new and fulfilling chapter of life. Whilst adjustment is related to a positive attitude, as we have just discussed (and which is indeed preached within most retirement preparation), a realistic outlook is possibly more valuable. This can be described as an approach that faces the imagined gains and losses of retirement, and acknowledges feelings about such changes. This need not be incompatible with generating enthusiasm for the future. Knowing oneself, one's strengths, weaknesses, skills, and the resources at one's disposal is probably the most valuable asset that can be taken into retirement.

Feelings may be largely bound up with the imagined contrast between the employed and non-employed situation, rather than with retirement as a separate idea in itself. For example, everything disliked about the work situation can be perceived as a retirement 'gain'; similarly everything valued and enjoyed about work can be seen as a loss. Feelings about freedom from work (the gains) are often summed up by people as 'independence'. Losses are more varied and complex, but can be summarised as financial, social or psychological (see Parker, 1982).

However, another process of adjustment is also at work in the individual or family thinking about separating from the world of employment. It is the longer-term adaptation known as 'ageing'. This is a dimension of the retirement transition that is rarely explored, perhaps because it seems to offer little of benefit to the immediate task of taking on a new lifestyle. Yet it contains important concerns for some, which present themselves as difficulties around retirement time, or as a refusal to engage in any preparation at all. Others 'go through the motions' of involvement in the preparation programme that is provided, but gain no real benefit.

These more fundamental concerns about onself can be raised within a good pre-retirement programme, but may require the back-up facility of a counselling function. This is another reason why employers should be clear about their aims in offering pre-retirement preparation, to keep within their capabilities.

The role of counselling

Potential retirees are likely to experience a range of reactions. Counselling would be beneficial in helping the individual manage and come to terms with the changes that are involved. The following are examples of areas where individuals may experience problems and where counselling might be successfully applied.

- Some people have difficulties despite pre-retirement preparation because they never quite grasped the issues involved.
- Some have difficulties because they have always coped badly with life changes, and retirement is no exception.
- Some have little personal insight, and do not 'know themselves well enough'; others have suffered but not resolved a mid-life crisis, and this is brought back into focus through retirement.
- Similarly, some find the ageing process difficult because of the increasing mismatch between their 'mental' age (how old they feel inside) and the way they are perceived by others on the basis of their physical age.
- There can be intimations of mortality – a feeling of only limited years left, and the realisation of the gap between youthful aspirations and actual achievements.
- They may have to cope with resentment from a spouse or children at home, either because of a loss of a family income, or because of anticipated encroachment on their previous independence. As one retiring executive's wife protested: 'I married him for better or worse, but not for lunch!'

Many of the factors outlined above can lead to difficulties in setting new life goals in a pre-retirement context, even during a course or other opportunity arranged specifically for this purpose. Again, specific attitudes can include rigidity of thought, fear of failure, feelings of isolation – of being 'left behind' in a modern and changing world. In some cases these uncomfortable feelings actually manifest themselves in psychosomatic illnesses of various kinds.

A few people, even when they have come to a point of knowing that they need help, cannot let go of unhelpful attitudes. 'I want help, but I'll make it as difficult as possible to be helped.'

Other general characteristics of the pre-retirement period relevant to counselling are the 'bereavement' effect of job loss, marriage and sexuality in later life, singleness and loneliness. People who, generally speaking, 'like themselves' do better at taking the further chances offered in these areas of life. It can be argued that it is healthier for people to grow to know themselves better through the 'crisis' of retirement, even if this is a painful process.

Potential problem cases

In terms of preventative strategies, certain warning signs can be observed, which give hints of potential difficulties in retirement. For example, is occupational status of prime importance? Retirement, where in one sense everyone is equal, may lead to feelings of vulnerability. Those leaving uniformed occupations may feel this most acutely.

Workaholics are another group who will have to find a substitute for their current job, or suffer withdrawal symptoms. Obsessive personalities who need routines and rituals will find the disruption and potential void of retired life very threatening. Those who find others' perceptions of them (as ageing) hurtful, will need to find a better way of dealing with such feelings than denial of the ageing process.

Summary

Counselling has an important role to play in the pre-retirement process. It is likely however that the benefits will only be brought into focus if a structure and process exists for the counselling to take place. The pre-retirement course can provide the opportunity for both practical and emotional issues to be addressed and resolved.

References

Battersby D. 'Education in later life, what does it mean?' *Convergence*. Vol 18 1985, pp 75–80

Parker S. *Work and retirement*. London, George Allen and Unwin, 1982

Further Reading

Books

Coleman A (ed Groombridge J). *Preparation for retirement in England and Wales*. Leicester, National Institute of Adult Continuing Education in association with the Pre-Retirement Association, 1982.

Employers and retirement. Incomes Data Services Ltd, London, Study No 350, November 1985.

Knight B. *Psycholotherapy with older adults*. Sage Publications, California 1986.

Lumbard J *et al* (ed Glendenning F). *The PRA manual of the retirement education*. Pre-Retirement Association of Great Britain and Northern Ireland, distributed by Choice Publications, Peterborough, 1986.

Toulson, N. *Preparing staff for retirement*. Gower Publishing Co Ltd, Aldershot, 1987.

Articles

Braithwaite V A *and* Gibson D M. 'Adjustment to retirement: what we know and what we need to know'. *Ageing and Society,* Vol 7, 1987. p1–12.

Wheeler T. 'Retirement planning : how it can protect business efficiency'. *Training Officer,* February 1988. p51.

Resources

Choice Magazine, monthly journal, Choice Publications Ltd, Apex House, Oundle Road, Peterborough PE2 9NP.

Pre-Retirement Association. *PRA Resources Unit News,* Quarterly newsletter, PRA Resources Unit, Dept Educational Studies, University of Surrey, Guildford GU2 5XH.

6 Performance Appraisal

Introduction

Performance appraisal is not a one-way process. It is a task which requires direct communication between two people. This communication may be constructive or damaging, beneficial or meaningless and the way in which it can be accomplished effectively is by means of counselling. Performance appraisal should be an open two-way dialogue, presenting an opportunity for any problems to be discussed, needs and objectives to be agreed and plans to be made to provide both career and personal development.

This chapter does not seek to cover the whole subject of performance appraisal. It will look at some of the major areas which those coming to it for the first time will need to consider, and at the structure within which counselling skills should be used. However, those who are already involved in appraisal should also find the chapter of value in comparing their own practices.

Anyone who directs the activities of others needs to be involved in some form of performance appraisal. They may not call it that but essentially they need mechanisms and the appropriate skills through which they can inform others what is expected of them, support them in the delivery of what is expected and be able to assess how well those expectations have been met. This will apply to a manager, chairperson of a local committee, a school governor, a private hotelier, even a parent. There are different levels of performance appraisal ranging from the very informal, such as parent to child, to the extremely formal, the latter depending on strictly laid down procedures.

Attitudes towards performance appraisal

The skills required in achieving effective performance appraisal extend beyond simply having a good system. As explained above, appraisal is carried out face to face. In the work setting this may often only be in the formal performance appraisal interview.

Knowing how to inform a person about their ability (or lack of it) to carry out particular tasks is a sensitive exercise which can either motivate or alienate the employee and will be dependent on good communication or counselling skills.

Managers often feel the need to collude with the employee by suggesting that the performance appraisal is an inconvenient process which just has to be done. Alternatively the manager may see it as the opportunity to use a company system to unleash all the frustrations and faults he or she has had to 'put up with' for the last year. Other managers may view the purposes and processes of appraisal as bothersome, difficult and time consuming. In these instances the appraisal is unlikely to succeed.

On the other hand the appraisal can be seen as something positive and dynamic, something from which both the manager and employees can benefit and grow. The manager's attitude, the extent to which sufficient plans and preparations for appraisal are made, are the keys to success in this area. The manager's attitude will either encourage or discourage the employee's confidence and involvement in the appraisal process. It is an important factor that the manager should consider and even discuss before beginning the task.

A manager in the role of appraiser may be experiencing a range of uncertainties, such as the following:

– Who am I to question the competence of others?
– We've tried this before and it didn't work then so why bother now?
– I know what others are up to. I don't need any bureaucratic systems to find that out. Why waste my time?

Negative attitudes towards performance appraisal will influence the tone and style of the interaction between appraiser and appraisee. It is therefore important to explain these aspects before commencing.

Employees on the other hand may ask:

– My manager never knows what I do. How can he or she comment on my performance?
– I know we're doing a good job. We never get any complaints.
– It's like being watched all the time.

Be aware of occasions when negative reactions are not really a means to block the scheme but rather are a plea for help. People, at all levels, may genuinely be feeling threatened by the scheme or worried about their competence.

The effective manager will attempt to recognise the range of feelings aroused by performance appraisal and create a climate in which these can be talked about and worked through wherever possible. There will be a need to demonstrate genuine acceptance of others by being prepared to listen, to paraphrase, to reflect feelings, and as appropriate to explain the reasoning behind the appraisal scheme. The appraisal process may lead to employees expressing strong emotions or revealing aspects of their personal life previously hidden. These should be dealt with sensitively and when appropriate left to be explored another time.

Benefits of performance appraisal

A well run performance appraisal scheme can have potential benefits for:

Staff
Managers
The organisation as a whole
Products/services
Customer relations.

What can effective performance appraisal do for staff?

Performance appraisal is about effective communication. It affords staff the opportunity to have planned time out with their manager to review performance together. It is legitimate time-out – not something that people should feel guilty about taking.

As a result, it enables staff to:
– have a clear understanding of the goals and standards that are expected of them
– know how they are valued in the organisation
– increase their confidence and awareness
– explain their needs and acknowledge any weaknesses in a positive context
– emphasise their own achievements
– generate their own solutions to problems and accept

responsibility for their own development
- contribute to operational processes – eg establishing policies, objectives, products ideas, procedures and so on.

What will a performance appraisal system do for the managers?

Many managers have found that well run performance review schemes have enabled them to:
- gain important insights into the work being done and those doing it
- improve the ability to plan, control and monitor work
- achieve greater openness in discussion with staff, thereby fostering good staff relations and morale
- develop a positive working climate in which effective staff communications and staff development is evident
- assess training needs
- operate on tangible performance rather than being judgemental about the individual's character
- introduce regular, purposeful appraisal sessions rather than rely on casual chats and annual 'mop-up' sessions.

What can performance appraisal do for the organisation?

If management and staff are benefiting as above, and provided they are working to clear policies and objectives agreed by senior management, then the organisation is likely to have:
- a staff whose abilities, talents, expertise are more effectively harnessed
- a staff who understand and work to clearly defined policies, aims and objectives
- a staff more able, and possibly willing, to manage change
- a more motivated workforce who may be less likely to need to resort to absenteeism or industrial action.

What can performance appraisal do for products or services?

It follows from this that an organisation which seeks to identify the strengths of its workforce and build on these is in a healthy position to analyse problems, to review the quality and range of its services and products and to seek and develop new ideas.

How can performance appraisal benefit customers/clients?

An organisation which builds into its performance appraisal scheme the facility for gauging customer reaction is likely to benefit its customers in that:
- some will have had the satisfaction of knowing that they have been able to comment on if not influence the organisation and its products and services
- the organisation is more likely to be in tune with changes and developments in consumer demand, so that consumers get what they want.

Many people view performance appraisal in the narrow sense of discussing only the individual activities of staff. However, staff belong to an organisation which is there to meet the needs and wants of a particular client group. It has been shown here that performance appraisal can encompass a wider perspective.

Objectives of an appraisal scheme

In introducing a scheme an organisation needs to define clearly its purpose. It can be helpful first to determine whether the need for a scheme is based on the desire to:

- improve the output of the organisation
- meet the needs of the organisation
- develop staff

From there these generalised aims can be converted into more specific objectives:

- to identify training needs
- to consider promotion/salary increase potential
- to monitor the achievement of policies and objectives
- to inform senior management on staff strengths, weaknesses, customer reaction etc
- to encourage staff development
- to let staff know how valued they are, where they stand in the organisation, to improve staff morale, communications etc
- to improve approaches to planning
- to identify underlying problems to staff development and abilities.

Closer examination of a manager's list may show that there is a danger of asking too much of the scheme. For some activities a separate but complementary mechanism may need to be established. For example, given that the object of performance appraisal is to provide a constructive vehicle for reviewing past performance and for planning ahead, the essence of this can be at odds with the style of discussion needed to tell a member of staff that they are not in line for promotion or a pay rise. Additionally, an activity like assessing training needs should not be made purely from performance appraisal.

The belief by some that appraisal is only an annual formal event needs to be shed. Appraisal is a continuous day-by-day week-by-week process, appropriate to the circumstances people work in. It is about constantly comparing results with expectations, assessing strengths and limitations, giving support and guidance, eg on completion of a project, or making interim review of a new procedure, or supporting a new member of staff, or member of staff undertaking something new. Regular appraisal provides opportunities to give and receive timely praise for achievement when it is appropriate or to take immediate action for unsatisfactory performance when it happens.

However, appraisal schemes should also provide a formal opportunity at least once a year to look back over achievements, or the lack of them, and to learn from that, with the aim of planning for the year ahead. The plans can be in respect of both personal and organisational goals.

Regular appraisal opportunities can be used as a basis for selecting key items for discussion at the annual formal appraisal meeting.

Whether the focus is on the annual formal appraisal discussion or the regular appraisal opportunities throughout the year, the process will be the same and consist, in simple terms, of the following cycle. (See Figure 6)

Figure 6
Appraisal process

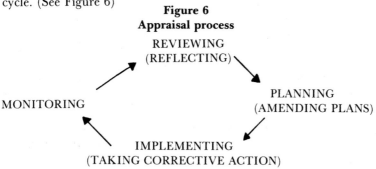

Structures and frameworks

If what is expected of the person or activity being appraised is not clearly stated in measurable terms then evaluation (ie knowing when it has been achieved and how well) will be difficult. The appraisal process starts when the parties involved (eg manager and member of staff) agree on what has to be accomplished. Various resources should be available to help with this, eg statements of company policy, objectives, job descriptions, although these are likely to be called different things in different organisations.

Whatever the terminology, there needs to be clear agreement on the following:

- the TITLE of the job – including any reference to grade, section position
- its PURPOSE – what is the job there for?
- the MAIN DUTIES – these cover the main areas for which the job holder is responsible and should indicate the relative importance of one against another, and any responsibility held
- the OBJECTIVE – these should stipulate, in 'do-able' terms what is expected of the job holder. They should be clear, concise, achievable and measurable. They should not be so easy that they provide no challenge at all: aim at stretching and developing the job holder as well as the job. The objectives can either be JOB RELATED, ie operational, or STAFF RELATED, ie personal/developmental, or both
- the RESOURCES – this clarifies any resources (eg staff, budget) for which the job holder is responsible and would indicate any responsibilities for cost efficient and effective use of resources.

This agreement provides a framework for planning and against which to monitor and review. Staff should not be presented with the framework already completed but should be involved in the process of deciding its content. Planning is about providing a pathway, not a mystery tour.

Setting objectives and criteria by which performance can subsequently be evaluated is often perceived as one of the most difficult tasks facing managers and staff.

In this chapter OBJECTIVE is the term used to describe the results which are to be achieved, eg:

– to prepare a feasibility study on the 'X' project
– to increase turnover in 'X' department, by 'Y' amount, by 'Z' date
– to introduce mechanisms for assessing consumer reaction to 'X'.

In these examples, it will be easy to judge performance because something tangible needs to be achieved. The manager and employee will both know when it has happened.

However, in many aspects of performance appraisal, evaluation will not be so straightforward, eg in measuring the effectiveness of customer relations by staff, or the quality of presentations by trainers. There are occasions, therefore, when the criteria used will need to be more subjective, and rely on an element of personal judgement. If such appraisals are likely, it is important to involve staff at the outset in deciding the criteria by which they will be judged. This will require the manager to set STANDARDS, eg:

'Errors in overbooking guests will not exceed 3 per cent of the total monthly reservations.'

'Visitors to reception should have their presence acknowledged immediately. Courtesies and standards of service are to be those defined in the staff manual.'

Making judgements on the effectiveness of staff in areas where the quality of work is assessed can be difficult. For example, how do you appraise the effectiveness of journalists, counsellors, teachers and the like? In most cases established objective criteria like the following are useful:

– number of reports to be written
– number of cases to be dealt with
– percentage of pupils achieving a certain pass mark in exams.

However, what is most easily measured may not be the most important aspect of the job. What about the quality of reports, the helpfulness of the counsellor? How are these to be measured? What of the pupils who did not pass their exams? Are we to conclude that it was because of the teacher alone? Sometimes, disentangling all the forces at play is impossible. In these cases all one can do is attempt to answer the question 'How will we know that this person

has performed efficiently and effectively?' and agree on whatever
criteria are chosen.

The formal appraisal discussion

We have already seen that appraisal should not be an isolated annual
event. Throughout the year various processes are at play and both
the appraiser and the appraisee need to be involved in these.
However, in order that the annual appraisal discussion can be as
constructive as possible, both parties can undertake certain activities
throughout the year.

Monitoring progress

Having agreed the objectives and the criteria by which the successful
meeting of these objectives is to be assessed, the appraiser needs to
monitor the position regularly, noticing and, where appropriate,
recording, events and behaviours which need to be and can be
meaningfully discussed. Those being appraised should be
encouraged to keep their own notes too, for reference. The notes of
both appraisee or appraiser might include:

- how particular projects were completed, and over what period
- the abilities required of the job and the extent to which they
  have been demonstrated
- tasks which went particularly well/not so well as might have
  been wished
- the effectiveness of training that has been provided
- factors which have prevented you/others from performing as
  well as you or others would have wished, eg ill-health, resource
  problems, shift of policy or deadlines, lack of direction, lack of
  training etc
- what is most/least liked about the job
- what would better enhance use of personal skills and talents
  more effectively.

Of course, neither appraiser nor appraisee should take notes simply
for the sake of it or to store information with which to get at each
other. If behaviours and events are causing undue problems or are
particularly praiseworthy they should be discussed immediately.

Preparing for the discussion

Taking notes throughout the year will enable both parties to engage in meaningful dialogue during the appraisal discussion. However, if time during the discussions is to be used to best effect there is a need for considerable additional planning by both.

The appraiser will need to plan by:

- putting time in the diary to prepare for the review discussion, conduct it, and follow it up
- arranging a date and agenda with the appraisee, giving at least three days notice for preparation
  agreeing and clarifying, at the planning stage, the activities to be assessed
- agreeing and clarifying the assessment criteria
- ensuring a place for the discussion is available, free from interruptions, and conducive to good communication
- having collated sufficient data on the activities being assessed and any job descriptions, plans and targets
- having sufficient data to support the points to be made. This means that for some activities staff will have had to be observed doing their job
- having data to hand – it devalues the process if there is a lack of preparation
- anticipating the likely reaction to the points to be raised
- identifying positive ideas and suggestions for improvement.

The appraisee can also prepare for the discussion by:

- using the notes they have taken throughout the year to identify those points they wish to raise and those which the appraiser is likely to raise
- having to hand any supporting 'evidence' they feel will add to the discussion.

Stages of appraisal discussion

Some people become very anxious about their formal appraisal discussion. This is less likely to be so where management has practised performance appraisal as a continuous process throughout the year. The structure of the discussion is usually in the hand of the appraiser but the appraisee can add to this and certainly, if the discussion is poorly led, suggest that it be restructured.

Whoever takes the lead, the interview will usually proceed through a number of stages:

The opening stage will include:

- an explanation of the purpose of the interview
- an explanation of the stages of the interview
- confirmation that it is a two-way dialogue with both parties being equally involved
- a sharing of expectation of the discussion and identification of the benefits to be derived from the process
- agreeing areas for discussion including, if appropriate, a summary of points raised at previous appraisal discussions.

The main part of the discussion will, in an appropriate order, focus on:

- review of previous year's performance, achievements (job descriptions, plans etc should be to hand)
- strengths/weaknesses
- difficulties/problems encountered
- opportunities used/to be built upon
- an agreed action plan for the future
- in some organisations, discussion of promotion potential/ training or transfer needs.

The conclusion will:

- summarise the discussion
- summarise action agreed upon by both, and other parties
- identify follow-up action.

The nature of the discussion

Given the anxiety that the appraisee may bring to the discussion, it is for the appraiser to create a climate which will encourage meaningful dialogue. In this role the appraiser will need to demonstrate effective listening skills, seeking clarification where necessary. Preparation should ensure that actual events and behaviours can be described and not left to generalities: for example, instead of saying 'That was a really good report you handed in', describe in what way the report was good, and how it benefited you/others.

Sometimes, in the desire to be supportive, appraisers may become dictatorial, and in the discussion of a problem may be tempted to say, 'Here's what you ought to do from now on' rather than, 'How do you think you might manage that in the future?' By all means offer help where appropriate but never forget the importance of allowing the appraisee to generate their own solutions, to accept responsibility for their own learning and development.

The appraiser may of course get some criticism from the appraisee. Rather than becoming defensive or taking the criticism personally, the appraiser should summarise what was said, and ask for examples, for instance promises that have not been fulfilled, and for clarification of any sweeping statements.

The appraiser should not listen passively whilst the appraisee pours out all that is good and bad in their life. There needs to be an evaluation of what is being said in terms of relevance to job performance, rather than its personal impact. The appraiser may also have to prompt the appraisee to keep to the point. Appraisees may be retiring, shy, reluctant to talk for some reason, and the appraiser will therefore need to develop skills in sensitive and attentive questioning.

In organisations where open communication is practised, both managers and subordinates will be used to discussing both strengths and limitations. The culture is likely to be one where weaknesses are something to be discussed and overcome. The appraisee will more often than not freely raise any 'negative' aspects.

However, there may be occasions when the appraisee does not raise the sensitive issue of performance which falls below standard. In this case the appraiser must do so by describing in non-emotive terms where the shortfall has occurred and by referring, where appropriate, to:

- previously agreed plans
- company standards for quantity and quality
- error rates compared to the organisational average
- time delays in meeting targets.

A corrective action plan should then be agreed. To fail to do so means that not only will the problem remain, but that others may see that they too can 'get-away-with-it', with the result that problems will be exacerbated.

If the problem remains because of apparent lack of co-operation by the appraisee, then disciplinary measures should be considered. These should always be dealt with separately from the appraisal process. (See chapter 14)

The appraisal discussion over, there may be the temptation for both parties to sigh with relief. But that is not the end of the appraisal. To be meaningful there needs to be a record of what was discussed, including a summary of the previous year's appraisal. Both parties should retain a copy. This should show the action both have agreed to undertake and by when.

Both parties should also engage in some reflection, either privately or, if the climate allows, together, on performance at the appraisal discussion. They could for example consider:

- what went well/not so well
- what either might do differently next time
- what was learned about self/each other.

Finally, and perhaps most crucially, it is essential to put into action anything that has been agreed to – either as appraiser or appraisee. To fail to do so completely undermines the whole appraisal process and stops the appraisal cycle. Having implemented, monitored and reviewed, it is now important to build on this and plan for the future.

Further reading

Anstey E, Fletcher C and Walker J. *Staff appraisal and development.* London, Allen and Unwin, 1976. 242pp.

Beveridge WE, *The interview in staff appraisal.* London, George Allen and Unwin, 1975. 132pp.

Fletcher CA and Williams R. *Performance appraisal and career development.* London, Hutchinson, 1985 (v). 166pp.

Lefton RE, *Effective motivation through performance appraisal: dimensional appraisal strategies.* New York, John Wiley, 1977, x. 348pp.

Long P. *Performance appraisal revisited, third IPM survey.* London, Institute of Personnel Management, 1986, xiii. 198pp.

Maier NRF. *The appraisal interview: three basic approaches.* (Rev ed). La Jolla, Calif, University Associates, 1979, xi 228pp.

Philp T. *Making performance appraisal work.* London, McGraw-Hill, 1983, xiii. 114pp.

Randall G, Packard P, and Slater J. *Staff appraisal: a first step to effective leadership.* London, IPM, 1984.

Stewart V and Stewart AM. *Practical performance appraisal: designing, installing and maintaining performance appraisal systems.* Aldershot, Hants, Gower Press, 1977. 182pp.

7 Psychological Testing

Introduction

Psychometric tests are used widely at work in order to ascertain different kinds of information about a person, ranging from their ability to put square pegs in square holes to sophisticated personality profile tests. Whatever their use, it is likely that each test is supported by technical data concerning validity, reliability, norm groups and so on. All these aspects are important and should be carefully considered before using a specific test, together with an assessment of the relevance of the test to the purpose it is being put to. Of equal importance is an area which is rarely examined: the need to attend to the person's anxieties and feelings about completing a test, and the subsequent feedback of results.

The use of counselling skills should play an important role from the moment a person is asked to take a psychological test to when the results are given back.

What are psychological tests?

The psychological test is one of a number of ways of acquiring information about a person. Typically other sources of information in an occupational context will include interviews, performance appraisals, references, application forms and CVs. Tests are believed however to provide 'an objective and standardised measure of a sample of behaviour'. The underlying assumption of all tests is that the way the person behaves or responds during a test is a likely reflection of the person's normal reactions and abilities.

How are psychological tests used?

The common usage for psychological tests is in the selection process including the selection decision, placement within the organisation, redeployment and promotions. Tests can also help in the identification and evaluation of training needs and objectives. Psychological tests are also widely used in career counselling in order to help people make informed decisions on the basis of increased insight and self-evaluation. (see Chapter 3 on Career Counselling).

The person's interests, values, aptitudes, abilities and behaviour can be assessed through the selective use of tests. On occasions such an assessment may be positive, that is they require within-the-person comparison. For instance, someone may be more interested in selling than in artistic pursuits, irrespective of anybody else. At other times assessments may be normative, when comparisons are made between people. The group of people against which the comparison is made is known as the normative group, for instance a group comprising people with similar characteristics, occupational group, sex, age. The specific aspects that tests are designed to examine are considered here briefly in order to illustrate the extent and depth of the test as it applies to its occupational purpose, eg selection.

Interests and values

This test produces a profile of the person's interests and values and provides useful information for a number of areas, especially career choice and development.

Aptitudes

An aptitude test is an assessment of the person's ability either (a) to develop a particular skill, eg a test of manual dexterity; or (b) to acquire knowledge or follow and use logical argument, eg reasoning ability (often referred to as intelligence testing).

Achievement

This type of test assesses how well the person is actually performing in a job. The test may be used to measure the effects of a specific training course or alternatively the person's level of readiness to undertake specific types of training.

Personality

A number of personality theories exist, and each has its own constructs. Anastasi (1982) writes that 'in conventional psychometric terminology 'personality tests' are instruments for the measurement of emotional, motivational, interpersonal and attitudinal characteristics, as distinguished from abilities'.

A great number of psychological tests exist to measure the above areas in respect to specific purposes such as career counselling. New tests are constantly being developed and care must be taken to ensure that the right test is used in the right circumstances for the right reason. Additional details are given at the end of this chapter on where information concerning tests can be found.

Introducing and running the test sessions

Poor test administration can lead to feelings of anxiety and a misunderstanding of what is required, resulting in the objective assessment of the test being distorted. Most commercial tests have a clear set of pre-written instructions that should be used. This is to ensure consistency in administration and conditions between candidates and test sessions.

Every test administration should include:

- advance notification of the need to take a test
- the purpose of the test
- the test procedure
- an opportunity to practice and complete examples
- a quiet atmosphere free of interruptions
- an opportunity to ask questions and clarify points
- a statement of time limits and/or expected time of test completion (for untimed tests).

In addition to these practical aspects of test administration the attitude and behaviour of the test administrator will affect the attitude and motivation of the person being tested. People will often have fixed attitudes concerning tests. Consequently, the mechanical aspects of test administration should be supplemented by further information and an acknowledgment of the probable anxiety and attitudes that exist. The test administrator may also be the first contact the candidate has with the organisation, and so it is important that a professional image is projected.

Thoughts and feelings before completing a psychological test

The very word 'test' is enough for some people to begin to feel anxious. Whilst every effort is taken to reduce test nerves, and most skilled test interpreters are aware that candidates who are especially nervous during tests may be very competent in a job situation, individual anxieties are often more broadly based than the test itself. Acknowledgement of these feelings, open information concerning the purpose of the test, clear communication and the encouragement of questions all help to ensure a positive approach to test completion by the individual.

Some of the more common fears and anxieties that should be addressed either before or during test administration include the following:

1 *Why am I taking the test?*
   People often feel that their experience, qualifications and track record are adequate information for a company to make a decision and consequently feel that a test is insulting and unnecessary. Senior executives, for instance, have been known to refuse to take personality tests or have only completed them grudgingly.

2 *What will happen to the information?*
   This is a common question which requires a clear and consistent answer by the test administrator, manager and personnel department. If the information is recorded and stored on a computer then under the Data Protection Act there are legal obligations to comply with. If the results are to go on to a personnel file or destroyed then this should also be explained.

3 *Will I get feedback?*
   Wherever possible and practical there is an ethical obligation to give people information concerning their test results and to discuss this with them. This can be done by providing a telephone 'hot-line' for candidates to follow up if they want to do so. If it is intended to give feedback then people should be told before taking the test, as this will result in a more motivated and accurate test completion.

4   *Who else will know about the test results?*
    This is often important to people, particularly where tests are
    administered for internal candidates. The potential circulation
    of results should be made known, the reasons for any circulation
    and when this will take place.

5   *When will the test results be known?*
    A straightforward question which should have a straightforward
    answer. If feedback is available people are often anxious between
    completing a test and gaining the results. It is beneficial to all
    parties to attempt to complete the exercise quickly.

6   *How does the test fit in with the total procedure?* (ie selection,
    promotion etc)
    Tests are often only one small part of the total process, an aspect
    which should be highlighted and reinforced. Where people see
    the test as the only criterion in the process they are more likely
    to feel that the process is unfair believing that it ignores other
    qualities. For some people the pressure to succeed will result in
    excess nervousness and poor, distorted results.
       Clearly in some situations tests will be used to screen applicants
    to find those most suited to the work or job being considered.
    Where this is necessary the reasons for their use should be
    explained, eg a test of manual dexterity or numeracy to a pre-
    specified level of ability, linked to the minimum requirements of
    the job, enables suitable applicants to be selected on the basis
    of aptitude or ability

7   *Does everything depend on the tests?*
    The underlying question to this is, 'Do I pass or fail?' The concept
    of pass or fail is implicitly associated with tests but should not
    be promoted in the work context. Where a person does not fit
    the requisite personality profile or reach the necessary skill level
    this should be explained to the person in terms of the specific
    job only. The person may be very capable in another area of
    work and should not be left feeling that they are a failure.
       People should be told the relevance of the test, the reason for
    doing it and how it affects the overall process the person is
    involved in eg. selection, redeployment, counselling.

The feedback of results

If care has been taken to alleviate the candidate's anxieties, and to answer questions and present a professional image, the groundwork will have been prepared for a constructive feedback session. The person giving the feedback should be thoroughly prepared. This means an understanding of the test purpose and the meaning of the results.

The task of test interpretation can only reliably be done by a trained member of staff. On some occasions the person who interprets the test may not be the person who gives the test results back to the candidate. In those circumstances where feedback will be given as part of a selection interview it is important that the interviewing manager understands the purpose of the test and will use the results positively. Simply paying lip service to the test will denigrate its value in the eyes of the candidate, resulting in resentment from the candidate and damaging the image of the organisation.

The rejection of psychological tests by a manager in, for instance, a selection process may be due to a number of reasons. The manager:

- may be suspicious of the process of testing, its mystical, 'crystal ball gazing' (particularly evident in the case of personality tests)
- may have experienced poor treatment in a test situation in the past
- may not have been involved in the decision to use (and choice of) psychological tests and consequently resent their use
- may not believe in the value or use of tests
- may not understand how the test results should be used in respect to their purpose (a crucial exercise in itself if the tests are to be valid)
- may feel uncomfortable at being required to give feedback, particularly if the test results appear to be unfavourable
- may not have been thoroughly briefed by the test interpreter. This will often be in written form and should be free of jargon. There should be time for clarification of aspects arising from the test results.

Establish rapport

It is essential in all one-to-one situations that the interviewer or counsellor establishes rapport with the other person. If this is not achieved then the remaining contact will lack the necessary involvement, interest and commitment to be constructive.

The person's expectations of the interview, and of its objectives should initially be jointly discussed and also reviewed at the end of the interview to check that there are no loose ends. The level of confidentiality should also be discussed at this stage, ie who will see the results etc.

Encourage involvement

Providing feedback is a two-way process and should not be used as a way of demonstrating power over another person. Tests are occasionally used in this way to elevate the position of the manager or counsellor and thereby perpetuate any mystique attached to the tests. Feedback should avoid the use of jargon.

The person receiving feedback should be encouraged to participate and discuss or question any aspects of the information they may wish to. This is particularly important in personality tests where the information arising from the test may lead to new self awareness.

Involving the person also leads them to accept responsibility for what they are hearing and presents an opportunity to elaborate or clarify areas. The final outcome is the product of their contribution to the exercise and not an abstract theoretical concept.

Explore feelings

As well as the factual aspects of any test feedback, the person should be encouraged to express and explore their feelings about taking the test and about subsequent feedback. Exploration will further enhance the quality of the interview and help both parties to gain a more accurate perspective of the person's needs, values and expectations.

Empathy

It is easy to use test results as a way of judging an individual. This should not occur. Developing empathy in the interview shows the person that there is understanding and an opportunity to respond.

Confront where appropriate

In order for the feedback to be constructive for both people it will be necessary to confront the person with some aspects of the test information. If a personality test indicates that the person is very anxious but they appear to be calm there clearly is a conflict in the information available, and this needs to be clarified with the person. Anxiety may occur in specific situations and be well controlled or well hidden, but it may nonetheless be an aspect which is crucial to the job or person's future goals. For instance, low as opposed to high anxiety may be a feature needed for air traffic controllers.

Avoiding feedback on what may appear to be 'negative' aspects of a test is of no benefit to anyone. Though it may be due to not wanting to hurt the other person, it is more likely to be due to a lack of confidence on the part of the interviewer. Confidence is needed to address the area and cope with the reactions.

Objectivity

It is important to maintain objectivity, not to project one's own values and attitudes. The manager needs to be aware of his or her own value system and avoid using this as a criterion to assess the other person.

A personal viewpoint of psychological testing

John had been asked to take a personality profile test as a way of helping to identify his career development within a local authority. The test was administered, interpreted and feedback given within a week, and was carried out by occupational psychologists from a professional consultancy. John's account typifies the range of emotions that are associated with psychological testing and illustrates why care and attention needs to be given to every stage of the testing process and why the use of counselling skills is important.

Reactions before the test

When I was first asked to take the personality test my immediate reaction was not to participate, because, I suspect, it seemed to be a self indulgent exercise that was going to tell me things I didn't really want to know. However my curiosity got the better of me and I ignored the 'voyeuristic' features of the testing – that someone else was going to be privy to this intensely personal information.

It suddenly seemed exciting to be able to discover or confront certain aspects of myself – maybe it would help me change. I then became very idealistic about the whole thing: it was 'a good thing'; 'a useful tool'; 'helpful to confront weak points'. I now saw the risk of self exposure as an exciting challenge.

After feedback

I felt horrible! Completely exposed, revealed for what I really am, 'undressed', vulnerable and insecure. I was very surprised at some of the results and felt slightly angry that this paper test could affect me in this way. I decided that maybe the results weren't accurate – where was the objective evidence as to their effectiveness and usefulness?

I felt I had to justify why I was as this piece of paper said I was, and was torn between feeling 'it must be right' and 'I don't believe in psychological testing anyway, so why worry'. The oddest feature was the fact that I felt my manager had used this measure to 'get to know me', and was this fair? It even made me have a cigarette, having given up smoking!

Six months later

I feel fine about it now. I haven't looked at the results in that time – in fact I've forgotten most of them. I feel 'dressed' again and the feelings of vulnerability and insecurity have gone. In fact, the experience was interesting and possibly useful in that I had to confront a few characteristics I had, which I felt could be changed and generally worked on. Self assessment presumably can assist in self-development which hopefully will be useful in all contexts, work and home and social.

Summary

Giving test feedback may appear to be a straightforward and mechanical process which can be achieved quickly and without complications. There are, however, a considerable number of aspects which need to be taken into account for the use of tests to be valid and beneficial. The manager should, for instance, check that the tests selected by the company are not contrary to the spirit as well as the letter of the Sex Discrimination Act 1975 and Race Relations Act 1976, nor contain any bias towards people who are disabled. Finally, the person's feelings, needs and expectations surrounding the psychological tests can only be successfully met by effective use of counselling skills in face-to-face contact.

Further reading

Books

Anastasi Anne. *Psychological testing.* (5th ed). New York, Macmillan, 1982, xiii. 784pp.

Cronbach Lee Joseph. *Essentials of psychological testing* (4th ed). New York, Harper and Row, 1984, xx. 630pp.

Holdsworth RF. *Personnel selection testing: a guide for managers.* London, British Institute of Management, 1972. 54pp.

Incomes Data Services Limited. *Psychological assessment.* London, IDS, 1985. 36pp (Study 341).

Pearn Michael A. *The fair use of selection tests.* Windsor, Berks, NFER Publishing, nd. 11pp.

Toplis John, Dulevicz Vic *and* Fletcher Clive. *Psychological testing: a practical guide for employers.* London, Institute of Personnel Management, 1987, x. 131pp.

Article

Fletcher C. 'Should the test score be kept secret?'(Job applicants who have been asked to undergo psychological assessment are entitled to have access to the results). *Personnel Management.* Vol 18, No 4, April 1986. pp44–46.

Resources

Independent Assessment and Research Centre, 17 Portland Place, London W1N 3AF. Tel: 071–935 2373.

NFER-Nelson, Darville House, 2 Oxford Road East, Windsor, Berkshire SL4 1DF. Tel: Windsor (0753) 858961.

Roffey Park Management College, Roffey Park Institute Ltd, Horsham, West Sussex RH12 4TD. Tel: 0293 851644.

Saville and Holdsworth Ltd, 3A. C. Court, High Street, Thames Ditton, Surrey KT7 OSR. Tel: 081–398 4170.

8   Relocation

Introduction

The prospect of moving home, even when the decision is one's own can result in a range of varying emotions. Feelings of excitement at the prospect of something new, apprehension at leaving behind the security of the old and trepidation at the potential turmoil that lies ahead. The decision to move is often based on an improved level of income, the need for a bigger home and the desire to improve one's standard of living. It is a decision to which is usually given considerable thought and planning, particularly since it frequently affects more than the person or family actually making the move. It is one of the universally recognised stress events that each of us enters into several times in our lives. For many people the pattern of what has taken place in previous moves will influence their emotional expectations and reactions to future moves.

Changing one's residence may involve leaving one's roots, family and friends, readjustment to a new culture (in the case of overseas appointments) and settling into a new environment. Very few people are able to cope with all the significant changes that take place. Indeed settling into a new area and home can take up to two or three years. Some people never completely settle, especially when they believe that another move may be required in the future.

The need to move home is most frequently associated with the demands of employment, and those most often affected are the managerial and professional grades. In addition, certain categories of people are required to accept moving as part of the terms and conditions of their job, eg certain kinds of engineers and salesmen. Responses to moving home will differ by degree rather than type. It is for this reason that it is important to consider counselling in respect to moving home as a broad concept and not to confine it to specific employment groups, eg managerial and professional.

The reason for moving home may therefore be due to any one of the following reasons:

1   as part of career progression
2   as part of the contract of employment
3   as a result of company relocation
4   in order to find employment (from an unemployed position)
5   moving house under 'normal' circumstances (self motivated).

Where the move is as a result of 1,2, or 3 practical help and support may be offered from the employer. This can include using a professional relocation company, providing temporary accommodation, offering financial relocation packages and financial compensation for any extra distance travelled or added difficulty experienced in the journey. These measures are designed to help with some of the financial and practical aspects of house moving but may do little to alleviate the emotional consequences for the employee and his or her family. These emotional consequences are rarely incorporated into the relocation plans of organisations. This is reinforced by a study of relocation practice conducted by the Institute of Manpower Studies (1987) which drew up a ten point 'prospectus of good practice' for managerial and professional staff. None explicitly dealt with the emotional issues involved in relocation although a number may indirectly alleviate the impact of a move, eg 'Open dialogue with staff in order to identify perceived constraints and disincentives and build up their expectations about mobility'.

   Moving home unavoidably affects everyone associated with it – husband, wife, children, in-laws, parents, work colleagues and so on. The problems are all pervading and insidious. The purpose of the following discussion is to illustrate the extent of and potential for emotional turmoil and the steps that can be taken to alleviate it, which can start from the moment the prospect of moving is introduced.

Announcing the need to move

The way in which the news of an impending move is conveyed to the individual can significantly influence his or her attitude towards the move. Where the move involves a company relocation and redundancies are a likely consequence, the company should ensure, as soon as possible, that it gives a precise time scale, details of relocation packages, and if necessary, redundancy packages. Early warning of the need to move will give the person time to discuss it with the family, consider repercussions and seek more information from the company. Providing such an opportunity will enable the company to respond to problems in good time and involve the person in the decision making process.

Deciding to move

Dual career couples

The last ten years have seen an increasing number of women in employment. This has led to a decline in the traditional family concept of the man determining his family's future by virtue of his career decisions. Now it is increasingly likely that there will be couples where either or both partners may be faced with important career decisions which have family implications.

There may be a reluctance to make job transfers, even with promotion (internal and external), if they involve geographical moves which could disrupt the other partner's career. This reluctance may be heightened if children's education is involved (and other factors discussed later).

Dual careers can increase an employer's relocation problems. It is questionable how tolerant or flexible an employer will be towards employees who refuse geographical moves. Employees who turn down these offers are often left feeling that they may be discriminated against in future promotional opportunities.

Sensitivity is needed, and the initiative is with the employer. Career counselling which incorporates both partners and takes account of both business and domestic aspects is one effective and practical step that can be taken (see chapter 3 for a full discussion of career counselling). Problems of one partner refusing to move may thus be explored openly, and future implications examined constructively.

An employer can also undertake to help the affected partner find suitable career development opportunities in the new geographical area they are asking the employee to move to.

Impact on children

People with children often plan moves around significant periods of children's education. Other practical aspects will include the availability of hospitals, nursery schools, day care facilities and so on. None of this takes into account how the child feels about moving home, but parents are very aware of how their child mixes with others, how readily he or she settles into a new school and makes new friends, and it is factors like these which can significantly influence the final decision to move. Including the child in the decision to move (once children have made friends they should be included) and discussing how he or she feels about it are necessary elements to a successful move. The ability of the parents to talk to their children in this way is one measure of the quality of the communication and relationship between them. A move requires the child to give up his or her roots, friends and familiar environment, all factors which contribute to the child's security, and all these aspects increasingly apply as children grow older. If an overseas move is being considered and the children have a particular interest in sports or music that are not available in the intended country then problems will emerge later.

Decisions to move may lead some parents to consider boarding schools and to question values and attitudes with regard to different forms of education, going for instance from state to private education for their children. Again it is important to introduce this aspect sensitively and give the child an opportunity to see and understand what, for instance, boarding or a change of school entails. There may in some circumstances be associated financial burdens.

The manager should respect the desire of an employee to involve his or her family in the decision making process, even encouraging this action. If the employee's 'home base' is unsettled this will ultimately affect the employee and organisation.

Impact on the person's partner

We have mentioned the difficulties associated with dual career families. Where dual careers do not exist it is still essential to consider the other person's thoughts and feelings about moving home. If the partner is not supportive, for whatever reason, then this will make the task of moving difficult and lead to considerable turmoil for all involved.

It is important to discuss the move fully and to identify and explore the anxieties and feelings of resentment that may exist. These may include a fear of needing to make new friends and of moving further away from family ties and support, or a desire to avoid the upheaval and other problems associated with moving.

Where it is possible to involve the partner in the decision to move, it is vital to do so. Employees who do not have a stable and supportive personal life are more likely to experience problems which affect job performance (see chapter 15). The way in which the news is communicated will be significant. In this respect the manager may need to encourage the employee to discuss it with their partner. An initial step may be to explore with the employee any fears and anxieties that may surround the task of talking to their partner. It is not uncommon for one partner to be excited by the challenge of a new position and location to the extent that they (inadvertently or purposefully) disregard the other partner's thoughts and feelings. Couples can quickly become entrenched and are unable to appreciate either person's perception of the situation. Where this occurs the couple may benefit from a third party, specifically a counsellor, who can facilitate communication between the two people. Where this does not occur and the move goes ahead regardless, the feelings of resentment and anger may begin to undermine the relationship. Feelings like these can also be focused on the employer.

General impact of moving

The prospect of relocating, particularly if overseas, will raise various stresses; tension may arise from unstable family relationships, and from the frustrations inherent in having to adjust to a strange environment and even the need to learn to communicate in a new language. The couple or individual will need help to consider all aspects of relocation. They may have failed to take into account feelings of guilt if they leave behind an ageing, widowed and perhaps ailing parent, or put their children into boarding school.

Some people may refuse to acknowledge that tensions of this kind exist. Reluctance to discuss a particular issue or denial that a problem exists are warning signs that should be investigated further before a final decision is made by the person, couple and employer.

The organisation may also be able to plan career progression moves to fit into the individual's changes in personal life – for instance children changing schools, partner giving up or starting work. Considerable planning is needed to achieve this but the benefits are seen in increased loyalty and commitment, as well as in reduced disruption to work performance.

Problems in selling the home

The constraints

The task of selling the home is one which can take several months. If the estate agent is not prepared to show people around the house, the need to be available can disrupt schedules such as meal times, erode one's social life and generally limit one's freedom. It can feel as if control has been given to a third party unless very specific and firm instructions are made. Even then there is inevitably someone who can only view at times different to those specified and if they are not accommodated there is always the thought that they may have bought the house. Very few people are able to tolerate these circumstances for long periods without becoming fed-up and frustrated.

There is also the problem of keeping the home 'presentable'. If the viewer does not turn up frustration and anger will be evident. If the person is married and the wife is not employed, often all of the above is left to the wife to manage which can lead to a strain on the relationship. She is left feeling resentful, particularly if he has already moved ahead of the rest of the family.

The uncertainty

Once an offer on the home has been made and accepted there is uncertainty as to whether the purchaser is serious, can raise the money, sell their own property, move as quickly as required, and generally cooperate with the whole process. Added to which, after the initial meeting they effectively become invisible as all the subsequent dealing takes place through various third parties, eg solicitors and estate agents.

Uncertainty is fuelled by the problems of communication that can exist between the parties. Perceived (or actual) lack of communication can quickly lead to mistrust and resentment. Feelings like these may initially be directed towards the partner who is pressured to find out what's going on, or may emerge in the workplace as upsets in relations with colleagues, changes in mood, and an increase in personal phone calls as the arrangements are carried through.

Some relocation companies will buy the person's home (third party purchase) which can reduce much of the burden already described. Companies may also offer bridging loans which are either interest free or at rates below the market rate, for specified periods of time. In the former situation, however, the person may be left feeling that they have undersold their home, despite several valuations to determine the guaranteed price. In the latter circumstance, however, the pressure to sell is still there. Practical assistance of this kind (shared equity schemes is another) is particularly useful for people moving from low cost areas, eg North to South, but does not remove the emotional side of moving (for a full description of services see references at the end of chapter).

Problems buying a new home

Finding the right area

We have already mentioned some of the practical aspects which people look for when they move home – even when relatively small distances are involved – eg schools, hospitals, bus and rail transport, availability of shops, pubs, sports centres etc. Alongside these needs may be efforts to avoid certain inappropriate or undesirable areas (although in some parts of the country areas previously thought of as 'less desirable' are now actively sought as investments).

These objectives warrant careful consideration when moving within the same borough but are more problematic when moving to a different part of the country or world. Many organisations provide time off for employees to visit new areas and pay the expenses for the individual and family. How much can confidently be achieved in what is often a short period of time is questionable. In addition, not many people are aware of how to find out the information needed to make the appropriate decision: for example the number of schools available, their quality, the teacher-pupil ratio, academic achievements, rewards etc.

Counselling can help the person assume responsibility for gathering appropriate information. This may consist of:

- providing the person with the information, eg costs of housing, climate, schools, employment opportunities, cost of living
- letting them know where it may be found
- encouraging the development of information gathering skills.

If adequate and appropriate information is available the person should be able to make better decisions, consider alternatives and implement their decision with greater confidence.

The company also needs to provide the person with adequate resources to collect this information. This could be in the form of extended time off, or, for people who are required to move overseas, educational seminars describing the country and culture. The opportunity to meet people who have worked or are currently working in the area or country would also enable specific fears and anxieties to be aired and discussed. These meetings should include the person's partner and should be conducted in total confidence.

Overseas appointments require particular trouble to be taken over obtaining information, eg sickness and disability care, travel arrangements, leave, laws of the land, cultural habits/taboos, etc. Issues surrounding the partner's career, implications for the family, future financial security and so on can be accentuated where overseas relocation is required. The family should also have the capacity, patience and desire to learn about a new culture and, in many circumstances, a new language. A rigid attitude and a rejection of the values of the culture the person is entering will lead to problems of acceptance and settlement.

Similar care and attention should also be given to the steps needed to reintroduce the expatriate. The adjustment back can be as emotionally and practically difficult as leaving the country initially.

Finding the right home

Assuming the right area is found, the next task is to find the right accommodation. The popular image here in achieving this objective is finding a home that has the 'right feel'. The reality is that many people do not really know what they want before looking at premises and the 'right feeling' is a crystalisation of jumbled thoughts and ideas.

Whenever possible help should be made available for the person and family to focus on what it is they want rather than relying solely on a pre-specified price range (although the price range is an important factor particularly when moving to a more expensive region). In some circumstances the person may need to come to terms with a drop in their standard of living because of a higher financial mortgage commitment.

Once this groundwork has been achieved then the task of visiting several premises begins. This can start with much excitement, quickly turn to disillusionment and end with feelings of boredom and apathy. When the right premises have been found the uncertainty described earlier relating to selling pervades the purchasing process. Disappointment will need to be coped with if offers are not accepted or are gazumped.

Financing a home move

A mortgage is the single, largest debt that most people will ever have. In addition to the type and size of mortgage are the associated costs of solicitors, surveys, stamp duty, estate agents, removals, repair work and so on. The financial burden of the move can be considerable even before the unpredictability of bills (gas, electricity etc) in a new home.

Financial support may be available from some employers in the following ways (as mentioned earlier):

- transaction costs: solicitors, estate agents, surveys
- bridging loans
- removal costs
- furniture storage
- excess housing costs
- disturbance allowances.

Where none of the above facilities exist it may be useful for some people to discuss the potential financial pressures and receive support with estimating and budgeting (see chapter 11). Many people buying a home for the first time will be unfamiliar with the hidden costs, such as stamp duty, and lack the confidence to ask estate agents or their solicitor. The relative ease of loans may have led some people to stretch themselves financially and support in coping with the financial demands may be needed. Care must be taken to use counselling skills in order to enable the person to take responsibility for their circumstances and decisions whilst learning from their situation for the future.

Settling in

Not only does the whole process, from start to finish, take a considerable period of time, but the 'settling in' phase can take much longer.

The efforts and support of the organisation and manager can make considerable inroads to smoothing the move but the person or family will need to establish new social networks and supports. Work will need to be done on the home to alter it to the specific tastes of the new owners. Some people never feel totally settled, and this may be exacerbated if there is a belief that the company will require them to move again in a few years time, or that the company is no more secure despite relocation.

If one partner is working and the other is at home the person working has daily access to a community – the workplace. This community can provide security, friendship, common interests and many other aspects to which their partner has no access and as a consequence the latter may feel lonely, depressed and resentful. Support and understanding should come from the other partner, although he or she may feel helpless to respond and only able to turn to the employer for help.

There may also be problems if the partner at home finds that they are taking on the responsibility for the social life of the working partner. This often happens if the home-based partner is a woman, possibly with children, who quickly becomes integrated in the local community through schools, local groups etc. It is also possible for a conflict to develop between the working partner's social life and the home-based partner's social life, leading to a distancing between the couple. All these aspects should be considered by the employer when assisting a relocated employee to adjust to the move.

Summary

Moving home is something which is familiar to each of us. Much of what has been written may be regarded as common sense. Indeed many people accomplish the move without any practical difficulties. The emotional problems will however certainly emerge during the move, and may linger for a significant time afterwards.

Managers should be aware of the impact that moving home at any time can have on an employee but especially when the move is required by the employer. The latter can result in more acute problems which if allowed to go unresolved will eventually affect the employee's job performance and relationships with colleagues. Problems are accentuated where overseas moves are required and sources of support in these circumstances may be severely limited or reduced.

Many of the areas mentioned in this chapter overlap with other chapters, eg career counselling and redundancy counselling, and reference should be made to these where appropriate.

It is important not to rely only on practical measures when a person moves home: although these do alleviate much of the stress, they are not the only factors involved. The manager should be aware of the emotional implications and pressures of moving home, particularly the sense of loss which may be felt. Be alert to ways in which help and counselling can alleviate the pressures. Simply providing an opportunity for the person to vent their frustrations and anger acts as an important safety valve. More specific counselling can benefit the individual and family where conflicts arise, and at these times referral to specialists would be appropriate.

References

Institute of Manpower Studies. *Relocating managers and professional staff.* Falmer, Brighton, Institute of Manpower Studies, 1987 vi. 142pp (IMS Report 139).

Further reading
Books and journals

British Institute of Management. *Transferring employees: policy and practice in the UK.* London, BIM, 1978. 40pp (BIM Management survey report 43).

Confederation of British Industry Employee Relocation Council. *Relocation News.* Quarterly publication.

Employee Attitude Surveys. *Employee attitudes to relocation.* Stone, Staff, Employee Attitude Surveys, 1976. 44pp.

Harris Research Centre. *Fourth annual study of employee relocation policies among UK companies.* London, Merrill Lynch, Relocation Management International, 1987. 35pp.

Incomes Data Services Limited. *Relocation.* London, IDS, 1987. 28pp (Study 399).

Shortland Sue. *Relocation: a practical guide.* London, Institute of Personnel Management, 1990.

Shortland Susan M. *Managing relocation.* London, Macmillan, 1987. xii. 222pp.

Articles

Cardwell J W. 'The other side of relocation – relocating the spouse; does your relocation programme meet the needs of dual-career couples?' *Personnel Administrator,* Vol 25, No 9, September 1980. pp 53–56.

Levenson M K *and* Hollman R W. 'Personal support services in corporate relocation programs; some helpful noncost services you can offer transferred employees. *Personnel Administrator,* Vol. 25, No 9, September 1980. pp45–51.

'Relocation and employment law'. *Industrial Relations Review and Report.* No 379, November 1986 (Industrial Relations Legal Information Bulletin. pp 2–9).

'Relocation' (factsheet No 5), ed Claire Hogg. *Personnel Management,* May 1988. 4pp.

9 Sexual Harassment

Introduction

Sexual harassment has for a long time been considered to be a trivial issue that only seriously affects very few people. However a number of surveys conducted in Britain to investigate the incidence of sexual harassment in the workplace have shown that it is an issue which needs to be taken seriously. One recent survey by a European Commission of 3,000 women asked: 'It can happen that women find themselves the object of sexual advances or propositions which are more or less a kind of blackmail. Have you experienced this kind of pressure?' Six per cent answered 'Yes' to this question.

Survey results do not however give an accurate picture. There is often a discrepancy between such percentages and the number of formal complaints made, which are usually very few. The low number of complaints may be due to the absence of a formal complaints or grievance procedure but is more likely to reflect the person's anxiety about complaining.

The incidence and assessment of sexual harassment is also dependent on the way it is defined by the organisation (if a definition exists) and the perception of events and actions by the 'victim'. Sexual harassment is described by the National Council for Civil Liberties (NCCL) as 'repeated unreciprocated and unwelcome comments, looks, jokes, suggestions or physical contact that might threaten a woman's job security or create a stressful or intimidating work environment. Physical contact can range from touching through to rape. It may also include personal property being defaced and vandalised, grafitti or the circulation of sexually explicit material making reference to employees.'

Definitions like the one above or similar outlines put forward by the employer ignore individuals' personal definitions and feelings. Equally, definitions which restrict sexual harassment to male behaviour towards women exclude the reverse situation (women's behaviour towards men) or behaviour involving people of the same gender. Sexual harassment may arguably become of increasing concern as the fear associated with AIDS spreads. Employees who are believed or known to be homosexual may be harassed by other employees, creating a stressful, intimidating, or unsafe working environment.

Why does sexual harassment take place?

A very simple perception of sexual harassment is to see it as the manifestation of sexual attraction. This can occur between work colleagues across hierarchies and work groups, and range from subtle displays of attraction to overt horse play or approaches.

Many of the reasons why sexual harassment occurs are associated with the sex role stereotyping of men and women. Male sex roles have traditionally encouraged men to be strong, aggressive, tough, dominant and competitive. Female sex roles on the other hand have encouraged women to be passive, gentle, submissive and receptive to the male initiative, particularly in sexual contact.

The opportunity to demonstrate dominance is also made possible by work structures. Men are often motivated by the need to exert influence and dominance over women and competitive advantages over male colleagues. Women similarly utilise work hierarchies to achieve the same objective – dominance – over men. Such behaviour need not involve sexual activity, but rather involves belittling the other person by emphasising their failings whilst associating these with their gender. Behaviour of this kind will also be more likely to occur where the person is in the minority sex, eg one man working with ten women.

What sexual harassment is not

Many misconceptions are held by both men and women about what constitutes sexual harassment. The following describes what sexual harassment *is not*, with a brief summary of each misconception.

Flattering
It shows polite attention to a woman's appearance or dress sense, nothing more. Women find it flattering, and use it to manipulate their male superiors.

Light hearted fun
Nothing harmful is actually said with intent and should be ignored or just accepted as the way of things.

Normal
Everyone makes comments about everyone else, men about or to
women and women about or to men, especially when people work
closely with each other. Anyone who doesn't isn't 'normal'.

A figment of a woman's imagination
It is commonly believed that sexual harassment probably only affects
very few women and the accusations that are made are done so by
women who want to get back at their boss for some reason.

Wanted or desired
The way some women dress is obviously designed to attract attention.
What do they expect?

Easily coped with
Men believe that women know how to take care of themselves, and
that they'd soon say if they didn't want the attention. Women enjoy
the chase, and 'no' invariably means 'yes'.

Consequences of sexual harassment

The consequences for the individual will range from irritation to
depression. The people who are subject to sexual harassment are
often least able to protect themselves. They may be young, lacking
in interpersonal skills, shy and inhibited. People in these categories
may already have low self-esteem and sexual harassment will further
inhibit their ability to develop self confidence.

Work is often disrupted since the 'victim' is unable to concentrate
on their tasks. Erratic timekeeping and absenteeism are common-
place. Tasks involving co-operation between people will suffer and
group cohesiveness will be lost.

Sexual harassment generates friction between employees, causes
productivity to fall, increases sickness and can ultimately lose the
organisation experienced employees. There may also be legal
implications if a person leaves on the grounds of alleged sexual
harassment.

How does the person feel?

People who are being sexually harassed can feel helpless. They
believe that nothing can be done to alleviate the situation and

consequently take no action. Most people believe that their complaints would be seen as trivial or, even worse, that they would end up being labelled as trouble-makers. The person can feel foolish that they can't cope with the situation. This is reinforced by the manager who laughs off problems of this kind with, 'I'm sure you can handle it'. This position is amplified if it is a man who is being sexually harassed.

Fear is another aspect of sexual harassment which seriously affects the person's ability to behave normally in the workplace. Fear can take several forms. Fear of doing things which can encourage the attention; fear and distress at realising that the person is being treated as a sexual object; fear at the consequences to job security and promotion and fear as a result of rejecting sexual advances. The latter is paticularly poignant when sexual harassment takes place when there are no witnesses, perhaps in the manager's office, in cars, in isolated parts of the factory, on business trips or at lunch times. On these occasions actual physical contact is more likely and the person is confronted with rejecting this behaviour in the knowledge that there is little that can be done to stop it continuing, since it would be one person's word against another.

The person suffering sexual harassment will feel embarrassed by the things that are said or the environment within which they work: crude jokes, pin-ups, sexual innuendo, whistling and so on. A workforce is quick to spot those people who will be particularly embarrassed by this behaviour.

Outwardly people will attempt to brush it off, stay calm and collected, but inside embarrassment quickly gives way to anger. This anger is also usually hidden. 'They make me feel so humiliated, my neck goes all red and I start shaking, and every time I think "one of these days"...' reported a young male clerk in a department of women, who'd disclosed (confidentially!) that his current girlfriend was his first and had subsequently become the focus of the daily round of jokes. The person is also likely to be angry even when they are apparently playing along with the sexual harassment. Jane found that the way men treated her was depressing and made her job even harder than she considered it to be as a woman in a male dominated system. 'But what can you do? If you're going to stand and fight you'd be doing it every day. It's easier to let them touch your bum, and to play up to their silly jokes. Superficially it's easier. It helps get you through, day to day, otherwise you end up getting very upset and very uptight. In the end, though, you're angry at the whole set-up and at yourself for playing the game.'

Sufferers will also feel guilty for a number of reasons. They may feel that they have contributed to the situation in some way and constantly review their behaviour, style of dressing and the content of conversation in an effort to pinpoint what initiated the attention. The reality is that they are unlikely to have caused the situation.

Feelings of guilt can become overwhelming and begin to be reinforced by conscious efforts to keep the fact that sexual harassment is taking place away from their husbands, wives, boyfriends, or children. The person being harassed will often feel that their partner wouldn't understand their feelings and would believe that they should be able to handle the situation and put a stop to it, or that the problem was being exaggerated. Alternatively, they may feel that either their partner would become angry and threaten to go into the workplace in order to 'sort it out', or prevent the partner from continuing to work in that environment. The partner may even blame them for attracting harassment and become angry if they refuse to leave or make a complaint. This may eventually lead to the harassed partner saying the problem has ceased when it hasn't, in order to relieve pressure on the relationship.

The tensions and anger, the fear and frustrations that build up can result in physical problems, which may include headaches, or nausea and depression, insomnia or hypertension.

The manager's response

Men are less likely to experience sexual harassment. As a consequence it may be difficult for a male manager to put himself in the position of a woman (or man) who has been sexually harassed. The manager may himself have indulged in female innuendo with female staff and not have considered this to constitute harassment.

The female manager may experience similar reactions particularly if she has prospered despite sexual harassment or if she has never been subjected to this type of problem. Either experience may adversely affect the objective response needed when discussing this problem with a female employee.

The manager may immediately experience feelings of embarrassment and guilt. Some managers may find the complaint titilating, especially when he or she finds the other person attractive. Care must be taken where this is experienced since the same problem may begin to emerge during the interview, through being overly sensitive and sympathetic. People are often very vulnerable after unpleasant stressful experiences and should not be taken advantage of. The manager is not there to provide a shoulder to cry on – metaphorically or literally.

The manager may also have friends or close colleagues among the work group (or individual) being discussed. This may result in feelings of anger and resentment towards the complainant and/or colleagues, feelings which will again interfere with the objectivity required in this situation.

The manager's actions

Sexual harassment is a sensitive and serious matter and should be treated accordingly. The manager should let the employee know they respect their belief and allow time for full discussion; it may be their last hope before they look for a job elsewhere.

The manager should:

- not be condescending, eg: 'Well, what do you expect when you dress like that?'
- not deny or devalue by making light of the situation; eg: 'Lots of people have this problem'; by sounding over-caring or over familiar; 'I'm sure you didn't do that' (implies disbelief)
- not jump to premature conclusions. The employee should describe the situation as they see it and enlarge on how it makes them feel.

Effective use of counselling skills will enable an accurate picture to emerge and decisions to be made. It is easy to sound disbelieving or patronising. Clarification needs to be sought sensitively and once this has been achieved the manager should not pressure the person to make a formal complaint. If they decide not to at this stage then he or she should look at other ways in which the person may be able to stop the sexual harassment.

1 Establish whether the person would feel confident in their ability to confront the harasser in order to:

- express how the person's behaviour is making them feel
- give statements of fact, eg 'I have a happy and secure relationship'
- be explicit and avoid using polite phrases which can leave the

person in doubt about the meaning or message being conveyed, eg 'I respect you and like you as a person and I hope we can have a professional relationship...(or)...we can just be friends.

2 Possibly role play to help the person in what he wants to say.
3 Encourage the person to be professional. They may want to make a formal complaint at a later stage.
4 Encourage the person to think how their work environment would change if the harassment ceased. How would it be improved? The person should be able to see the benefits of taking control in changing their circumstances.
5 Consider with the person whether they would benefit from an assertiveness training course.
6 Help the person assess the risks involved in following a course of action. This will enable the person to evaluate the options and consider in advance their reactions if things do not go as hoped.

Check list of information needed if disciplinary action is to be taken

If a formal complaint is made the manager will need to have collected specific information before talking to the harasser. This should include:

1 The substance of the complaint – action, abuse, comment etc
2 The name of the person against whom the allegation is being made
3 Were there any witnesses – who are they?
4 Where or when or how often has the harassment happened?
5 What are the effects on the victim?
6 Has the person making the complaint taken any action already – have they complained to or told the alleged harasser they will not tolerate such behaviour?

Finally, the manager should summarise – check that he or she correctly understands the nature of the complaint. The manager will have to speak to the person against whom a complaint has been made. Disciplinary action should be taken for inappropriate behaviour such as sexual harassment; simply having an informal chat with the harasser is insufficient. The principles outlined in chapter 14 concerning disciplinary interviews should apply.

Organisational measures to reduce sexual harassment

1 A policy statement should be developed, to determine the company's definition of sexual harassment – the NCCL definition given earlier may be a useful guide – and if sensitively handled and not rushed can be thorough without inducing paranoia in employees.

2 Managers and supervisors should be responsible for their own workplace and employees they supervise, and lead by example. All supervisory personnel should be made aware of what constitutes sexual harassment and that some individuals or groups are more susceptible to harassment than others. Both supervisors and managers must become aware of their responsibility to treat their workers as individuals and to make their working environment as safe and gratifying as possible for them.

3 The policy statement should describe the procedure that employees should use to report any instances of harassment. This should take account of the fact that the harasser may be the person's boss, and that an alternative grievance route may therefore be needed. This should then be fully communicated to employees. The TUC's guide issued in August 1983 contains a sample clause that may be inserted in an equal opportunity agreement. It reads, 'The union and the employer recognise the problem of sexual harassment in the workplace and are committed to ending it. Sexual harassment shall be defined as: (1) unnecessary touching or unwanted physical contact; (2) suggestive remarks or other verbal abuse; (3) leering at a person's body; (4) compromising invitations; (5) demands for sexual favours; (6) physical assault. Grievances under this clause will be handled with all possible speed and confidentiality. In settling the grievance, every effort will be made to discipline and relocate the harasser, not the 'victim'.'

4 Where a complaint of sexual harassment has been made, it will be the employer's responsibility to investigate the complaint and to take disciplinary action against the harasser if the complaint is considered well-founded.

Legal implications

The Sex Discrimination Act 1975 includes the following areas:

- Discrimination
- Harassment
- Employer liability.

Discrimination – The Act (Section 1,(1)a), makes it illegal for a person to receive 'less favourable' treatment from an employer on grounds of sex. Thus if an employee receives 'less favourable' treatment than would be the case if they were members of the opposite sex, they are being discriminated against unlawfully.

Harassment – In law harassment is called 'detrimental treatment' – again, to differentiate on grounds of sex is unlawful. However, the law has been interpreted to include within 'treatment' conditions in the work environment.

Employer liability – Under Section 41 of the Act, an employer will be held liable for any act of discrimination or harassment committed in the course of employment by an employer. However, an employer cannot be held liable if it can be shown that 'reasonably practicable steps' have been taken to end discrimination and eradicate harassment.

Summary

Sexual harassment is another area where the organisation can provide a policy framework for reducing and/or dealing with the occurrence of this disruptive behaviour. Managers should lead by example, and avoid indulging in game playing or jokes which can result in a member of staff feeling belittled or excluded. They should accordingly reflect on their own behaviour and feelings concerning sexual harassment in order to be able to deal objectively and fairly with any complaints that may be raised. This will include appropriate disciplinary actions when required.

Margaret Mead, an anthropologist, held striking views on sexual harassment in the workplace. She maintained that taboos against sexual relations between people whose jobs require them to work closely with each other should be developed to match the taboos in most societies against incest. She argued that the social fabric of the workplace, like the home, depends on a deep abiding trust in one another. Workplace sex, like incest, is based on exploitation rather than a desire for real intimacy. Trust, consequently, is destroyed.

References

Alfred Marks Bureau Limited. *Sex in the office: an investigation into the incidence of sexual harassment.* London, Alfred Marks, 1982. 11pp (Supplement to 'Secretaries and clerical salaries', April 1982. pp 25–36.

Sedley Ann and Benn Melissa. *Sexual harassment at work.* London, National Council for Civil Liberties (Rights for Women Unit, 1982. 32pp.

Trades Union Congress. *Sexual harassment at work: a TUC guide and workplace programme for trade unionists.* London, TUC, 1983. 15pp.

Further reading

Books

Davidson Marilyn J and Cooper Cary L. *Women Managers: their problems and what can be done to help them.* Sheffield, Manpower Services Commission, 1983. (i), iii, 36pp.

Equal Pay and Opportunity Campaign. *Guidelines for employers and trade unions on preventing sexual harassment at work.* London, BNA Communications Europe, nd. 2pp.

Greater London Council. *Sexual harassment at the GLC and how to challenge it.* London, GLC, 1984. 6pp.

Neugarten Dail Ann and Shafritz Jay N, eds. *Sexuality in organisations: romantic and coercive behaviour at work.* Oak Park, Illinois, III, Moore Publications, 1980. ix, 166pp

Articles

Collins E G C and Blodgett T B. 'Sexual harassment...some see it...some won't. *Harvard Business Review.* Vol 59, No 2, March-April 1981. pp 76–95.

'Sexual harassment at work'. *Employment Digest.* No 117, July 6 1982. p1.

'Sexual harassment at work' *IDS Brief* 282, August 1984. (Employment Law Briefing No 69, pp i-iv).

'Sexual harassment at work' *Industrial Relations Review and Report.* No 384, 20 January 1987. pp2–6.

Remick J C. 'Sexual harassment at work: why it happens and what to do about it'. *Personnel Journal.* Vol 59, No. 8, August 1980. pp 658-662.

Rubenstein M. 'The law of sexual harassment at work'. *Industrial Law Journal.* Vol 12, No 1, March 1983. pp1–16.

Resources

Equal Opportunities Commission (EOC), Overseas House, Quay Street, Manchester, M3 3HN. Tel: 061–833 9244.

National Council for Civil Liberties (Rights for Women Unit), 21 Tabard Street, London SE1. Tel: 071–403 3888.

Women against Sexual Harassment (WASH), 242 Pentonville Road, London N1 9UN. Tel: 071–833 0222.

10 Counselling in the Youth Training Scheme

Introduction

The Youth Training Scheme (YTS) has been in operation since 1983 and is now a permanent feature of the employment scene in Britain. It offers training in work skills to people aged 16 and 17: two years to the former and one year to the latter. The emphasis on 'training for skills' extends to personal as well as strictly work-related skills.

The scheme is sponsored by the Training Agency formerly the Manpower Services Commission (MSC), and is managed by 'Managing Agents'. These have to meet specified standards in order to operate as Approved Training Organisations.

Managing Agents may either be based within an organisation, providing its own work experience, or be independent training agencies who place their trainees within companies offering suitable work experience. In addition, all schemes should provide agreed training away from the workplace, and the opportunity to gain a qualification.

Within the workplace, the trainee is attached to a workplace supervisor and, depending on the scheme, this key person will have some responsibility for the welfare of the trainee, as well as for training the young person in acceptable standards of behaviour. This is in addition to the task of helping the trainees to acquire work skills.

The need for counselling

Trainees joining YTS may have experienced a period of unemployment before recruitment to the scheme. This alone may lead to a decline in self image and consequent loss of self confidence. One of the main rules of YTS is therefore to give these young people successful experiences at work and on courses in order to increase self confidence.

Some trainees have problems which are more deep-rooted and are therefore less easily solved. Lack of self confidence may be the consequence of many years of failure at school and at home. At times, a teenager may seem determined to prove that he or she is a failure, in spite of any efforts that the workplace supervisor may make, but most young people do respond positively to appropriate praise and encouragement.

Other trainees may present more specific problems which require some action. It is quite common for a trainee to express problems at work when they are unable to do so at home. Often, the supervisor is the first to notice the problem but may not have the skills or knowledge to help.

While such situations may be seen as a challenge to some supervisors, there is a limit to the amount of time that can be spent on a trainee, without neglecting one's own work. There is a point at which even the most dedicated supervisor must call in specialist help.

This chapter aims to give workplace supervisors an indication of common problems experienced by YTS trainees and some guidelines regarding agencies that can be called upon to assist in the solution of such problems.

It must be emphasised at this stage that all schemes are different and many have their own systems for dealing with problems encountered by trainees. There are also regional differences in the facilities provided by statutory and voluntary organisations.

Identifying a problem

The first thing that the workplace supervisor will notice is unusual behaviour or lack of concentration, or a change in behaviour on the part of the trainee. For instance, a reliable trainee may suddenly start arriving late, cease to turn up for work at all or behave in an uncharacteristic fashion. More often than not, these changes in behaviour are symptomatic of a problem unrelated to work, but since the behaviour of the trainee affects everyone in the workplace, as well as the young person's ability to learn, it is best dealt with at the earliest opportunity.

The first step is to take the trainee to a room where you will not be disturbed and to attempt to find out what is wrong. Depending upon the relationship with the trainee, this may or may not give rise to an honest answer. It will also depend on the seriousness of the problem itself. Often, young people are so relieved to have someone with whom they can share their problems that they will trust the supervisor with feelings that they have not shared with either parents or peers.

Informing the Managing Agent

All YTS Managing Agencies are required to provide counselling and advice to their trainees and each young person should have one person on the staff of the scheme to whom he or she is able to speak confidentially about personal difficulties. Therefore, rather than attempting to deal with the problem alone, it is important to involve the Managing Agency. In an ideal world, all schemes would employ trained counsellors who would be able to appear within a few hours and discuss the problem. Indeed, depending on the seriousness of the situation, some assistance and advice should be expected from a representative of the scheme. This may be gained from a telephone call, but may necessitate a personal visit by a representative of the scheme at the earliest opportunity.

Even though not all Managing Agents employ counsellors themselves, they usually have contacts in a range of local organisations offering advice and counselling. Thus the supervisor can often work in partnership with the Managing Agent and the outside agency to help the young person through the problem. Although it could be argued that the Managing Agent may have a financial interest in the trainee, this should never be the case. In fairness the chief aim of these organisations is to help young people towards a career, rather than to make money out of them. The people employed by the agencies should all be committed to the personal success and well-being of the young persons on their scheme.

The workplace supervisor will quickly learn the limitations of the particular Managing Agent. Some schemes pay more attention to the personal needs of trainees than do others. If help and advice is not forthcoming from the particular Managing Agency, then the supervisor may wish either to insist on more help or to deal with it personally, depending on time available and the limitations of the service offered.

Clearly, the confidentiality between supervisor and trainee should be respected, and so it is essential to gain the young person's consent before speaking to the Managing Agent's representative about the problem, or to arrange for the trainee to meet this representative in order to share the problem in person.

All schemes are also required to provide training for their

workplace supervisors, and this can be arranged at no cost either to the work experience provider or to the Managing Agent, through the local Accredited Training Centre. It may be possible for the Managing Agent to arrange training specifically on the subject of counselling young people, if it is felt that this represents a training need.

Summary

1. Discussion between trainee and workplace supervisor
2. Contacting the Managing Agent
3. Discussion between trainee and representative of the Managing Agency, probably involving the supervisor
4. Contact with outside agency or agencies
5. Possible continued counselling by supervisor, managing agent, outside agency, or various combinations.

The problem may be alleviated after any of the first four stages, and a move to the next stage may not be required. All stages should take due regard of the need to observe confidentiality.

Some general comments

As a general guideline, it is advisable to listen with an open mind and it is important to avoid being judgemental, particularly in the early stages, when the trainee has actually summoned up the courage to share the problem. Often the supervisor will be the only person to whom the young person has been able to speak about the cause of the worries. A judgemental attitude will only serve to confirm any feelings of guilt and block further progress on the subject. Progress is more likely to be made with judicial questioning encouraging the young person to analyse the problem and come logically to the right solution for him or herself. This solution may in some cases be to seek further help, possibly with the supervisor's support.

Weighed against this understanding approach is the danger of being too lenient and allowing the trainee to use personal difficulties as an excuse for poor attendance and poor performance. It is often hard to be an employer and a counsellor at the same time, as the two roles can conflict, with the result that neither role is performed satisfactorily. If this dual role is to be attempted, then the ground rules should be agreed with the young person at the outset. The trainee's side of the bargain must be that their attendance and performance meet the employer's standards, and the employer's side of the bargain is that they offer opportunities for discussion and/or time off for agreed appointments with professionals. Only when this has been agreed can any progress be made.

The harsh truth is that employers do not wish to employ unreliable people on a permanent basis, and the sooner the teenager learns to put personal problems to one side whilst at work, the more acceptable he or she will be as a potential employee. Some help may be needed in making this transition, and many YTS workplace supervisors find this a very rewarding aspect of their work with young people.

Common problems

Problems with a boyfriend or girlfriend

We may all have experienced the pain of a broken relationship. However, young people experiencing this suffering will feel that they are unique. It will not help to hear that the supervisor has had the same feelings, miraculously 'got over' them and lived happily ever after. To acknowledge that rejection is painful is helpful, but to share memories is only to diminish the young person's own grief at being rejected. Listening can help, but if the supervisor does not have time, the Managing Agent, local Youth and Community Service and parents may have more time.

Agencies:

Referral should not usually be necessary. National Association of Young People's Counselling and Advisory Services, 17–23 Albion Street, Leicester LE1 6GD. 0533-558736. Activities include provision of local youth advisory services.

Unplanned pregnancy

This is, unfortunately, a frequently occurring problem, in spite of modern birth control methods. The symptoms are surprisingly often detected by the workplace supervisor before the parents. Absence, lateness and lack of concentration are just as reliable indicators as the telltale morning sickness. If a trainee is suspected to be pregnant, it is best to ask her directly as soon as possible. Then, if she fears that this is the case, there is time to help her to carry out the necessary tests, through either the chemist, the general practitioner or the local family planning clinic. If her suspicions are confirmed, she then has time to consider the various options available and to make a decision as to whether or not and how to keep the child. She can also be referred to the appropriate agencies for medical assistance and counselling, and decide whether or not to inform parents and boyfriend. All these must be her own decisions, but the supervisor's crystallisation of the problem at an early date can increase her options.

Agencies (also offering contraceptive advice):

British Pregnancy Advisory Service, Austy Manor, Wootton Wawen, Solihull, West Midlands B95 6DA. 05642 3225. Provides advice and treatment, whether or not treatment is decided upon.

Brook Advisory Centre, 233 Tottenham Court Road, London W1P 9AE. 01-323 1522. Gives the young and unmarried advice on contraception, pregnancy and emotional and sexual problems.

Let Live Association, 56a Kyverdale Road, London N16. 01-806 1984. A caring organisation for girls and women who have decided to continue with their pregnancy. Telephone referral service 20.00 – 22.00 hrs, befriending scheme and help with accommodation.

Lifeline UK – Pregnancy Care, 39 Victoria Street, London SW1. 01–222 6392. Helps women who are facing an unintended pregnancy. Counselling and care: post-abortion, miscarriage, adoption, helps in obtaining support from statutory bodies, list of approved private accommodation.

Pregnancy Advisory Service, 40 Margaret Street, London W1. 01-409 0281. General aims similar to those of Lifeline UK above; assists those with legal grounds for abortion to obtain it.

Problems in relationships with parents (or parent substitutes).
This is a perennial problem for teenagers. Time to listen without judgement might be all that is needed, either from you or from any other understanding adult, if they have time. Some local authorities have a Youth and Community Service which offers counselling for young people and their parents concerning their relationships. Local services vary enormously.

It seems fairly common that friction between parents can give rise to absence from work by the son or daughter. Some young people have acknowledged a fear that if they go out of the house, then they may return to find that one or other parent has left. It is understandable that the trainee will be preoccupied and unable to concentrate on work, if he or she does attend. Preoccupation with family tensions has quite possibly hindered the offspring's progress throughout school life, resulting in frequent absences and consequent gaps in abilities and knowledge. In their teens many youngsters are able, with suitable encouragement, to think of their own futures and to consider that poor attendance and performance will have permanent consequences for themselves, while making very little difference to the family problem.

Agencies:
National Association of Young People Counselling and Advisory Services (address page 131)

Identity Counselling Service – the Viva Trust (IDENTITY), Beauchamp Lodge, 2 Warwick Crescent, London W2 6NE. 01 289–6175. Counselling for those struggling with relationships and for those for whom self expression or sexual orientation pose problems.

Unauthorised absences due to 'babysitting'
It is worth mentioning at this point that parents can often make unreasonable demands on their daughters. Teenage girls are often called upon to look after siblings and their own mothers when needed, without any consideration for their own future at work. The reality is that this is not a reasonable explanation for absence, and many schemes deduct pay pro rata. As with the previous type of problem, however, a discussion of personal goals and priorities can help a young person to realise that a career cannot be helped by dropping all work-related responsibility in favour of family demands.

Problems with accommodation
Family tensions can ultimately result in the young person leaving home. Obviously, an unplanned departure is to be discouraged, as this leads to problems concerning suitable accommodation, finances and clothing. Moreover, young people leaving home in a hurry invariably forget to take with them paper documentation. Due to the lack of funds and to ignorance of how rented accommodation operates, they may run into problems such as threatened eviction. In some cases, the young person's home life may be so intolerable that departure is the only solution, but tolerance should be encouraged until the young person is in permanent, full-paid

employment. Research into the financial situation regarding allowances and the local availability of suitable rented accommodation often leads to the young person reassessing the advantages of staying at home. Nonetheless, if a move is planned, the local Youth and Community Service may be able to refer the young person to landlords offering accommodation to young people with little money. The Local Authority Social Services Department will also give advice, assistance and in some cases, sheltered accommodation to teenagers starting out on their own.

Agencies:
National Women's Aid Foundation, 51 Chalcot Road, London NW1. 01–586 0104. Aims to provide temporary refuge for women and their children who have suffered mental or physical harassment; helps them to decide upon their own future.

DSS Linkline 0800 666555. For advice regarding benefits etc.

Problems with money

On a YTS allowance, a trainee should have sufficient funds to buy the clothes and basic necessities for work and social life, but may need some help in budgeting. Most parents charge the teenager a small amount for board and lodging, and it is worth pointing out that some parents are alarmed to find that they do not receive Child Benefit for an offspring on YTS. This can lead to friction in some families and may result in a great deal of pressure on the teenager to 'get a proper job', even if it's a dead-end job without prospects or training. If the trainee offers to pay some rent, then this problem can often be overcome.

The only situation in which the money does not stretch is when the trainee is not living at home. In such cases, the DSS will provide additional funds, but these are often unreliable, which can lead to delay in paying rent and bills. A call from the Managing Agent to the DSS can sometimes iron out any hitches in the payment of allowances. Trainees should be prevented from borrowing from colleagues at work, and made aware that this will lead to poor relationships. The individual supervisor must, however, make decisions based on knowledge of the personality of the trainee and the nature of their relationship.

Problems with drug abuse, including alcohol and tobacco

The Department of Health issues a very useful leaflet (DM4) entitled 'Drugs: What you can do as a parent'. The advice is very sound, and applies equally to YTS supervisors. The leaflet gives illustrations of drugs commonly used by teenagers, and describes briefly their effects on users. Getting angry and expressing disgust at the use of drugs may worsen the problem. An understanding approach will increase the likelihood that the trainee will share the reasons for taking the drugs, rather than just dealing with the drug problem itself. They are then also more likely to take up suggestions about seeking help from advice centres and other local services.

A high proportion of YTS trainees start to smoke heavily, probably because they now have the money to buy cigarettes, or because they see this as a symbol of adulthood, or because they are not prevented from doing so by school teachers. If the trainee is at all motivated to give up cigarettes, the supervisor can help by suggesting a sponsored 'give-up'. Encourage the selection of a charity and discuss how the trainee might organise sponsorship. The young person's doctor can help too. Making contact with ASH is really the last resort (see below).

Agencies:

Al-Anon Family Groups UK and Eire, 61 Great Dover Street, London SE1 4YF. 01–403 0888. Helps the families and close friends of alcoholics; teenage branch is Alateen.

Alcoholics Anonymous, PO Box 514, 11 Redcliffe Gardens, London SW10 9BG. 01–352 9779. Group meetings and a programme of recovery for those with a desire to stop drinking.

Action on Smoking and Health (ASH), 27–35 Mortimer Street, London W1N 7RJ. 01–637 9843. As well as working to influence the public regarding the dangers of smoking, carrying out research and providing educational materials, ASH maintains a register of smoking withdrawal clinics.

Helping Hand Organisation, 8 Strutton Ground, London SW1P 2HP. 01–222 6862/3. Aims include the provision of therapeutic counselling for those suffering from drug or alcohol addiction.

National Campaign Against Solvent Abuse, Box 513, 245a Coldharbour Lane, London, SW9 8RR. 01–733 7330. Offers counselling and advice for those with a solvent abuse problem within the family.

Dealing with bereavement
If the trainee needs help in coping with the death of a close relative, then this may need more counselling than the supervisor is able to offer, and the local branch of the charity Cruse may be able to help. This is an organisation helping people of all ages through bereavement, rather than being a charity solely for teenagers. The national address for Cruse is given below, but the general youth counselling service provided by the Local Authority Youth and Community Service or one of the agencies listed on page 201 may be more useful.

Agencies:
Cruse (National Organisation for the Widowed and their Children), Cruse House, 126 Sheen Road, Richmond, Surrey TW9 1UR. 01–940 4818/9407. Offers a service of counselling and opportunities for social contact to all widows and widowers, whether alone or with children.

Problems in relationships with adults at work
Teenagers can often be intolerant of adults at work who, they feel, are patronising or give them menial tasks to do. Listen to the trainee before dismissing the problem, as the young person is quite often honest and very perceptive about shortcomings in colleagues. On the other hand, the trainee may need help in examining views of authority, and ways of dealing with conflicts with older colleagues in a way that improves relationships rather than causing them to deteriorate further. The trainee may benefit from role plays as part of personal effectiveness training, and the Managing Agent may be able to arrange this.

Problems in relationships with peers
Arguments with people of their own age can cause considerable distress, but can often be resolved quickly, if the trainee is encouraged to make the right approach to the person with whom the quarrel has taken place. The Managing Agent may have time to discuss this with the trainee, and may be of more help, as he or she may know both of the protagonists and therefore be able to deal with the situation when both are together, perhaps on a course day. If the young person has problems relating to peers in general, then counselling by an outside agency may be helpful. The local Youth and Community Service may be able to help or one of the agencies listed on page 133.

Summary

Teenagers often ask their supervisor for an answer to their problems, and are frustrated when encouraged to find their own answers by considering various options. Nonetheless, this is the only way that they will learn to take responsibility for their own lives. Learning to make decisions and to become self-reliant is one of the most important steps towards maturity. The hardest job for the supervisor may sometimes be to let them take this step, so that they do not become dependent. It is a risk, but the reward will be in seeing the trainee develop confidence and the ability to cope with problems as they arise.

Further Reading

Books

Engineering Industry Training Board. *The two-year YTS*. Watford, EITB, 1985, 3, ivpp (Information paper 78).
Forrest A. *The Youth Training Scheme: a practical handbook.* London Industrial Society, 1984. 47pp.
Incomes Data Services. *The two-year YTS* London. Incomes Data Services, 1987. 42pp (Study 387).
Incomes Data Services. *Young workers and trainees.* London, Incomes Data Services, 1987. 30pp (Employment law supplement).
Morrison John. *Youth Training: principles and practice.* London Hutchinson, 1984. 187pp.

Article

Johnson R *and* Singer E. 'Working with young people'. *Personnel Executive*, Vol 4, No 8, February 1985. pp21–23.

11 Debt

Introduction

The pressures of today to compete in the ownership of consumer items – cars, houses, appliances – and access to easy credit mean that debt is now a common problem. How many of us have a mortgage, an overdraft, or a consumer durable on HP? We probably all have a debt in some form, small or large, socially acceptable or unacceptable. For some people debt can quickly and easily become unmanageable, with adverse affects on all aspects of their personal life. In the workplace managers will find many problems presented by their employees, but debt is insidious.

Historically debt was seen as being vulgar and degrading and debtors in Victorian times were treated as criminals. The word debt still has a Dickensian ring about it. Unfortunately the attitudes that prevailed in Victorian times have not totally disappeared and it is important to rid ourselves of the stigma associated with debt before being able to deal with it objectively.

Why debt counselling?

When a debt has become unmanageable the repercussions can be very distressing. People are often unaware of the best way to cope with the situation and can only see a bleak and unhappy outcome. This may lead to total inertia: 'It will be alright', 'I'll get the money somehow', 'They'll never repossess the house', or to extreme anxieties: 'We'll lose the house, car, everything', 'How will we eat?'.

Debt does not need to assume large proportions before affecting personal relationships. An unusually large telephone or heating bill can result in domestic arguments or concern at how it will be paid. Employees with children may find it difficult to cope with the increased drain on financial resources, particularly if there had previously been two incomes contributing to the household but now there is only one.

Concerns and worries arising from these circumstances may be manifested in the workplace through signs already discussed in

Chapter 1. Aditionally employees may start to ask for pay advances or ask their colleagues for loans, or resort to stealing.

Counselling can be used effectively at this time to help the person talk about the pressures they feel and to encourage them to look at their financial management. The latter is especially necessary where it is revealed that the person is experiencing an unmanageable or multiple debt, when they may have become caught up in a debt spiral. A debt spiral takes different forms and can involve a person borrowing more money in the form of expensive loans with very high interest to pay off other loans (usually the one they feel most pressurised by).

Another form the spiral may take is for the debtor to resort to expensive means of trying to forget and release the tension caused by the debts. This could mean drinking heavily, increased smoking and gambling – all leading to more financial outgoings and only increasing the anxiety. The debt may also be symptomatic of a more serious problem, eg alcohol or drug misuse, or gambling. Where this emerges more specialist help will be required. Feelings of loss of confidence and inadequacy will be strong and despair at being unable to unravel the debt spiral will be acute.

The employee's position

The person with a debt problem will expect to be judged by his or her peers. A personal debt will be seen as their own making and an indication of poor management, careless spending or extravagent lifestyles. The reality may be totally different. If, however, it is believed that a judgemental attitude will be the response of the manager then the employee is more likely to withdraw and be unable to articulate his anxieties. Debt causes and increases insecurity.

Employees who are in debt may feel isolated, helpless, guilty, embarrassed and confused. The support and guidance of a manager acting in a debt counselling role can be crucial, in a) money management and b) counselling.

The manager's position

The manager will need to come to terms with his own thoughts and feelings concerning debt. He may find it difficult to imagine how debts can accrue and become unmanagable and be angry that an employee can 'allow' this to happen and that it is interfering with his or her job. The manager may feel a sense of responsibility and want to do something practical. An advance on wages would be simple but ineffective until the employee has seriously assessed his circumstances.

Practical help for debt management

The steps needed to help an employee assess his circumstances are relatively straightforward and the manager can therefore offer at least a first level of debt management. This usually involves the initial gathering of all information regarding the debts; prioritising the debts, taking into account the level of pressure the employee feels regarding each debt and the possible repercussions of non-payment of certain debts (see page 144); helping the employee produce a financial statement detailing income and outgoings and working out a programme of possible repayments and/or holding letters.

Before doing this, however, the manager should consider the following:

a) The time involved in supporting an employee in this process may ultimately be greater than for other types of help. Once begun it would be disruptive to back out at a later stage if this aspect became a problem.

b) Whether or not there are appropriate local agencies that the employee may be referred to for debt counselling. This decision should be weighed against the quality of the relationship that exists between manager and employee. This includes the degree of trust that exists and whether the employee (or indeed manager) would feel it was appropriate to discuss and have detailed knowledge of an employee's personal financial circumstances.

c) The size of the debt – for instance, large multiple debts or a debt on a secured loan (often using the employee's home as security) – may require the manager to be particularly sensitive to the employee's needs, and in some cases referral to a more specialist agency may be necessary at the outset.

d) Is the debt a presenting problem for some other underlying problem? If this is the case then referral should be made to the appropriate agency, eg alcohol, gambling, marital problems.

Having made decisions about the above, the Manager should now be in a position either to refer or to begin the initial stages of helping the employee manage their debt. The approach must be systematic, and an accepted method of debt management has been established in other debt/money advice contexts. This pragmatic approach encourages the employee to develop an overall picture of their circumstances leading to a financial statement which consists of their a) income (including child benefit, wages, maintenance payments etc.) and b) essential outgoings.

Initial stages

The manager should:

1 First, gather all the information regarding all the debts. An overall perspective of the extent of the problem is vital.
2 Identify any emergency measures that need to be taken, eg bailiffs coming the next day, fuel supply being disconnected today, and work out a priority order for dealing with those debts.
3 Encourage the employee to deal with immediate emergencies.
4 Discover what action the employee has taken, eg any letters/ contact made with creditors or offers of repayments made.
5 Discover what action the creditors have taken.
6 Advise the employee to write to all the creditors a 'holding letter' explaining how the situation is being managed and that the employee now has a support structure from their employer/ manager (examples on page 145-6).
7 Encourage the employee to co-operate with the creditors through offers/negotiation to restore a viable working relationship and confidence between them.
8 Be sensitive to any indications of harassment and be aware that harassment of debtors can be a criminal offence. The manager should always ask the employee if they feel undue pressure has been put on them to pay a debt. Section 40 of the Administration of Justice Act 1970 makes illegal any practices by debt collectors that give rise to alarm, humiliation or distress.
9 Constantly encourage and reassure the employee that the problem can be managed. Encouragement can be in the form of regular meetings and discussions regarding the steps the employee is taking and reassurance in the form of support and understanding of the problem.

Once all the above steps have been followed a clear picture should now be emerging of the employee's financial circumstances and a relationship based on trust, understanding and co-operation will be developing.

'Drawing up the employee's financial statement

Drawing up a financial statement is vital since it is usually sent to all creditors in order that they may understand the employee's situation. It also encourages acceptance of the offers suggested by the employee for repayment.

All expenditures must be taken into account and consist of essential and less essential outgoings:

a) Fuel – electricity, gas and any other fuel the employee may use.
b) Housing costs – rent, mortgage, rates (general and water rates), insurance relating to the home (household contents and house insurance).
c) Household items – food, cleaning equipment, etc. including items for children, eg nappies, childminding, etc).
d) Travelling expenses including costs of car – tax, maintenance and insurance.
e) Television rental, television licence, telephone.
f) Court fines, maintenance payments.
g) Any other items that may take lower priority.

Once this has been done the total expenditure for each week or month can be calculated and compared against actual income. This procedure excludes the debts at this stage. What money is left – the difference between income and outgoings – is then available to be distributed on a *pro rata* distribution basis to all creditors ie an offer of regular payments to creditors on a proportional share basis, as shown below:

Example of pro rata distribution of remaining income to creditors
Mrs X has 3 debts:

> £200 – a credit card
> £100 – finance company (HP)
> £150 – gardening catalogue
> £450 Total

If we assume that at the end of each month Mrs X has £30 disposable income to divide between the three creditors, the calculation to obtain the repayment for each of the creditors will be:

$$\frac{\text{amount owed to each creditor} \times \text{disposable income to pay debts}}{\text{total owed to all creditors}}$$

$$\frac{£200 \times 30}{450} \qquad = £13.33$$

$$\frac{£100 \times 30}{450} \qquad = £\ 6.67$$

$$\frac{£150 \times 30}{450} \qquad = £10.00$$

By this stage the person should have written holding letters to creditors in order to establish whether interest may be frozen or action delayed (example on page 146). Repayment is therefore for the amount loaned only.

Opportunities to maximise income

At the same time as a financial statement is being established and payments to creditors prioritised the employee should be helped to look at ways in which he or she may increase the amount of money coming in each week. The manager should ask the employee to check:

a) Tax code and entitlement to tax allowances, tax rebates.
b) Entitlement to DHSS benefits, eg child benefit, single parent benefit, Family Credit.
c) Entitlement to health benefits, eg sickness benefit, attendance allowance if looking after a sick person, free dental treatment, free prescriptions.
d) Wages – that any overtime has been recorded properly etc.
e) Housing requirements, eg claiming rent/rate rebates (standard housing benefit).
f) Position with regard to maintenance if divorced or separated.
g) If they can do more overtime.
h) If their partner can take on any more work.
i) If they can take a lodger.
j) If they have assets they can sell or insurance policies that can be cashed.

k) If any relatives or friends may be willing to help out.
l) If they can extend their mortgage.
m) If they can get a second mortgage.
n) If the type of mortgage can be changed to reduce payments, eg to a low start mortgage.
o) If they have a loan on which the interest is extortionately high. Under the 1974 Consumer Credit Act interest charged on credit over a certain limit can be challenged in the courts – legal advice is advisable if this occurs.

Once the employee has been encouraged to look at the above points they will have completed a very necessary exercise that may have enabled them to increase their income.

Priority debts – checklist

For different debts there are different ultimate sanctions and it is worth checking what action creditors can take so the employee can plan how to deal with specific debts.

a) Fuel debts – electricity and gas boards have the power to disconnect the supply without going to court.
b) Mortgage arrears – arrears can ultimately lead to eviction and sale of the house, although this will be after a long legal procedure.
c) Loan secured against the home – the creditor may be able to force an eviction and sell the home.
d) Rate arrears – the Local Authority can order that goods be seized with a Distress Warrant granted by the Magistrates Court. This is known as distraint. Imprisonment is also possible but very rarely happens.
e) Rent arrears – these can eventually lead to eviction via the courts but can take a long time. In some cases landlords can impose distraint.
f) Water rates arrears – usually the Water Board will pursue an action in the County Court but the supply can be disconnected without a court order.
g) National Insurance Contributions – arrears of up to two years are dealt with by the Magistrates Court but time is usually given to pay before this happens, if the DHSS is kept informed.
h) Income Tax arrears – depending on the size of the arrears the Inland Revenue can either impose distraint or seek an order in the County Court for immediate payment. If you are taxed through PAYE then your tax code can be adjusted to incorporate your arrears.

i) Loans (other than HP, mortgage and secured) – the creditor can take court action for the recovery of the debt.

j) Hire purchase – goods can be repossessed without court proceedings if less than one-third of the payments have been made.

k) Unpaid fines – in theory distraint can be imposed or the debtor can be imprisoned but in practice it is nearly always possible to contact the court and arrange a method and amount of regular payment.

l) Maintenance arrears – again in theory a debtor can be imprisoned but in practice usually distraint is imposed or the court may order 'an Attachment of Earnings' – an order allowing the court to make direct deductions from an employee's wage.

m) VAT arrears – distraint can be imposed.

Example of holding letter

Holding letters can be written by the employee to stave off any threat of legal action. The letter necessarily refers to a third party, in this case the employer, in order to show serious intent to deal with the debt.

Name of Creditor   Date

Address   Reference

Dear Sir/Madam

Re: Employee's Name/Address

I am writing to inform you that, due to my financial circumstances, I have now sought advice from my employer as to how to manage my commitments to you. At present we are looking at my overall financial situation to assess what offer I may be able to make to you to resolve my debt. I will be offering a firm proposal for settlement in the near future.

I would be most grateful if you would kindly confirm that at this stage no further action will be taken.

Yours faithfully,

Example of letter to 'freeze interest'

On most debts where there is interest it will be accruing quite quickly, so it is important to try to have the interest frozen whilst negotiating a reasonable offer of payment. To do this the employee should be encouraged to write to the creditor. The creditor is not obliged to conform to the request but it demonstrates a responsible attitude towards managing the debt and may be looked upon favourably.

Name of Creditor   Date

Address   Reference

Dear Sir/Madam

Re: Employee's Name/Address

As you are aware my account with you stands at £   and I am finding it difficult to manage to pay this off all at once/in instalments. As interest is accruing at the rate of £   per month, I would be most grateful if the interest element can be frozen to enable me to offer a reasonable amount on a regular basis to pay off the debt. I enclose a financial statement showing my position and other commitments and hope this enables you to appreciate my position. I will be writing to you shortly with a firm proposal for settlement. I have destroyed my credit card as suggested by my employer who is assisting me to manage my debts.

Yours faithfully,

Example of repayment letter

Finally the employee must be encouraged to write an offer for repayment letter. This will be sent to all creditors after a *pro rata* distribution has been worked out. The formula for calculating this is illustrated on page 143.

Dear Sir/Madam,   Date

Re: ....

Further to my previous letters to you of .... and .... I now enclose a copy of my financial statement together with an explanation of the distribution of repayment proposals to my creditors. This has been worked out on a *pro rata* basis.

I would be grateful if you would confirm that this offer is acceptable to you. I feel it is a realistic offer which I will be able to pay on a regular basis. If my financial circumstances change for the better I will of course inform you and increase my repayments to you.

Yours faithfully,

If after these letters the creditor still refuses the employee's offer, they must be encouraged to write again, perhaps in more detail and suggesting it is the best offer they will get. The manager should point out that if the creditors take the employee to court they will be involved in extra cost, and the court might in any case consider the offer reasonable. In other words, it is in their best interest to accept it.

A second stage of debt counselling would be for the manager/ employer to write the letters, and perhaps even be the employee's representative in court. If the manager feels unable to do this the employee may have to seek legal advice or more specialist advice from an independent debt counsellor. The Office of Fair Trading (O.F.T.) is obliged under the 1974 Consumer Credit Act to be notified if someone is acting as a debt counsellor/adjustor to the extent of negotiating with a creditor on a debtor's behalf as their main activity. It is always important to check whether the debt agency has been licenced by the OFT.

It is worth noting that 'Credit Reference Agencies' keep records of people who have been sued for a debt in the courts and have judgements against them, also records of bankruptcies. If an employee is unreasonably refused credit he is entitled under the Consumer Credit Act 1974 to know the name and address of the agency that has information on him/her and to be sent any records they may have in relation to the refusal of credit. If the information is wrong the employee can insist it be corrected. The Office of Fair Trading will give further information on this.

Summary

Debt counselling is now a very necessary and specialised area of help. It requires specific knowledge and the application of counselling skills. It also requires a commitment on the part of the debtor and encouragement and support on the part of the counsellor/manager. It is a working relationship which may at times be very stressful for both parties. *But* it can play a very important part in allowing an employee to resolve a distressing personal crisis. Equipped with the above information a manager can fulfil the first stage of debt management and counselling.

Further reading

Andrews A *and* Houghton P. *How to cope with credit and deal with debt.* Unwin Paperbacks. 1986.
McQueen T. *What to do when someone has a debt problem.* Elliot Paperfronts. 1985.

Resources

Association of Bankrupts, 4 Johnson Close, Abraham Heights, Lancaster LA1 5EU.
Banking Information Service, 10 Lombard Street, London EC3V 9AR. Information about banking matters and acts as a referral agency.
Building Societies Association, Information Department, 3 Saville Row, London W1X 1AF.
Child Poverty Action Group: addresses in phone book or contact: 1–5 Bath Street, London EC1V 9PY. Produces excellent

publications on a wide range of issues with a particular emphasis on Welfare Benefits and the Social Security System.

Citizen Advice Bureau: addresses in phone book or for local branches contact: National Association of Citizens' Advice Bureaux (NACAB) 115–123 Pentonville Road, London N1 9LZ. Will give free and impartial advice in the strictest confidence.

DSS Freeline – 0800 666555. Free phone advice on DSS benefits.

The Housing Debt Line Project at Birmingham Settlement, Tel: 021 359 8501. Debt Advice Line and useful leaflets.

Office of Fair Trading, 15–25 Breams Buildings, London EC4 1PR. Produces free leaflets on a wide range of consumer issues, including debt and credit.

12 Substance Misuse

Introduction

Substance misuse is the term commonly used to describe both drug and alcohol misuse. Many of us think we understand what the term 'alcoholic' or 'addict' means, but our understanding tends to rely more on stereotypes than on reality. It is easier for us to believe that an alcoholic or addict is someone unable to hold down a job and who is easily identifiable by their behaviour, than it is to understand someone who can mask their problem for many years, only showing obvious signs of their dependency when it has reached a more chronic stage. We also tend to believe that people with substance misuse problems are weak, undisciplined, pathetic characters whose problem is self-inflicted. Many personnel managers still adhere to the belief that employees can and should leave their personal problems outside the workplace.

Employees are, perhaps, the greatest investment a company will ever make, but an employee with a substance misuse problem is likely to lower overall productivity and morale, decrease the quality of work within a department and put customer relations at risk.

Unfortunately, employee problems involving substance misuse are unlikely to disappear and, given the growing complexity of the society we live in, are likely to increase. Many employers believe that sacking employees provides an answer. However it is estimated that the cost of dismissing an employee and hiring and training a new person can cost three times as much as helping an existing employee deal with their problem.

A historical perspective

Alcohol and industry have a long history of mutual collaboration. Throughout much of the first half of the 19th century workers in practically all occupations drank either on the job or at specific times set aside, often at the employer's expense. Today, many companies have limited access to alcohol during working hours, and provide employees with guidelines regarding sensible drinking. To counter this, alcohol is more easily obtainable in a wider variety of settings, the price having declined quite dramatically in real terms.

Laudanum, a mixture of alcohol and opium, proved to be particularly popular in the 19th century and was freely available as an over-the-counter remedy. Many poorer families who could not afford a doctor would use laudanum for pain relief. The introduction of the Dangerous Drugs Act in 1920 restricted the sale of morphine and heroin to those with a medical condition. The majority of people being prescribed these drugs were older and middle class and such people were referred to as 'therapeutic addicts'.

Medical advancement has meant that numerous drugs have become available to the general public and, in turn, we have become a society that believes that all pain or discomfort can be alleviated by some remedy or other. The majority of people in their 20s and 30s have either experimented with drugs or know of someone who has, and access to illicit drugs such as amphetamines, cocaine or cannabis has increased. Access to prescribed drugs and their misuse has also increased and many people who would not consider themselves 'drug users' experience problems with tranquillisers and antidepressants.

A statistical perspective

According to current information, approximately 1,000,000 people in the UK are no longer able to drink in a controlled way and are misusing alcohol: this means that it is statistically possible for up to one in ten of an organisation's employees to have an alcohol related problem. The Royal College of Psychiatrists, in a report entitled *Alcohol – Our Favourite Drug*, stated that alcohol problems are as likely to occur in the boardroom as on the shop floor. Many business executives working under pressure turn to alcohol as the most socially acceptable stress management technique.

The CBI in its publication *Danger – Drugs at Work*, states that at least 30 per cent of the population under the age of 40 have at some time experimented with cannabis, and that 25 per cent of clients applying for help at drug centres were currently in employment. The Addictions Research Unit of the Institute of Psychiatry produced a report which stated that GPs were seeing no less than 40,000 heroin users each year.

A number of publications advocate the need for business and industry to take the implications of substance misuse seriously and, in particular, the need for workplace policies. It is interesting to note that the TUC publication *Problem Drinking*, found that only 25 per cent of the organisations looked at had a formal policy, 16 per cent had an informal understanding, 7 per cent were negotiating a policy but that 50 per cent had no intention of introducing a policy at all.

As mentioned earlier the most favoured way of dealing with substance misuse in the workplace has been to discipline those found to be affected. The Labour Research Department (LRD 1987) found that this kind of action took place in 40 per cent of cases and in 13 per cent the outcome had been dismissal. It is worth noting that cases of unfair dismissal relating to alcohol misuse have been upheld by industrial tribunals based on the view that an alcohol problem should be viewed as a medical condition. Tribunals are free to treat cases 'in accordance with equity and the substantial merits of the case' (Employment Act 1980, S6).

An Income Data Survey (IDS) in 1986 stated that between three and 14 million working days a year are lost as a result of alcohol abuse alone and that few companies can hope to escape the problem completely.

Some myths about substance misuse

Alcohol is not a drug
Because it is accepted socially, people do not like to think of alcohol as a drug – it is. Alcohol acts on the central nervous system, is addictive and alters a person's perception of the world around them.

Alcohol is the cause of alcoholism
If it were, all of us who drink would develop alcohol problems. No one knows what makes some people more susceptible to becoming dependent than others. What we do know is that it is a mixture of physical, behavioural and psychological factors. Recent research suggests that heredity may strongly influence a person's susceptibility to alcohol.

Alcohol is a stimulant
Alcohol is a depressant and we often confuse the lowering of

inhibitions as a sign of a stimulant. Alcohol anaesthetizes the brain and, as the blood alcohol level rises, bodily functions slow down. Large enough doses of alcohol can result in death.

Cannabis and cocaine are not addictive
Because of the growing acceptability of these drugs in our society, many people wrongly believe that these drugs are not addictive. All drugs produce both physical and psychological dependency. The physical dependence of cannabis and cocaine is considered non-existent. However, both create a strong psychological addiction which is not easily overcome.

Most people are dependent on one drug only
The majority of people entering treatment programmes admit to misusing a combination of drugs and alcohol. For example, if cocaine causes someone to feel over-stimulated and agitated, they will have a few drinks to calm down.

Women are less at risk of becoming dependent
Dependency is likely to affect either sex and 30–40 per cent of people entering treatment programmes in recent years have been women. Many women do not admit to their problem as readily as men, either due to society's attitude or because they have children.

There is no cure for people with substance misuse problems
People with substance misuse problems can be assisted to overcome their problem. Although dependency is a chronic disease and one where a policy of total abstinence must usually be adhered to, it is perfectly possible to return to normal living whilst taking sensible precautions against relapse.

A person who does not have the willpower to stop their substance misuse or who does not ask for help cannot be helped
Motivation plays a substantial part in overcoming a substance misuse problem. However, for many people, fear of losing their job, family or friends can provide the background on which to build successful treatment. Treatment has assisted many people develop the willpower and motivation required to deal with their particular problem. External pressures, whether from family, friends or via the workplace can be equally successful.

Action a company can take to protect itself against substance misuse

If employers are able to recognise the emergence of substance misuse problems amongst the workforce at an early stage, it should be possible to take action before job performance or employee behaviour deteriorates to the extent that dismissal becomes the only option or damage is caused to the company due to human error.

It is important that the company adopts a specific, open and consistent approach to substance misuse. This must include the equipping of managers and supervisors with the skills necessary to identify and confront employees suspected of substance misuse. If this is accomplished effectively, many of the ill-informed but typical behaviour adopted by managers and supervisors in these situations can be avoided. Ignoring the situation or collusion with the employee as often as not leads to additional problems for the personnel department. They will be left to deal with problems as they arise and the only solutions may then be to dismiss employees, fight out appeals in tribunals, accept poor quality work and low productivity and deal with employee theft and security problems.

Drug policy: guidelines and features

Substance misuse policies generally contain the company's philosophy regarding the problem of substance misuse together with relevant procedures for dealing with individual substance misusers. Several guides have been published which are referred to at the end of this section.

A number of guidelines have been identified by Knox and Fenley (1985) as essential components in the implementation of such a policy.

1 The policy needs to apply equally to all grades of employees.
2 The policy should apply to the dependent substance misuser, thereby excluding the employee who gets drunk once in an isolated incidence. Boundaries need to be made to preclude an employee escaping disciplinary action by blaming their unreasonable behaviour on a substance misuse problem.
3 The policy should be in writing and brought to the attention of all employees. It will carry more force if it is seen to be supported by both management and trade unions.

4 The guidelines relating to referrals should be clear and consider what will happen in each of the following three cases:

    a) where an employee requests assistance VOLUNTARILY
    b) where an employee is challenged or ADVISED to seek treatment
    c) where a MANDATORY REFERRAL is made as part of a disciplinary procedure.

5 It must be clear that no stigma will be attached to employees experiencing a substance misuse problem and that career prospects will not be affected, provided that work performance is satisfactory.
6 The rules that will apply to statutory sick pay and time off whilst an employee is receiving treatment need to be stated.
7 It should be made clear that the company is within its rights to intervene where job performance is affected, but that there is no intention to interfere with an employee's private life.
8 All records relating to an employee with a substance misuse problem should remain confidential.

Education and training

1 Every effort should be made to communicate the existence and content of the substance misuse policy to all employees. This can be achieved through posters, articles in in-house magazines, seminars and discussion groups.
2 It is important that those responsible for the implementation of the substance misuse policy are trained in the identification of misusers and, most importantly, the procedures contained within the policy itself.

Identification

The company position should be one of assisting an employee with a substance misuse problem *before* work performance deteriorates to such an extent that the employee cannot be retained.

To enable identification of a substance misuser, consideration should be given to those issues relating to:

    a) behaviour
    b) attendance
    c) job performance.

Note that a line manager can only describe what they *see* with regard to behavioural issues. They are not competent to make a medical diagnosis. For example, a line manager might record that 'Marie's speech seemed to be slurred during yesterday's meeting'.

It may be that employees will not exhibit obvious signs of dependency because their substance misuse takes place only during out of office hours. However, work performance and attendance may still be affected.

The skills a line manager needs to deal with employees exhibiting work performance problems are not new. They are used every day in assessments of work performance and subsequent evaluations for salary and promotion purposes.

The company will already have performance indicators in place. However, the two factors given below should be useful.

1 Know the employees – how does this person typically behave or perform?
2 Know the organisation – what is expected in the way of attendance, efficiency, work patterns and employee relations?

The first point may simply seem like common sense, but it is worth stressing that what is normal behaviour for Jim may be abnormal for Jeff. Many experts cannot tell whether a person is a substance misuser or not as most substance misusers are able to maintain consistent behaviour on a day-to-day basis for long periods of time. Eventually, though, substance misuse will take effect and signs will be observable by others.

Some behaviour patterns to be considered are:

– a pattern of Monday to Friday absences
– excessive lateness
– excessive use of sick leave
– unauthorised leave
– unexplained absences
– improbable excuses for missed time
– other people telephoning with reasons for absence
– failure to meet deadlines
– failure to meet quotas
– inaccuracy
– wasted resources, eg excessive computer time
– inappropriate customer relations
– accidents and safety-related issues.

Documentation

Observing and documenting an employee's work performance is one of a manager's primary responsibilities. Some examples of documentation are:

- If a manager receives a report from a project manager that a highly efficient programmer has taken twice as long as the budget allowed to produce a software product.
- If a manager notices that a secretary who was previously a steady worker is now producing memos in fits and starts between long periods of inactivity.
- If a manager hears from the testing department in an assembly area that there has been a high failure rate for one worker's output during a particular week.

Documentation should depict facts related to an incidence or series of incidences. This allows for the collection of information on an employee. If information is recorded it is less likely to be forgotten, disputed or distorted. The consequence of this is consistent application and adherence to personnel policy and procedures and a greater understanding between managers and employees.

Documentation should include:

1 Specific job-related behaviour – explain what the employee did or did not do in relation to the duties indicated on the employee's job description.
2 Situational content – record both the circumstances and the individual(s) involved in the incident.
3 Verified events only – if the manager did not personally observe the incident, explain where the information came from. It is unwise to document hearsay or gossip.
4 Outcome of the incident – accurately describe the results of the event.
5 Accurate dates for the incident – provide dates and times for the event. Document incidents as soon as possible after they occur.
6 Manager's interpretation of the incident – record whether the employee behaved appropriately and effectively.
7 Action to be taken – what is the next step, eg further observation, an interview etc.

Intervention

If a situation occurs where the manager is concerned about an employee's possible substance misuse problem, he or she will need to hold an interview with the individual concerned. The following is a set of guidelines:

1 Hold the interview in private and communicate with others on a 'need to know' basis only.
2 Make sure the facts are reliable.
  Confront the employee with the facts only, and then the company policy and consequences.
3 Listen carefully to the explanation given and document this.
4 Limit the discussions to job performance related issues only, eg attendance, attitude, behaviour, relationship with manager and co-workers.
5 Acknowledge the employee's positive contributions both past and present.
6 Consult both prior and after the interview with another manager, eg personnel, company doctor, counsellor etc.
7 Make sure all records are held securely and remain confidential.
8 Make it clear to the employee that help will be offered and in what form and encourage the employee to use this.
9 Ensure the employee understands the consequences of repeated poor work performance.
10 Explain what action will be taken, ensure that the employee understands this and attempt to seek a positive commitment from the employee.
11 Set a date for a review meeting.
12 If necessary follow normal disciplinary procedures.

The manager should not:

– Jump to conclusions
– Make accusations
– Try to be a doctor diagnosing the problem
– Assume facts
– Moralise or preach to the employee
– Be unfair or inconsistent
– Get involved in a verbal battle in an attempt to 'prove' right or wrong

– Lose his or her temper
– Take responsibility for solving the employee's problems
– Become overly sympathetic
– Give advice
– Leave room for uncertainty about the employee's situation
– Make exceptions
– Neglect to follow up the interview with a review meeting.

Treatment

Once an employee has been identified as having a substance misuse problem, the next step is to consider the treatment options available. The manager may choose to develop links with treatment services and the scope and range of these services are very broad. These are drop-in services, NHS alcohol treatment services and drug dependency units, private clinics and self-help groups.

External resources are needed from time-to-time to provide medical treatment such as detoxification or to deal with associated physical and psychological illnesses. However, in the majority of cases a course of out-patient treatment in the form of counselling or psychotherapy at a specialist service will be of greatest benefit. Some forms of treatment are covered by private medical insurance and a list of referral addresses is given at the end of this chapter.

Where the employer recognises the root problem to be substance misuse, he or she should make it clear that if the employee refuses treatment, and job performance or behaviour continues to be unacceptable, disciplinary action will be taken.

Dealing with someone with a substance misuse problem is not easy and needs to be tackled on a professional basis. Professional services may adopt a variety of helping strategies. There are two main schools of thought. The first is that drug misuse is simply a symptom of an underlying psychological disturbance, eg depression. The second believes that substance misuse is an illness in its own right. Both approaches work well for many people and, as always, it is a case of matching most closely the individual's personality and circumstances to the most appropriate form of treatment. All treatment agencies tend to hold a rigorous belief that their approach is best.

Companies may wish to consider setting up an Employee Assistance Programme (EAP). The basic concept of an EAP is that the company employs either trained counselling personnel or an external specialist EAP organisation to offer professional assistance to employees experiencing a range of emotional problems including substance misuse.

Return to work after absence for treatment

Returning to work tends to be a delicate time for managers and supervisors as well as for the employees themselves. Questions arise on how to deal with this aspect. The following may prove helpful:

1 On or prior to an employee's return to work, a meeting between the employee and the employee's supervisor should be arranged. This meeting should outline the expectations of the company. It should be stressed that future evaluations and promotions will depend on work performance and will not be influenced by past events.

2 The employee should be treated upon their return as after any other illness.

3 The supervisor should avoid making an issue of past performance problems and should not allow personal feelings or biases to interfere with good supervising practice.

4 In general the company has the right to expect improved work performance upon the employee's return to work. However, certain considerations should be kept in mind:

   a) As with any other illness, expect an adjustment period.
   b) Don't expect perfect performance immediately. Patience and support may be all an employee needs.
   c) Monday and Friday absences occur, even in recovery, and it is important not to jump to conclusions.

5 If a relapse should occur, the action taken should be consistent with the company substance misuse policy and be handled in the same way as any other chronic illness.

6 Any difficulties that may arise should be directed to a professional resource such as the employee's treatment centre or other specialist agency.

References

McDonnel R *and* Maynard A. 'The costs of alcohol misuse' *British Journal of Addiction. 1985, pp 27-35*

Further reading

Alcohol Concern. *Workplace advisory service information pack.* London, Alcohol Concern. 1987.

Allsop D T. 'Dealing with problems of alcohol in an employment setting'. *Health Services Manpower Review.* Vol 12, No 4, February 1987, pp 20–22.

Breeze E. *Women and drinking,* London, HMSO, 1985.

Confederation of British Industry. *Danger – drugs at work.* London, CBI. 1986 31pp.

Dickenson F. *Drink and drugs at work: the consuming problem.* London, IPM. 1988.

Hyman J *and* Beaumont P B. 'Identifying the problem drinker'. *Occupational Safety and Health,* Vol 14, No 11, November 1984. pp26–29.

Incomes Data Services Limited. *Protecting employees' health.* London, IDS. 1986, 23pp (Study 371).

McNeill Andrew. *Alcohol problems in employment: a British perspective.* London, Institute of Alcohol Studies. 1982, 13pp (occasional paper No 1)

Trades Union Congress. *Problem drinking: TUC guidelines for a workplace policy.* London, TUC. 1986. 25pp.

Resources

Alcohol

Alcohol Concern, 305 Grays Inn Road, London WC1X 8QF, 071–833 3471. A national agency which provides lists of established regional councils on alcoholism in the UK.

Alcoholics Anonymous, PO Box 1, 4th Floor, Stonebow House, Stonebow, York, YO1 2NJ, 0904 644026. A network of support groups nationwide for those with alcohol problems.

ACCEPT, 200 Seagrave Road, London SW6 1RQ, 071–381 3155.

Help, advice, residential and non-residential services for people with alcohol and drug-related problems.

Turning Point, 4th Floor, CAP House, 9/12 Long Lane, London EC1A 9HA, 071–606 3947/9. A leading service provider in the field of alcohol and drug misuse, operating residential and non-residential projects.

Drugs

Standing Conference on Drug Abuse (SCODA), 1/4 Hatton Place, Hatton Gardens, London, EC1N 8ND, 071–430 2341. A national body for voluntary and non-statutory organisations working in the drugs field.

Turning Point. See 'Alcohol' above.

ACCEPT. See 'Alcohol' above.

13 Violence

Introduction

There are many parallels to be drawn between an individual's emotional response to bereavement and to violence. Clearly violence can potentially lead to death or bereavement and it is this awareness of vulnerability and lack of total control over one's environment, following a violent episode, that links the individual's responses with those following a bereavement.

Indeed, one model that management could use for assisting employees traumatised by violence is the one outlined in the section on bereavement, especially where only one or two individual employees are involved.

Any model for action needs to be adapted to take account of the nature and type of organisation. For example, professional helpers such as firemen, security guards, police and even nurses may be subject to overt or hidden pressures within their organisation that make the employee feel they should be unmoved by the violence and 'take' it as part of their job. These pressures can make it difficult for the individual to come to terms with a sense of personal vulnerability. The worker may attempt to deny feelings normal to victims of violence, and as a consequence fail to find ways of understanding the strange and frightening reactions they believe to be abnormal. The effects of this will be explored more fully later.

A clear definition of 'violence' in the workplace is important at this point. It is generally accepted as meaning 'physical force used so as to injure, damage or destroy'. But consider the social worker, threatened by a potentially violent father of abused children, or bank clerks threatened in a robbery. None may be harmed physically but these incidents are clearly deeply disturbing and are bound to have a profound effect on those involved. The common definition therefore is clearly inadequate.

There is a more useful definition of violence for purposes of this discussion: 'any act of physical abuse or verbal, psychological or physical threat on an individual that results in physical and/or psychological damage'.

It is not likely that an individual exposed to violence at work will emerge unmoved by the encounter. If the person does, this may itself give cause for concern. The employer and managers must find ways of helping the traumatised employee assimilate the experience in order to reduce the likelihood of permanent psychological harm.

The Labour Research Department published in its journal, *Bargaining Report* (July 1987), results of its survey on violence at work. It discovered that only 45 per cent of the workplaces where violence had occurred had any system of monitoring violent incidents. The Health and Safety at Work Act 1987 requires the written reporting of accidents where physical injury occurs. But this does not cover violence at work; even where physical injury occurs it is not seen as a work-related accident. Nor does this legislation help employees bring prosecutions against their employers when injured through violence at work.

There are signs of an increasing incidence of violence at work, and its true extent is becoming more widely accepted. This can be seen in an increasing number of publications addressing this area (see end of chapter). All examine the problems of prevention and of protection from violence, but less attention is given to the problems of managing individual workers following a violent incident.

Emotional responses to violence by victim or eyewitness

The responses can be divided into four stages. The first stage involves shock, denial and disbelief. This may occur at the time the violence is happening and can exacerbate the situation. Some individuals may freeze, unable to move their muscles. A supermarket cashier held at gun point may be unable to hand over the money. This can lead to later feelings of remorse and guilt.

The sense of disbelief can be strong and last beyond the initial incident. The employee may seem unsettled and begin to show signs of dysfunction after some weeks. There may be a drop in work performance, increased absenteeism, and/or illness, increased or excessive drinking. This could also be a sign that the employee's confidence has declined and they can no longer believe in their own work. This will be discussed further.

In the second stage the victim can become clinging, pleading, dependent, even towards the perpetrator of the violence. In their desire to protect themselves they may do things which provoke considerable guilt afterwards. They can behave totally selfishly, even destructively towards other victims, or they can sob or plead in a way which later seems unacceptable.

Once the incident is over the victim is subject to a variety of behaviour and feelings which are all normal responses to the trauma. This third stage can bring with it:

- depression
- weepiness
- shell-shocked apathy
- tension, headaches
- irritation
- anxiety and fear including claustrophobia, agoraphobia
- lack of concentration
- insomnia
- nightmares
- fear of being alone
- fear of being with others
- paranoid thoughts.

All these are potentially damaging to work performance if they are prolonged. It is this stage in which people can become enmeshed. The common response after any shocking event is to replay the situation, reviewing one's behaviour. People cannot accept what they did to survive. Self image can be damaged: eg the husband who was caught with his wife and family in a bank robbery by a gang of violent armed raiders, who managed to escape leaving his wife and children trapped. His image of himself as protector was shattered; the wife forgave him, but he could not forgive himself. The parallel with grief reactions is clear here. Extreme situations reveal aspects of oneself hitherto unexposed. The need to accept oneself as different from the way one was or thought one was is paramount to the process of resolution and personal growth.

The fourth stage, resolution, comes when the victim or eyewitness of the violence integrates the experience into his or her view of life, accepts their own vulnerability and mortality and thus experiences a reduction in the fear and anxiety, back to a level which, for them, allows normal functioning.

Abnormal responses to violence

The previous descriptions are of 'normal' behaviour following violence. Abnormality is where these behaviours are prolonged, continuing to disrupt work or increasing in intensity after an apparent resolution. If these behaviours do reappear after weeks or months then the individual may be suffering from post-traumatic stress disorder and needs help from psychologists or counsellors trained in helping with such disorders.

A person's entire life may be upset. A previously well functioning individual, if a victim of violence at work, can develop problems associated with job performance, and with family and other relationships to such an extent that he or she may be unable to go about daily tasks.

The incident can bring to the surface feelings about other long forgotten incidents of violence which may have been left unresolved; these re-aroused feelings, added to the 'normal' responses, may lead to substantial dysfunction. Should this happen, the manager will be able to observe it clearly in the workplace, and the employee will need help, perhaps prolonged, in the form of skilled counselling assistance.

There may be legal consequences following the violence which can present problems for the victims and witnesses if called upon to take an active part in the proceedings. For some, the procedure itself can be therapeutic and aid the resolution and reintegration of the episode. But for some the involvement can be an intimidating experience, and can exacerbate their dysfunction if they are suffering from post traumatic stress disorder.

The National Association of Victim Support Schemes is an organisation which encourages the development of local schemes where victims of crimes are visited at home and counselled. They are also offered assistance and support through the legal procedures. Managers can make use of these organisations, which are locally organised. The police often work with these groups.

Another problem is that victims may become callous and hardened, which may make them less sensitive to the cues that signal a potentially dangerous situation. They may therefore themselves contribute indirectly towards the further provocation of violence. Such insensitivity is one of the significant causative factors of violence in the workplace in service industries, and comes about because, first, employees often do not consider themselves to be at risk of violence, especially where the organisation itself has failed to address the possibility directly. Therefore these employees, if attacked, do not accept that they are vulnerable, or do not perceive themselves as victims. The result is denial of the feelings that are normal to victims of violence. This process of de-sensitising themselves can have the effect of making them unresponsive to the feelings of others. They may also come to accept the blame-the-victim attitude which sometimes exists. The result is a hardened insensitive employee; the personal and organisational costs of this are high, particularly in respect to interpersonal relationships.

General guidelines for helping the victims of violence at work

As already indicated, the differing natures of organisations means that there will need to be variations in helping the victims of violence at work. For example, the West Yorkshire police force has an established procedure for their workforce when involved with violence. Counselling facilities are part of the standard service offered to their staff, and employees are obliged to use the service in circumstances where senior management has deemed it necessary. Not all police forces are as well equipped, and it may be seen to be counter-productive to expose the fact that an individual may need help to cope with the violence which is an inevitable part of the job.

The first way that managers can begin to help the workforce is to monitor accurately the level of violence at work. Guidelines exist for this, published through the Health and Safety Executive, October 1986: *Violence to staff: a basis for assessment and prevention.*

The second way of helping is by ensuring good general standards of management. Communication within the organisation should be clear and accurate, and regular and sensitive supervision should also ensure any incidents of verbal violence are known about: it should be standard practice that nurses, teachers, social workers, and DSS officers, should receive supervision which encourages them to express their feelings. Such procedures are supportive and also identify those workers who are becoming susceptible to the de-sensitising process mentioned before, when their ability to handle potentially dangerous situations declines.

The third way of assisting with the problems of violence at work is for management to take all steps to reduce the risk of it. It is not possible to explore this in detail here as these requirements will be specific to each organisation, but some simple and general guidelines include: reducing the handling of cash, avoiding situations where staff are working alone, improving communication with public particularly about delays in the service (whatever they may be), providing physical aids, eg barriers between staff and public, and alarm buttons, and training staff in understanding the causes of violence.

In addition to the general guidelines above, a specific procedure that managers may adopt in the aftermath of a violent incident, eg an armed robbery or a fight in the workplace, is now outlined.

1 Managers should accept responsibility for the victims, including witnesses and their families, and make it clear that their physical safety and the psychological well-being is of prime concern, even if this means that valuable stolen goods have to take a low priority.
2 In the event of a major incident, the senior person at the site should have responsibility for initiating a response to the event, eg summoning medical attention, police, fire brigade, the alerting of relatives if necessary.

   This requires the need for continuous in-service training at all levels, as there is no guarantee of who will be the senior person on duty at the time of any incident.
3 Organisations with medical departments should alert them immediately and discussions held as to the necessity for involving help from specialists.
4 There should be formal authoritative information given to all employees at the specific location about the incident and plans to assist, regardless of who was directly involved. This should be given verbally and in writing and up-dated regularly for days and weeks following the event.
5 Communication with the media should be the duty of one person and all external communication should be made through that individual.
6 There should be rapid communication with immediate relatives of victims and eyewitnesses by someone who has good knowledge of the situation and who has the power to authorise transport where necessary.
7 There should be encouragement for all employees to contact their relatives to reassure, stem false rumours, and activate informal support networks.

8 With professional counselling support, small group meetings may be convened for those most closely involved: eyewitnesses, victims (if medically fit), friends and colleagues of victims. These should take place as soon as possible, and be held regularly over the ensuing weeks, to express fears and update information.

9 These meetings should also be available for management, who will suffer the same effects as any other victim or witness.

10 Open meetings should be held for whoever wishes to participate. People should be allowed to express their fears, and receive accurate information.

11 At all such meetings, brief presentations can be given about what likely emotional responses can be expected and the normal patterns of coping and adjustment.

It is important that meetings should include counsellors or employees trained in group work techniques, to prevent or curtail some of the less constructive aspects of group interaction.

12 Individual counselling sessions with a specialist should be provided on site with an experienced counsellor and should be used and encouraged by managers.

13 The families and friends of distressed employees could be specifically invited to individual and family counselling sessions.

14 It is beneficial to keep the work group together in the immediate aftermath of a violent incident. The group structure can be very supportive. But there may be witnesses or victims who have to go home. They need to be given specific time off, with pay, but the length of time should be fairly short, a few days or a week initially with subsequent renegotiations if necessary. The workplace, group discussions and support are important. Witnesses and victims could find it harder to return to work after a long absence. Feelings of guilt which accompany the 'play back' process can begin to undermine the employee's self esteem, and they may begin to believe they are abnormal. If the employee does seem to need time off, individual counselling should be offered at the employee's home. It may also be necessary to seek medical help.

15 Managers should review the event and the response to it some weeks later – not immediately. Conclusions should be communicated to the workforce.

It is not helpful for managers, in the immediate aftermath, to state that procedures will be reviewed immediately, as this runs counter to the principle that victims are the prime concern. It

is easy to forget the victim, and to want to bolster management
control and self image by telling the staff that an immediate
enquiry will be held into what went wrong.

16 Managers should continue to enquire informally for weeks and
months into the well being of their employees.

17 There may be a need for adaptations to victims' work patterns,
as with those of bereaved employees. For example, they may
need to be relocated in an area where poor concentration would
not be a hazard, or a nurse may need to avoid a violent patient
for a while. It is hard to generalise here, as it may indeed be
important that nurse and patient do confront each other.
Employers need to be flexible: small concessions can signal care
and concern to the employee which can be beneficial.

Summary

The incidence of violence at work is under-recorded and often
inadequately handled by managers. Companies should be responsive
to the problems associated with it.

The need for accurate monitoring and recording of such incidents,
whether major or minor, is important. Risk must be weighed in
individual cases: nurses, teachers, social workers, Citizen Advice
Bureaux workers, and all those dealing with potentially violent
people, often need a system whereby they feel safe to report threats,
so that risk is identified without inducing a sense of failure. Good
management is required, and also in-service training.

The blame-the-victim attitude will not help prevent violence
because it overlooks the causes of it. Individual characteristics can
contribute towards violent outbursts, but the causes will also be in
the social fabric and the personality of the perpetrator and all these
must be regarded as significant factors.

Work practices must be continually reviewed not only to protect
vulnerable staff from physical damage, but also to relieve frustration
in the general public. Respect for the individual, whether it be the
employee or a member of the general public, is something which
needs to be emphasised while maintaining physical safeguards of
the highest order for the workers.

It is not possible to stop all threats and acts of violence. Therefore
good practices of care should be made available in the aftermath of
violence, including counselling on a group and individual basis, good

communication, the inclusion and the acknowledgement of the family and support systems of the individual, and flexibility of work arrangements where possible. The foremost message that should be communicated to the victims is that the workplace itself accepts responsibility for them and for what has happened, and that the employee as victim is of prime concern. By these means the victim will emerge intact, scarred but not damaged by the incident.

References

'Comprehensive survey on violence at work'. July 1987, Labour Research Department Journal Bargaining report.

'Violence to staff: a basis for assessment and prevention'. Health and Safety Executive. 1986.

Further reading

Department of Transport. 'Assaults on bus staff and measures to prevent such assaults'.April 1986

Duckworth D. 'Professional helpers in disaster situations'. *Bereavement Care (Journal)*. Winter 1987

Hill C. 'Protecting employees from attack'. *Personnel Management,* February 1988.

Symonds M. 'Victims of violence, employers can help'. *Employee Assistance Programmes Digest,* July/August 1987.

Health and Safety Commission 'Violence to staff in the health service'. May 1987.

Walsh J A *and* Ruez JF. 'Murder in the workplace: responding to human trauma'. *EAP Digest.,* July/Aug 1987.

Resources

Rape Crisis Line, 071–837 1600   24 hour counselling service.

Victims Support, National Association: Cranmer House, 39 Brixton Road, London SW9. 071–735 9166. See telephone directory for local branches.

14 Disciplinary Interviews

Introduction

The majority of people in work organisations obey the rules most of the time. There will however always be people who will see how far they can go before the manager makes a stand.

Many managers prefer to tolerate poor performers and erratic behaviour in order to avoid conflict and possible repercussions on future working relationships. Some managers will go to great lengths not to enforce work rules, or will do so inconsistently and, in their efforts to please everyone, they please no one or are accused of favouritism. Rules and standards incorporated in policies, and applied fairly and consistently, provide a sense of security for all employees and help them to concentrate on their own work.

Counselling skills can be used to ensure that the appropriate behaviour and standards of work are understood by an employee. The effectiveness of discipline seldom has anything to do with the severity of the punishment, but is to do with correcting behaviour and standards.

If the correct behaviour is not achieved by co-operation, as described in this chapter, then appropriately graduated sanctions may of course have to be applied. These sanctions will not be arbitrary, but will have been incorporated into the management policy of the organisation and their existence should be explicit in the contract of employment. It is the manager's responsibility to ensure that employees are aware of these sanctions as well as any rewards, promotion, bonuses etc, which may be available – and that they understand their relationship to performance and behaviour.

The legitimate cause for disciplinary intervention by a manager or supervisor will be an adverse change in the employee's job performance or behaviour.

The following provides some counselling skills guidelines appropriate to a disciplinary interview. They are not confined to those situations where a formal disciplinary process has been instigated but apply to all situations where corrective action is instigated by a manager or supervisor to influence a change in an employee's work performance and/or behaviour. The specific emphasis of this section is on using the disciplinary interview to motivate an employee to acknowledge that a problem exists, and to take responsibility for coping with it. This could range from the apparently trivial, eg repeated careless errors, to the potentially serious, eg alcohol misuse.

Characteristics of the disciplinary interview

In chapter 1 we discussed the effort that a person will go to in order to prevent other people from knowing about personal problems. In some situations, however, the problem may be revealed through changes in the person's job performance or behaviour. There is then a legitimate reason for the manager to intervene and it is part of his responsibilities to raise the subject with the employee.

It is important that the line or personnel manager tries to discipline the employee in a way that motivates and is positive rather than negative, in order to reduce the likelihood of resentment from the employee. This can be achieved by ensuring that discipline is immediate, predictable, impersonal and consistent.

Immediate
Many problems can be solved easily if they are dealt with at an early stage. Noting the evidence of a problem and talking about it as soon as it comes to light and the full facts are gathered can be crucial. Deliberating about what, whether or when to do something can only erode the manager's position and add to the employees' uncertainty.

Predictable
There should be predictable consequences of following and not following the rules. People are more likely to follow the rules where they are familiar and understood, and where the consequences of not doing so are known.

Impersonal
This means that the focus of discussion should be on the problem and not the person. Where the rules are known and understood the employee will be more likely to accept the consequences of a breach of rules, ie it is an issue of specific behaviour or actions, not of personality.

Stewart (1982) has identified seven reasons why it is essential that the problem and not the person is the focus of the interview:

1 It is easier to alter behaviour than to alter personality. If someone is shy, they can learn to behave as if they were not, and perhaps some of the shyness will disappear. But a full frontal attack on a shy personality is unlikely to help.

2 By the same token it is easier to counsel someone about how to behave differently than about how to be a different person. For instance a shy person can be given a short list of things to do next time he finds himself giving a talk, which will help him cope tactfully with hecklers. If the problem does seem to be outside the employee's control then more in-depth counselling or referral to a specialist may be necessary.

3 It is easier for outside observers to agree about behaviour than about personality. What one person may classify as 'aggressive' someone else may say is 'assertive' and another may describe it as 'anxious'. It would be much easier to agree on the number of times the person had interrupted someone else and the number of times he had refused to give way when interrupted himself. This point is particularly important if there will be more than one person involved in trying to improve the poor performance.

4 Personality terms will cause problems at an industrial tribunal if things get that far. There are a number of judgements making it clear that industrial tribunals are most unhappy when people are dismissed in a case describing not what they did wrong, but how their personality did not fit.

5 Talking to someone about what he or she has done wrong can be done in such a way that it indicates a basic acceptance of and regard for him or her as a person. When the conversation is in personality terms, he or she will feel challenged and rejected, and is more likely to be antagonised.

6 The discipline involved in handling the problem and not the person is good for the manager, who cannot usually afford the luxury of taking personal dislikes to people who work for them – or, more realistically, they can only afford that luxury at the time of initial selection. If someone's performance is not up to standard the manager has every right to try to correct it; but if it is a matter of personal dislike then the manager should recognise that the problem is partly his or her own.

7 Finally, if the problem is handled and not the person, both manager and employee stand a much better chance of being able to measure the success of any changes that come about as a result of a joint effort. Behavioural change is much more easily measured than personality change.

Consistency
This is fundamental to the behaviour of people in positions of responsibility. Inconsistent behaviour increases stress in others and, in the context of discipline, can increase resentment and a sense of being singled out.

These are the four basic principles of disciplinary actions. The actual interview, like many counselling interviews, should pass through various stages with a clear start and finish point.

Stages of the disciplinary interview

In order to enable the person to understand what changes are expected, four features are important. The employee needs to:

a) know what it is they are being asked to do
b) understand and appreciate the reason for change and the final objective
c) know how to take the first step towards this objective
d) be motivated to initiate change.

Hill (1981) has outlined the procedures and techniques believed to be necessary in progressing a person from a) to d).

Correcting procedures and techniques

Procedures	Assessment questions	Techniques
State problem	What work rules have been violated? What standards of performance are not being met?	State position briefly, boldly, clearly, unemotionally.

State the evidence	Refer to the documented observations of performance or behaviour. Give dates etc.	As above
Listen to other's point of view	Are there extenuating circumstances? Is the person denying a problem exists? Are there reasons or excuses behind the explanation?	Clarifying questions. Active listening.
Summarise both perspectives	Is there agreement that a problem exists regardless of who may be responsible? How far apart is the manager's perspective and the employee's perspective?	Paraphrase
Explain what is expected from the employee	Does the employee know the manager is serious about this? Can the manager articulate what specific changes need to be made?	Contracting
Ask what the employee would like from the manager	Is the employee willing to take some responsibility for improving matters? What resources does the employee need to improve matters?	Problem focusing
Agree on action steps	Who is going to do what? When will both parties discuss this again? Are the action steps realistic and attainable?	

It is useful to look at each of the procedures in more detail to appreciate how they relate to counselling skills.

Notify the employee

Where the formal disciplinary procedure is to be used any written organisational rules should be followed carefully. The employee should be notified in advance of the purpose of the interview. This will allow the employee time to compose and prepare him or herself for the interview and also consider whether or not they wish to be accompanied by a third party. Notification should include information about the date, time and place of the interview. The time between notification and interview should be as soon as is reasonably possible.

State problem

The first thing the manager should do is state the purpose of the interview and the problem as he or she sees it. If the issue is poor performance the manager should be certain that changes in their own standards or in externally imposed standards have not resulted in a previously proficient employee being labelled a poor performer. The use of open or leading questions before stating the problem is inappropriate in a disciplinary interview, and is likely to alert the employee to a hidden agenda, consequently eliciting only guarded and defensive replies.

Where the manager is able to state the problem objectively the interview is more likely to be successful. When a manager becomes personally involved or shows too much emotion the employee's reflex reaction may be of a similar type.

Listen to other's point of view

The manager should allow the employee equal time to explain his or her point of view. The employee will then feel that the full picture has been given. Additional information can also be discovered at this stage which may influence the final outcome: for instance, poor performance may be a result of inadequate or incomplete training, an inaccurate perception of the job and its requirements, or personal problems impinging on the person's normally good job performance.

The manager should produce documented evidence of the employee's poor job performance. The employee is nevertheless likely to offer excuses or alibis to defend his or her actions. If denial is put forward by the employee, this should also be heard fully before referring the employee back to the documented occurrences as evidence of what has actually taken place.

It is important to hear the employee's point of view without showing agreement or disagreement. The manager will in this way demonstrate a willingness to listen to both sides of the story and sensitive probing to establish the root cause of the problem will also enable a complete picture to emerge.

Summarise
At this point the manager should summarise the employee's perspective of the situation. This illustrates that the manager has listened to what has been said, that it has been noted but that a problem remains that needs to be corrected. This process also enables the manager to put the interview back on course.

Explain what is expected from the employee
The behaviour or job performance that is required of the employee should be explained fully in order that he or she understands what type of change is required. An explanation of this kind should reinforce the rules or standards expected whilst motivating the employee to achieve this. The manager should consider explaining why such standards exist.

Both should discuss and agree what the employee can do to change. This needs to be carried out carefully without attempting to patronise or criticise. There is often a narrow divide between encouraging an employee to improve job performance and accusing him of laziness. The interview must centre on the employee dealing with the problem at hand, rather than being dictated to or preached at. If the interview gets stuck at this stage the employee could be asked what they would do if faced with the same situation. This will help them to distance themselves from the situation and look at it in perspective. Once this has occurred the person is beginning to take responsibility for the problem.

What can the manager offer the employee?
The manager can then offer to help the employee achieve an effective change. The focus of the discussion is now on *how* the situation can be improved without involving blame or justification. The manager does not take responsibility for changing conditions but agrees to be a supportive resource.

Various aspects of the employee's personal life may be revealed during the disciplinary interview which will necessitate the employee to contact a specialist or to manage their situation so that it does not interfere with their job performance or behaviour. The manager or supervisor may agree to support the employee during this period through time off from work, a reduction in work load, a suspension of disciplinary action or any other appropriate or supportive actions.

Action steps
Whilst asking the employee what the manager can do to help, the responsibility for change must remain firmly in the employee's court. Agreement should be reached between the manager and employee on what should happen next to improve the situation. This makes it clear that improvement and not punishment is the objective.

Future action steps should not be agreed lightly. They need to be realistic and achievable within a stated time period. Regular reviews should be built in, in order to monitor progress. Also needed is a clear indication of what will happen if progress is not achieved. The manager may encourage the employee to finish the interview by asking him to summarise its outcome.

It should be remembered that the objective is to restore the employee to his or her former productivity, not to become involved in the employee's personal problems.

References

Hil N C. *Counselling at the workplace.* McGraw-Hill, 1981.
Stewart V and Stewart A. *Managing the Poor Performer.* Gower, 1982.

SECTION TWO

This section examines problems which are principally non work-related but which are known to have a significant impact on the individual's performance at work. All these areas are likely to require referral to a specialist counselling agency.

15 Marital and Relationship Problems

Introduction

We have already seen that sources of stress outside the workplace will be reflected within it. The reverse is also true. If someone is experiencing a stressful time at work and is unable to discuss or improve the situation, it is likely that they will take home frustrations and other emotions. These may then be vented in a variety of ways, perhaps constructively if support is good at home; alternatively it may generate adverse pressure in home relationships.

If an employee's job has a strong destructive impact on family life, the two extreme options open to the employee are giving up the job to preserve the family, or relinquishing the family to continue the job. To protect themselves from having to make such a choice, many employees report that they try to maintain a psychological separation between work and the rest of their lives by 'leaving the job at the office'. This is rarely possible and the cycle in which job-induced tension leads to family disruption, which in turn feeds back to affect work performance is easy to imagine though difficult to record.

This chapter reviews the complex area of marital breakdown and its consequent impact on the individual and workplace.

Effects of relationship breakdown

Britain has the highest divorce rate in Europe. One in three of more recently occurring marriages are projected to end in divorce, ie involving 300,000 adults per year, a total of about four million by 2000 AD. These figures do not take into account the increasing number of people who live together in stable relationships: if the relationship ends, they will be subject to the same emotional responses as those whose marriage is ending. The National Marriage Guidance Council (NMGC – now RELATE) reports that the secondary effects of broken and unhappy marriages are reflected in growing alcoholism, drug abuse, domestic violence and crime.

Robert Chester of Hull University has made a study of the incidence of divorce and its effects on the individual and consequently the workplace. He has also drawn attention to the relevance of wider familial problems. For instance, there are around one million single-parent families (one in eight of all families with children) – mostly headed by women, but 13 per cent headed by men. In addition, one marriage in three is now a remarriage, and there are often many associated difficulties.

Chester reports that the physical health of the divorced and separated is frequently affected. They have a higher death rate and higher incidences of heart disease, car accidents, cirrhosis of the liver, cancer of the lung and stomach and suicide. Psychiatric hospitalisation rates are also higher. However, large-scale statistics like these lose sight of the detailed picture, which is best revealed by smaller social and clinical studies. These show that in general the ill-health associated with marriage breakdown is less spectacular, but is nevertheless widespread and has a significant effect on individual performance.

People who are divorced and separated may exhibit a number of complaints, including sleep problems, weight loss, irritability, mood swings, tiredness, excessive worrying, disordered eating patterns etc. Such items are suggestive of depression, anxiety and tension, with their various physical symptoms and behavioural expressions. Some individuals cope with marriage breakdown and rebuilding a new life without manifesting strain. However, studies suggest that the majority do not, and of the various stages of marriage breakdown the time around the actual separation and its aftermath may produce the most trauma. The separation involves not only the loss of a key relationship but also a great change in daily routines, problems of accommodation, financial difficulties, and disruption of parental, kinship and social relationships. Throughout this process there may appear not only recurrent illness, anxiety and depression but also emotional turmoil, poor judgement, accident proneness, self-depreciation, morbid preoccupation, social withdrawal and loss of interest in life.

In the workplace this leads to the following:

– lost time; days off as a consequence of ill-health but also to see solicitors, look after children, attend welfare hearings

- lack of motivation
- lack of concentration at work
- job change and job loss: these have been reported as frequent outcomes of divorce.

Marriage: what every manager should be aware of

Many managers may not be aware of the many demands that family life exerts on their workforce, or the vulnerable times in a relationship when these demands can be at their greatest. Employees who are happily married or in a stable relationship are productive and effective. They gain much benefit and support from their partner. Jobs which have peaks or especially busy periods, such as stocktaking, can put great demands on a family as the employee spends more and more time at work, or brings the work home. A good relationship can bear these pressures as long as they are not continuous. Conversely managers need to be aware of the demands which marriage, cohabiting or any permanent relationship have on their workforce. The demands, like those of a business, can vary, at times needing greater or lesser input. The danger times are when the relationship is experiencing major changes, especially if they are compounded by external circumstances such as relocation.

A relationship between two people is a very complex activity and one which requires give and take from both people. The complexity arises from the close proximity of two different personalities, each with its own needs and expectations. Each person will also bring their own life experiences and learning. Many people are able to recognise and accept these issues and work through them strengthening and bonding their relationship.   Issues and changes which seem quite small and insignificant can have a devastating effect on a relationship. It is the number of such changes and not necessarily their severity which can affect the relationship. Some (by no means all) are listed below:

Change in responsibilities
Employment problems/demand
Change of employment or geographical location
Financial difficulties
Loss of single status and independence
Illness/accidents

Accidents and sickness of children or partner
Loss of child, eg miscarriage
Arrival of first and subsequent children
Illness or disability of family/relation
Bereavement
Children – starting school
          – taking exams
          – failing to meet expectations
          – starting college
          – leaving home
          – taking drugs
          – poor family relationships
Feelings of – resentment
          – neglect
          – jealousy
          – isolation
          – poor esteem
          – guilt
Changes in emotional quality within the relationship
Recurrence of dysfunctional patterns of behaving
          – alcohol abuse
          – violence
          – child abuse
Inability to recognise or express emotions appropriately.

Marriage is for many people the most important relationship in their lives. It can confer status and social acceptability along with emotional fulfilment. When problems affect this relationship and the work performance of one or other partner suffers, managers may find this a most difficult situation because it tends to be accepted that everyone should sort out their own marriage problems. However, it is possible to understand and sometimes to help subordinates (and peer group colleagues) to acknowledge and cope with such problems.

Social and economic changes, both in marriage and work, have contributed to problems which are now fairly common, which may not have been apparent years ago. For instance, where previously women did not work for long after they married, had children, brought them up and expected to move wherever and whenever their husband's company required, nowadays many women have their own careers. This can cause much stress within the marriage if either partner's company asks them to move. Although changes have occurred over the last 30 years, it is still deemed more difficult, socially and emotionally, for a man to give up his own job and move 200 miles to accommodate his wife's promotion. It may happen, therefore, that the wife does not accept this promotion – with resultant feelings of resentment which, if not resolved, will affect the marital relationship.

Relocation is high among the problems causing stress, but nevertheless is now a common feature of work and marriage. Relocation can have positive benefits although it is sometimes hard for the employee to see the positive side of a move unless his company explores relocation in a realistic way, as many now do (see chapter 8). The employee, however, moves into an environment which has some familiarity; the partner and family do not. This may cause the employee to feel guilty about the unhappiness caused to the family. Consequently performance at work could suffer, since the employee may adapt less quickly to the new work situation.

Heavy drinking may be a symptom of both marital and work stress. People with these problems are usually the last to acknowledge that they are in difficulties, and therefore pose a problem for partners and colleagues. (see chapters on alcohol – in chapter 12 – and mental breakdown, chapter 20.)

Impact on the individual

In order for a manager to be aware of and to appreciate the problems resulting from a breakdown of a relationship it is necessary for him to have some understanding of what can go wrong and how the employee is likely to react under these circumstances.

The experience of a relationship break-up affects some people so deeply that the emotional pain can become a kind of paralysis. Their feelings are so badly affected that they find it almost impossible to trust anyone afterwards and may withdraw into themselves and shut off new relationships. Regret and bitterness are normal after such an experience, especially if the sufferer is now in difficult circumstances as a result. A period of withdrawal can allow a healing process to occur. The danger is that regret, bitterness and withdrawal can harden into permanent attitudes of distrust which undermine every aspect of life.

The likely impact on the individual undergoing the breakdown of a relationship is that the person becomes distracted or irritable. Mistakes may be made. Absenteeism may increase or, conversely, a tendency not to want to go home, becoming a 'workaholic' as a defence against the problems at home. So a clue for a manager might be a distinct change in the employee's working pattern.

The impact on the individual is likely to accord closely with the employee's early childhood experiences and can activate earlier unresolved situations, leaving the employee with feelings of being worthless and abandoned. Fear of rejection can lead to utter despair, even suicide. Anger and guilt at the failure of the relationship can also be a massive block to recovering from the break-up. There may be great confusion as to why it has happened, particularly if one partner genuinely believed the marriage to be satisfactory.

Many desperate 'last attempts' at reconciliation may be made, despite an underlying realisation of a lost cause. A d for the divorced there may also be a deep sense of failure, shame ai d betrayal. Divorce involves a long drawn out process of disengagement. When a marriage fails, a divorced person may experience feelings of mourning as if bereaved, and this applies not only to the spouse who defines himself as having been 'left' but also to the person who initially does the 'leaving'. There may be an inability to accept the reality of the end of the marriage.

The process of mourning after a bereavement, when taking its due course, may take two years. After a divorce, it may well take up to five. Why, when a marriage is unhappy enough for one or both partners to *want* to leave it should the process of recovery from its ending take so long? Certainly one of the characteristics of divorce is the persistence of the continuing sense of attachment of the husband and wife to one another. In addition to relinquishing what was originally invested in the marriage, there are other major losses to be mourned, eg the loss of the social status that is associated with marriage, loss of a familiar life style, loss of income and, for some, loss of companionship and sexual intimacy. There can be loss of a familiar network of married friends, leading to social isolation. In divorce, one or both of the partners faces loss of the family home, and perhaps prolonged separation from the children.

After the end of a marriage both the man and the woman may no longer feel themselves to be quite the same people they had been when they were married. But while they experience some loss of their former identities, they have not yet gained new ones. They may feel abandoned and isolated and alone with feelings of both anger and sorrow.

Sometimes the anger may be unconsciously maintained to ward

off the grief and emptiness that might otherwise ensue. The 'fight' can be used by the separated partners to preserve their relationship. The fight and the feelings associated with it may then be re-directed to the problems of custody and care of the children, or access: If there are children the marriage cannot be neatly 'ruled off'. In bereavement, the person dies; in marriage bereavement, the protagonists don't go away.

Taking decisions

People find many reasons for not taking the steps to free themselves from a marriage they believe is empty. Their knowledge that the marriage has effectively ended is opposed by all kinds of thoughts and principles which make them reluctant to leave. For example, strict beliefs that a marriage should never be dissolved may itself be a rigid attitude which traps them. Some people strongly resist any idea of ending a marriage because the loss of status and standard of living is unthinkable to them. Others often put off the decision because they think it unfair to deprive the children of a mother or father.

Common feelings over marital breakdown are fears of the unknown and of being alone. The person may be afraid to face the disapproval of family and friends, and worry about the children's future. They may also want to cling to the home and lifestyle they have become accustomed to over the years. If the marriage is intolerable it is helpful to understand that the doubts and insecurities the person has may be blinding them to how things could change and improve outside the marriage.

The fear of being alone does not necessarily mean that will happen – new friends will emerge even if some old ones are lost. The belief that there can be no happiness elsewhere is not only being pessimistic but denies the chance of creating a happier life elsewhere. Leaving what is familiar is harder the older the person is, but it may still have to happen.

Impact on the manager

The difficulty in dealing with any type of personal relationship is that the manager may be influenced by personal experiences. Marital breakdown is, however, an unfortunate fact of life and will inevitably impinge on the workplace. Therefore, it is essential that good management is capable of recognising and addressing this problem whenever it occurs.

Managers may feel unwilling to invade the employee's personal privacy. But if they are told why work performance and/or work relationships are suffering, then they can find out by using counselling skills what it is their employee needs. For instance, no more may need be done than just to accept the information given; on the other hand, the manager may need to listen to a lot of angry words about the marriage and the other partner. This can be done without offering comment, which may exacerbate the situation.

The manager may be asked for advice and practical help and, as any manager knows, this is where the situation can become extremely difficult.

A manager interested in working with counselling skills will have decided how appropriate it is to give practical information, ie the probable need to consult a solicitor rather than attempt to advise the employee what to do about the marital situation. In situations like this it is helpful to have set the limits of involvement, because the manager can if necessary make it plain that he or she is willing to listen but not comment and, in terms of practical information and support, will give this only in a generalised fashion rather than in specific detail.

A difficult situation into which many unwary people fall when dealing with marital problems is to become too involved. This means that the necessary and constructive distance during work hours which helps a manager in his job is eroded, and both employee and manager suffer from such inappropriate behaviour. It would be wise for a manager with counselling skills who wishes to use them effectively to make it plain to an employee who reveals marital problems during, for instance, an appraisal that the appraisal will be used for appraising and time taken afterwards to talk of the marital problems. For this a time limit should be set, and agreed, by the people involved. It can be very distressing for the person with marital problems to spill it all out, with no prospect of resolution, and no idea how long the interview will go on for. However a manager using the skills of attending and active listening, and working to a three stage model of exploration, understanding and goal setting will be able to help an employee use a time limit in a constructive way.

It can be quite hard when listening to someone who is living in a situation which they find distressing and/or stressful not to feel that something should be done very quickly. Possibly the employee will be urged to see a solicitor immediately with a view to divorce. It might even be argued that this could be seen as the goal setting in the three stage counselling model above. However, the type of action required is more gentle – maybe a suggestion from the manager that the couple might try to acknowledge together that something is wrong, and where do they go from there. A crisis in a marriage will emphasise the fundamental differences between the two people. It could be useful to suggest that one, or preferably both, visit a counselling agency. It is also possible that the manager may have to remind the employee that working hours are for work, and an action plan could be drawn up to help keep this distinction.

An exception to the less vigorous course of action are where children are troubled, or seen to be in some danger. It is sometimes felt by the partner who feels they have been badly treated, that the children will suffer from their other parent in the same way. The situation may need to be talked through very carefully to make sure that angry imagination has not heightened the situation. Health visitors can be contacted and are very helpful where younger children are involved. The NSPCC, whose particular care and expertise centres around endangered children, are listed in telephone directories.

Summary

The manager should not take on the role of a marriage counsellor but should offer support and reassurance in difficult circumstances. Basic listening skills should be used to allow the employee to talk if he or she wishes. The manager should resist giving 'good advice' but rather allow the distressed employee to find their own solutions.

It might be possible, if necessary, for the employee's workload or responsibility to be reduced. This would need to be carefully worked out with the person concerned and arrangements made to review the situation from time to time.

The manager needs to be aware of any physical problems resulting from stress and to encourage the employee towards a constructive attitude.

The employee should be encouraged to seek professional counselling in order to reach a greater understanding not only of the problem but of the person's own contribution to the situation.

References

Chester Robert. Paper given at 'Domestic stress at work' seminars organised by the Marriage Research Centre. January 1987.

Further reading

Belshaw Chris and Strutt Michael. *Couples in crisis*. Gollancz. 1984.
Black Jill. *Divorce: the things you thought you'd never need to know*. Elliot paperfronts. 1972.
Parents are forever, RELATE booklet.
Shapiro Jean. *On your own*. Pandora Press. 1985.
Skynner Robin and Cleese John. *Families and how to survive them*. Methuen. 1983.
Williams Angela. *Divorce and separation*. Sheldon Press. 1983.

Resources

Catholic Marriage Advisory Council: Clitherow House, 1 Blythe Mews, Blythe Road, London, W14 0NW. Telephone: 01-371 1341. Offers marital counselling to all, regardless of religious persuasion.

Jewish Marriage Council: 23 Ravenhurst Avenue, London, NE4 4EL. Telephone: 01-203 6311. Offers counselling for any kind of relationship problem. Centres in London, Manchester and Glasgow.

Parents Anonymous: 9 Manor Gardens, London, N7. Telephone: 01-263 8918. Available for parents who fear they may abuse their children – can be used anonymously. Enquire for other areas in the UK.

RELATE: National Marriage Guidance Council Headquarters, Herbert Grey College, Little Church Street, Rugby, Warwickshire, CV21 3AP. Telephone: 0788 73241. Branches throughout the country offer relationship counselling. There is also a bookshop and comprehensive mail order book list on relevant topics.

STD: Association of Sexual and Marital Therapists, PO Box 62, Sheffield, S10 3TS. Send S.A.E. for information both about NHS and private treatment in the locality.

Westminster Pastoral Foundation: 23 Kensington Square, London,
W8 5HN. Telephone: 01-937 6956. To make appointments for
marital counselling ring and ask for the Intake Office. The cost
varies according to income but nobody is excluded from
counselling on grounds of income. Centres and associated centres
throughout the country.

16 Bereavement

Introduction

An essential principle for managers to understand when dealing with bereaved employees is that mourning is something which has to be worked through before the person can achieve a state of adjustment. Grieving should be seen as a process of healing through adaption to loss.

There are four stages in mourning; these can be identified clearly but may vary in sequence and intensity in each person. Unresolved grief can impair the development of an individual and it will benefit employer and employee if a manager both understands and as far as possible is instrumental in aiding the natural progress of grieving.

The stages of mourning are as follows:

When someone dies, and even when the death is expected, there is usually a sense of disbelief, of numbness, denial, or all three, so that the first step in mourning is to come to terms with the reality of the loss.

The second stage is to experience the pain of the loss fully. It is essential to feel and admit to grief, or other symptoms may eventually manifest themselves.

The third stage in mourning is to adjust to an environment in which the deceased is missing. The survivor is not normally fully aware of all the roles which the person fulfilled until after the death has occurred. The bereaved employee may have to take on new roles: learn to cook, fix electric plugs, fill in the income tax form, take the children to school. The loss of a child can be even harder to bear than the loss of a spouse.

There is often a diminution in the employee's role which can be very hard to come to terms with. Abortion and miscarriage can also arouse strong feelings of loss that are often insufficiently acknowledged.

This third stage can take months or several years. Its successful completion will involve a change in self image in the bereaved individual and often a redefinition of the goals in life.

The final stage of mourning is to withdraw the emotional energy associated with the dead person, be it negative or positive, and to reinvest it in other relationships or goals. It may take several relationships or several new objectives in life to fill the gap, even where the relationship with the dead person contained many negative aspects. The survivor has to change permanently to adjust to the loss healthily.

Common patterns of behaviour in a grieving individual

Immediately following the death of a close relative, friend or partner, there will obviously be unavoidable disruptions in the work pattern: the employee may have to attend the hospital, funeral, or inquest.

The employee might seem initially to behave automatically, distractedly, or excessively calmly, perhaps as if nothing has happened. This behaviour is a manifestation of the numbness and unreality that they may be feeling. This phase can last days or weeks, but if it lasts for months, the employee may need specialist help to come to terms with the reality of the loss.

The employee may talk in an off-hand way about the dead person, they may shock colleagues or friends by under-playing the significance of the relationship. This denial can indicate an inadequate resolution of the first stage of mourning. If it dominates an employee's conversation, he or she may need to seek specialist attention.

Somebody newly bereaved may be confused and lacking in concentration. They may talk of reunion in heaven or contact through spiritualism. This also is normal as long as such ideas do not dominate the behaviour of the individual for longer than the first three to nine months following bereavement.

The employee may be subject to poor time keeping, absenteeism, and diminution in the quality of relationships with workmates. These manifestations may indicate that the employee is 'stuck' in his or her grieving process if they persist at length or start to recur after a period of apparent stability. But they are normal initial manifestations of grief.

Alternatively the employee may wish to immerse himself in work, and produce at a prodigious rate. This can often be an avoidance mechanism. One of the common observations made by bereaved individuals is that work saved them. This is not likely to be the whole truth. It may have saved them facing their pain but may actually have delayed their progress through the four stages of mourning.

The employee may decide to move house, job or both fairly soon after the bereavement. This may be essential for practical reasons, but can be an attempt to forget, or block out the pain.

There may be an increase in sick leave of an employee. There are many reasons for this. Sleep disturbance is common following bereavement, and fatigue and stress can make the individual more vulnerable to infection. Contributory factors to this may include a loss of desire for food, a reliance on tranquillisers, anti-depressants or alcohol.

Bereaved individuals can experience real physical symptoms, such as tightness in the chest and throat, difficulty in breathing, excessive sensitivity to noise, stomach pains, continual sighing. These can be symptoms of panic and anxiety, but may be sufficiently acute to make the individual feel he or she is suffering a serious illness. Hallucinations are common; they may see the dead person sitting in their normal chair, walking down the street, or hear them speaking. Such manifestations and the afore-mentioned physical symptoms are common and do not necessarily herald mental or physical illness.

Anger is frequently experienced after a loss and is one of the most confusing feelings for the survivor. It can be directed against other members of the family, friends, doctors, hospitals, the police, even employers. Often this anger ought to be directed at the dead person, as it can derive from feelings of helplessness at being abandoned or real and imagined deficiencies of the deceased. Yearning feelings often accompany these angry thoughts. The anger can, however, become misdirected and may need to be worked through with skilled counselling.

Guilt and self-reproach are common experiences of a bereaved individual: guilt that one did not do enough, care enough, behave well enough. The individual may feel that there is no chance of reconciliation once the death has occurred. This guilt can manifest itself by depression, withdrawal, over work, fatigue as well as by constant reference to it in conversation.

Depression, sadness and withdrawal are normal responses to bereavement, but where they continue for more than a year and seem to be persistently impairing the functioning of the individual, the individual may require specialist help. Acute depression can lead to suicidal behaviour. Suicidal thoughts are common, but attempts at suicide are not. Every attempt should be made to enlist medical help if the manager feels the individual is potentially suicidal.

Action to be taken by the manager

Where possible, be as helpful as possible about allowing the individual time for the practicalities surrounding the death: time for inquests, funerals, to recover from the initial shock. Full involvement in such matters is the first step towards facing the reality of the loss.

The manager should also inform work colleagues of the bereaved individual verbally or by written communication. If necessary, a notice can be posted on a board: it is perfectly acceptable for the employee to see this notice as long as it is removed after a period of two weeks, and not left indefinitely as if forgotten. This procedure helps to actualise the loss for the bereaved employee; it paves the way for work colleagues who are less likely to make tactless remarks; and it may also mobilise an informal network of support for the employee.

Also, the place of work should contribute some sort of formal acknowledgement of the death, for example flowers or a wreath sent to the funeral, or a card of condolence, signed by as many colleagues as possible.

Immediately following the bereavement, and for sufficient time afterwards, an employee should be allowed to move to an area of work which will accommodate lapses in concentration, and diminution in powers of judgement. Physical responses can be slowed after shock, and fatigue, stress, anxiety and panic can make it dangerous for the employee to remain in certain situations.

The manager must inform himself of the facts surrounding the death. Some forms of dying leave the survivor with a much harder burden of grief to resolve. Sudden deaths, deaths where no body is recovered, death of a child and suicides all present greater difficulties for the survivor to overcome. Also individual survivors of horrific accidents, such as the Bradford and Kings Cross fire survivors, can experience excessive feelings of guilt and anger. All these forms of bereavement may need more help than can be offered in the work place. A list of agencies to which the manager can refer an employee is included at the end of this section.

Managers should encourage the employee to talk about what happened surrounding the death both informally and formally, if time permits. Avoid euphemisms for the word 'death'. Ask the employee how he or she is, how are things going at home, whenever chance meetings allow. The employee will respond in the manner in which he or she feels safe; even if the individual is uncommunicative, it is important that the opportunity is presented.

Many managers will be afraid of upsetting the individual by making them remember the pain. They will worry that the employee will break down, or they may even be angry that the employee has put them in this position, and there will be embarrassment on all sides. People experiencing normal grief often do resort to tears when reminded, but they regain their composure fairly quickly. This reaction is an essential part of acknowledging the loss and feeling the pain.

Managers acting in this way are breaking the bounds of accepted behaviour: in our society we tend to avoid topics of conversation which arouse strong emotion, especially death. These attitudes reflect our own feelings of helplessness and fear in the face of death; when we avoid addressing a bereaved individual, we are protecting ourselves. But such attitudes cause great hardship for bereaved individuals. The manager should be aware that other colleagues may disapprove and even oppose taking such an open attitude to discussing the death. They will tend to support their case by pointing to the fact that the employee gets upset!

Problems that might be encountered by the manager

As suggested before, short formal discussions with the bereaved individual on a regular basis would be helpful if the structure of the organisation allows for it, perhaps once a month. However, such meetings can present difficulties. The employee/manager relationship may be uneasy. There may be insufficient trust so that the employee has great difficulty in expressing anything of their feelings. If the employee has had their job altered to allow for the situation, he or she will accept the need for formal meetings to review the situation even if they are unable to use the session to the full extent. They might view such a procedure as an intrusion, maintain that they are coping and that there is no need to make a fuss.

These attitudes can stem from four sources. The first is that industrial relations within the company are such that there is a poor record of trust between employee and managers, so that the employee will be concerned that any sign of 'weakness' on their behalf will render them vulnerable. In this situation it may be very difficult for a caring manager to provide the forum for a bereaved employee to move through his grief satisfactorily. But there is every reason why the manager should still attempt on a formal basis to allow the employee to talk, even if the process is not fruitful in the short run, and must ensure that the employee has written information about the sources of help, practical and counselling, for bereaved people.

The second source of difficulty in this situation may stem from the anger that has been aroused in the bereaved individual following the death. As we have noted before, anger is a common but confusing emotion following bereavement. Its source is often anger with the bereaved person for leaving the survivor with unfinished business, but it is too painful and indeed too illogical to express this feeling towards the correct source. It is also associated with guilt – the guilt the survivor feels at his own failures. Death often brings with it a great sense of injustice, the question 'why?'. God can be seen as impotent; disasters such as the Zeebrugge ferry disaster and the Bradford fire disaster can arouse great fury because an element of negligence and human error contributed to the deaths; the feeling that those deaths were avoidable is deeply disturbing.

Because it is sometimes too difficult to express the anger towards the right person, the employer might become the target. The manager might feel threatened and bewildered in the face of hostility from an employee who they are trying to help, who 'ought to feel grateful'. The manager might be tempted to act defensively and indeed aggressively. Past deficiencies as an employer may be raised. The manager should try to bear in mind what happens to bereaved individuals, and try to avoid being drawn in to replying to the accusations. The employee should be encouraged to talk, eventually the anger will subside, or may even turn itself towards its correct object.

Some of the basic counselling techniques should be used, such as commenting on the force of the employee's anger, and asking what else is contributing to this attack? The employee who has been encouraged may well become much better able to talk about their total situation.

Where there are genuine complaints which the employee insists on pursuing, they can be directed through the normal complaints procedures. But at each stage, the manager should encourage discussion, and be aware that the hostility and anger, although apparently justified, may have another source.

The third source of difficulty for a manager who is trying to encourage an employee to talk over their bereavement constructively can lie deep within the personality of the employee. For reasons unconnected with bereavement, she or he may be hostile, deeply withdrawn, evasive, or totally ill-equipped for examining and revealing feelings. This may arouse exasperation, anger and impatience in the manager. Help cannot be forced on someone who is not ready to receive it. People grieve at their own pace, in their own time. The manager can only insist on interaction with the employee if their work is persistently falling below standard: even months after the bereavement the manager may have to involve an outside agency skilled in coping with such problems. Employer and employee may have to agree mutually that the employee undertakes counselling and, at the end of a defined period, say six months, that the situation will be reviewed.

Where the company is smaller, and does not have the resources for this process, it can still make known to the employee the counselling resources available within the community, suggest that the employee makes use of them and their GP and agree to review the situation within six months. Other sources of help are listed at the end of this section.

This is much the same process that would occur with employees who have a severe drink or drugs problem. The employer would attempt to help from within their own resources, offer information and advice and other helping resources and set this within a time period. All that can be done eventually has to be done by the individual, once the framework of care and concern has been established.

The final source of difficulty about formal (or informal) talks with bereaved individuals can lie in the manager's own reactions to loss and bereavement. The manager himself may have been bereaved and have inadequately grieved, and may be using the talks to work through his or her own grief. The manager can even generate hostility and anger in the situation because of the arousal of previously buried, unresolved feelings. It is important for managers to look at themselves and at their own emotional responses to situations, particularly loss, before they can properly manage their employees.

During these discussions, if the employee gives indications of wanting to change his or her job, or move house, encourage him or her to talk through these ideas, as the perceptions involved may not be realistic, nor the judgements sound. If at all possible, major changes should be avoided for at least one year after bereavement.

The manager should encourage the employee to keep in close contact with the GP to monitor any physical symptoms and give reassurance. The bereaved employee may have fears about his or her own death. Should normal depression become more acute, the GP will have an important role. The risk of suicide is increased in those who have a previous history, physical or mental illness, or where family patterns are known to be unusual, or where the bereaved individual is living alone. Tell the employee you are going to inform their GP if you are anxious for the employee's safety. You can feel justified in doing this even in the face of objections from the employee (see also chapter 17).

References

Bowlby J. *Attachment and loss.* London, Penguin, 1969.
Parkes C M. *Bereavement: studies of grief in adult life.* London, Penguin, 1983.
Worden J William. *Grief counselling and grief therapy.* London, Tavistock Publications Ltd, 1983.

Further reading

Lewis C S. *A grief observed.* London, Faber. 1961.
Torrie M. *Begin again: a book for women alone.* London, Dent, 1979.
Morris Sarah. *Grief and how to live with it.* London, George Allen and Unwin, 1971.

Resources

Citizens' Advice Bureau: to provide information on practical problems and where to find help. For area offices and local branches see telephone directory.

CRUSE: The National Organisation for the Bereaved, Cruse House, 126 Sheen Road, Richmond, Surrey TU9 1LR. Telephone: 081–940 4818/9047. Cruse has many local branches: ring Head Office or see local telephone directory. It offers counselling for all bereaved people, advice on practical problems, social contact to ease loneliness, parent circles.

The Samaritans: 24 hour listening and befriending service for the depressed and suicidal. For local branches see telephone directory.

The Society of Compassionate Friends, 6 Denmark Street, Bristol BS1 5DQ. Telephone: 0272 292778. Self help group of bereaved parents offering help and understanding to those who have recently lost a child. Telephone answering service in almost every county in UK.

Tranquilliser Support Groups: see local telephone directory or ring local CAB for local branches. They provide self help groups and some counselling to help individuals who have become addicted to tranquillisers.

17   Suicide

Introduction

A manager may encounter suicide in the workforce in the following ways:

1 An employee may succeed in taking his or her own life
2 An employee may attempt but fail to take his or her life
3 An employee may be bereaved because a member of his or her family or a close friend has committed suicide.

Managerial response needs to take account of the fact that suicide is a particularly difficult form of death for those close to the dead person – family, friends or work colleagues – to grieve over and come to terms with.

Suicide is almost always connected with other disturbances. Those who suffer from depression, drug or alcohol dependence, schizophrenia, severe marital and relationship problems, severe physical problems, major financial problems, exposure of previously hidden crimes, significant loss of any kind, especially bereavement, those with a history of previous suicide attempts, those who have been punished or rejected recently or consistently, are all at greater risk of attempting suicide.

It is not uncommon for suicides to take place when a hitherto depressed or agitated person seems to be getting better. They may seem calmer and more tranquil. Family and/or friends may relax at just the moment when the suicidal individual is calm either because they have made their decision or because strength has returned sufficiently to make them take action against an intolerable state.

It can also happen as if by accident. Flirting with danger can produce an addictive thrill and this sometimes accounts for the deaths of young people particularly.

The manager's responses

Where there has been a successful bid by an employee, the manager should inform the remaining workforce of the death of the employee (without pre-judging any outcome of a post mortem or inquest) in verbal form if the workforce is small and/or by means of written information posted on a notice board.

It is important to contact the family, if there is one, of the dead person, to express the sympathy of the organisation. The wishes of the family in relation to funeral arrangements, the sending of flowers and so on can be enquired about, and then communicated to other members of the workforce. But this process is also the first step towards the usual grieving process which the work colleagues, management included, may need to undergo. Any method of facilitating the channels of communication between potentially sympathetic work colleagues and family will be important for both groups. Management lead here will be beneficial.

Almost inevitably, guilt will be a component in the reactions of some in the workforce, as it will be in the close relatives and friends. How did he/she get so low as to do this? What could I/we have done to prevent it?

Shame is another of the predominant feelings in the survivors following suicide. Shame originates from feelings that they should have done something (or more) to help or prevent the death, and also from the death itself and the way it occurred. The tendency to deny or suppress the nature of the death may be strong. In these circumstances effort should be made to present open, and factual information about the death.

Managers should allow other members of the workforce opportunities to discuss their own responses to the death. If possible make clear formal arrangements for this to take place and for it to be available to any member of the workforce.

Management needs to be alert to signs of distress in other employees who were close to the dead one. They may need to allow for some variation in the work performance or behaviour of these individuals. Friends as well as family can feel bereft by the death of an individual. Where the bond was one of friendship however, the grieving process is unlikely to be as disruptive or prolonged as when the bond was a familial one.

Managers need to be alert to the true nature of their own feelings surrounding the suicide of an employee. Managers, too, may feel guilt and shame especially where the dead person was known to have had other problems, which is almost always likely to be the case. They need to take account of the anger they may feel towards the dead employee whom they may have been trying to help. If that anger is insufficiently acknowledged, it may become a barrier to the expression of normal grief within the remaining workforce, especially in small companies.

The normal supervisory process may not be able to accommodate the manager's expression of his or her own feelings, or the manager may feel threatened by his shame and guilt and feelings not always commensurate with the normal management profile. In other words, it may be outwardly unacceptable to explore such feelings within the normal structure of the organisation. This sort of supervision may need to be sought out from a specialised division in personnel which aims to handle 'welfare type' problems, or from an outside counselling resource.

The unsuccessful suicide bid

The second way in which managers may encounter suicide is when confronted by an employee who has attempted suicide but failed, and has returned to work. Managers may have intellectual and moral objections to suicide and suicide attempts. As mentioned above, it is important for a manager to understand precisely what these beliefs and feelings are, to seek help to explore these, and to make attempts to put aside their own responses and look at the employee clearly without fear and prejudice.

One dominant element that lies behind suicides and suicide attempts is that of an inability in the individual to express their anger freely, except self destructively. Any unconscious anger emanating from a manager trying to manage such an individual can further block the employee's attempts towards a healthier form of expression.

Suicide attempts, as mentioned before, are rarely isolated gestures. They are often a symptom of profound depression with an overwhelming sense of hopelessness; factors that contribute to suicide have been listed, but the elements that need to be offset are the sense of isolation, the increasing inability to take up help, and the unexpressed anger.

All possible channels of communication to the employee, formal and informal, should be maintained. It is important for managers to encourage the employee to maintain all links with the medical profession and other support systems which may have come into operation following the suicide attempt. Hospitals refer patients suspected of having inflicted injuries on themselves to their social work departments or psychiatric departments, who will then attempt to ensure there is ongoing support following discharge from hospital. A GP should refer the patient for psychiatric help where the attempt did not result in hospitalisation.

The employee's job should be reviewed to ensure that safety standards in the workplace are maintained, and also to ensure that the stresses of work have not contributed to the depression and hopelessness. Work performance of someone who has attempted suicide is likely to be diminished as most of the factors that contribute to suicidal tendencies will adversely affect concentration, memory and motor functioning.

If work performance continues to fall below standard then the employer could justifiably confront the employee using the guidelines described in chapter 12. It may be necessary to agree on a programme of treatment, to be carried out over a realistic time scale. The workplace would therefore tolerate the diminished efficiency of the individual for a while in return for the attempt of the employee to make real efforts to help him/herself.

Responses to employees at risk of committing suicide

If the manager is confronted by an employee who is talking of suicide, there are various possible ways of handling the situation. The manager should concentrate on the feelings of the individual: it is not helpful to engage in philosophical or intellectual arguments about the course of action. A manager should ask whether the employee has made any plans: the difference between suicidal thoughts and suicidal plans is considerable. The manager should not hold the view that real suicide risks do not talk of their plans: most people who attempt suicide have spoken of it several times and usually shortly before the attempt.

Should the manager feel there is a real risk of an imminent suicide attempt he or she should invoke medical help as soon as possible. Calmness but not coolness should be maintained. Company doctors should be called, or the GP of the individual or doctor on duty, or mental health care team or the local psychiatric hospital, and meanwhile the employee should not be left alone. all this activity should be explained to the individual and their consent sought. But should they resist it is still appropriate to invoke medical help and is also important to seek the help of all other professionals who may already be assisting in the treatment of the individual: psychotherapists, psychiatrists or any other.

One final note, it is important for managers to realise they are not omnipotent, and where they have become closely involved with a suicidal employee, they may not be able to prevent or postpone suicide. Someone who wants to commit suicide will eventually be able to do so.

The manager's responses to employees affected by the suicide of a relative

The final way in which managers may encounter suicide is through the death by suicide of a close relative of an employee. In this case the employee should be treated in the same way as any other bereaved employee as discussed before (see chapter 16.) It should be noted however, that the guilt, anger and shame is likely to be even stronger in such an individual and that the grieving process may be more intense and prolonged.

Further reading

Alvarez A. *The savage god: a study of suicide.* New York, Random House, 1972.

Kennedy Eugene, *On becoming a counsellor.* Gill and McMillan, 1977.

Parkes C M. *Bereavement: studies of grief in adult life.* London, Penguin, 1983.

Warr P B. *Work, unemployment and mental health.* Oxford, Oxford University Press, 1987.

Wordes J William. *Grief counselling and grief therapy,* London, Tavistock Publications, 1983.

Resource

Samaritans: local emergency numbers are listed in the telephone directory.

18 Disability or Chronic Sickness

Introduction

A look at some possible causes of disability or disabling conditions provides a reminder that disability is no respecter of age, sex, social class, race or religion. The following list is not intended to be exhaustive:

- accident at work, home, on the roads, during sport or recreational activities
- traumatic illness such as stroke, coronary, thrombosis
- degenerative illness such as multiple sclerosis, Parkinson's disease, Aids (Aids is dealt with separately in chapter 19)
- other illness with potentially disabling effects such as arthritis or cancer
- the normal process of ageing can have an extreme effect on someone who had only a very slight disability previously. For instance, a weakness in one leg can put an additional strain on the other, which can lead to osteoarthritis in a hip, making walking very difficult in middle or later life.

You will see from the above that the onset of a disabling condition can be swift or gradual. The psychological effects on the individual will depend on many factors including age, type of disability/illness, importance of those activities that the person is unable to continue, degree of support available from friends and family, financial circumstances, security of employment, living conditions, and in general the number and nature of difficulties that have to be confronted.

It is important to emphasise that people with disabilities are exactly the same people as they were before the disabling event. It is too easy to fall into the trap of regarding disabled people as different, and using terms like 'the disabled' does little to help.

Definitions of disability

Three terms are commonly used to refer to disablement or disability: 'impairment', 'disability' and 'handicap'.

Impairment refers to the medical condition or lack of functioning: for instance, paraplegia.

Disability refers to the effect that the impairment has in relation to normal human expectations: unable to walk, lack of control over bowels and bladder.

Handicap refers to the problems encountered when faced by the environment: unable to climb stairs, to turn round in a limited space, use an ordinary toilet, and so on.

If a person with a disability cannot perform a task that an able bodied person can perform due to some environmental obstacle such as a step or a high shelf, then the 'fault' is as much, or more, a feature of the environment as it is of the person. Nothing can be done by an employer or colleagues to alleviate the disability. However, a considerable amount can be done to remove the handicap by removing obstacles in the environment. Practical steps which the employer can take are reviewed at the end of this chapter.

Emotional responses to disability or chronic sickness

The psychological effects of the diagnosis of a potentially disabling condition, or the onset of disability itself, can be as debilitating as the physical effects themselves.

The actual experience of a disabling condition, whether as a result of a loss of limb or the encroaching disability due to a degenerative illness, will result in a range of strong emotions. Whilst practical measures can help the person cope with their situation, specialist counselling may be needed in order to provide emotional support and adjustment.

The type of emotions associated with a disabling condition will vary from one person to another in much the same way as people differ in their response to other traumatic experiences, eg bereavement. A detailed examination of all responses is beyond the scope of this book. However, examples of the type of reactions that may be experienced are reviewed here.

The introduction to this chapter outlined the various ways in which disability may be experienced, ranging from accidents to ageing. Disability in whatever form will evoke a considerable amount of psychological stress. One person may experience stress much sooner than another but every person will experience it at some stage of the disabling condition; for example, on diagnosis, during the treatment and its results and any of the side effects, or during confrontations with the medical organisation and/or employer and reactions of friends and family.

Stress may be more subtle in form, due for example to the worried expression on the face of a doctor, friend or work colleague, the lack of speed with which things happen or conversely the speed with which things do take place. In addition the person is likely to be faced with four pervading emotions.

- uncertainty
- negative feelings
- loss of control
- threat of loss of self esteem

Uncertainty

The future becomes very unpredictable. Questions about the outcome of the disabling condition on the person, their family and job will pervade the person's thoughts. Questions will include: Is treatment possible? What is the best form? Will it help? Who provides it? How will it affect me? How far will I recover? How long will it be before I can be independent again? How should I react? Will I be able to carry on working? How will my family react?

Negative feelings

People will often feel ashamed and withdraw from their existing support network. This, coupled with feelings of anxiety, fear, guilt, anger, apathy, sorrow and depression contributes to long periods of loneliness and desperation. Negative feelings may persist into periods of remission or, in the case of cancer, even when it has been cured, particularly where it has involved surgery. Women for instance who have had mastectomies begin to view their bodies with distaste and their self confidence declines, and as a consequence interpersonal relationships become more difficult.

Loss of control

This is related to several events. Loss of control relates to the inability to manage or influence the course of the disabling condition, the way it is treated or the future in general.

Threat to self esteem

The person's self image is often closely aligned to how one feels about one's body; and about the ability to be independent and lead a 'normal' life. The disabling condition can significantly affect all aspects of a person's life.

As already mentioned, where surgery is a requisite of treatment the person will mourn the loss of that part of the body. Mastectomy may lead a women to feel that she has lost her attractiveness, femininity or womanhood.

Disability of any kind continues to carry a stigma. People tend to focus on the disability and forget the person. The able-bodied individual feels embarrassed and impotent and is reminded of his or her own vulnerability, death and dying.

Reactions of others to disabled people

The following case studies illustrate how people in the workplace may inadvertently react to people with disabling conditions.

Labelling

John was looking forward to returning to work after a break of 18 months. He had been employed by his company, an engineering firm, for ten years. Up until the time of his accident he had taken no sick leave. Following a car accident, however, his left leg had been amputated below the knee.

John had come into work to discuss with his foreman the type of work he could return to. John recognised that he wouldn't be able to do parts of his existing job, which required heavy lifting and carrying. He was keen to continue to use his manual skills on bench and machine work. The foreman listened to John's expectations but his responses concentrated on John's disability rather than his ability, which had been demonstrated during ten years of service. 'I really don't know how we'll cope. What happens if there's a fire? You're bound to get tired quickly.'

The 'disabled' label prevented the foreman from looking at John's assets, preferring that John should conform to the perceived limitations and potentials of that label, and disregarding personality. In the foreman's mind John was now an amputee, and amputees were not capable of doing the same work as the able-bodied.

Labels encompass the whole range of disabilities, eg the deaf, crippled, the handicapped, the blind, spastics and so on. Since how we perceive ourselves, value ourselves and attempt to enhance ourselves is significantly influenced by interactions with others, the ability of the individual to cope with stress or disability will depend in part, on how their family, friends and work colleagues react to them. Over-protection either at work or at home or preventing efforts to return to work can contribute to an inadequate self concept as much for the able-bodied person as the disabled person.

Managers should keep in mind when talking to someone like John that person's personality prior to the disability. The person with a poor self concept and accompanying feelings of inadequacy before the disability may exhibit an increase in these feelings afterwards (and of course the reverse will also be true).

Pity

Simon, a successful solicitor in a major London firm had been diagnosed with multiple sclerosis (MS) two years previously. Since that time Simon has experienced a slow decline in his general motor abilities. During remission no one would know that Simon experienced any difficulties.

On this particular day, Simon had completed his client's work early and decided to take the next day (Friday) as a holiday. He felt satisfied with a hectic and successful week of negotiations. Simon therefore looked into the senior partner's office to let him know he was going early and would not be back until Monday. The partner immediately became very concerned and with a pained expression and a gentle slow voice asked: 'How are you feeling?' Simon replied: 'Fine, thought I'd have a long weekend', smiled and went on his way. As Simon left, another partner entered the office and, seeing the sad expression on his colleague's face, enquired what was wrong. The reply was: 'Simon used to accomplish so much; it's a real shame to see him this way'.

Pity is probably the most common feeling people in our society have for people who are physically disabled. Managers are not likely to be any different in their reactions.

The senior partner in the law firm focused disproportionately on what he saw to be the negative aspects of Simon's life: pain, suffering, difficulty, frustration, fear and rejection. Simon is typically believed to be fragile, hopeless, despairing and a victim of misfortune. Although the partner may be aware of these negative feelings and thoughts and try not to show them, the feelings still emerge through his tone of voice and facial expressions. The partner overlooked Simon's success with his client and his pleasure at the opportunity of a long weekend. In fact it seems likely that Simon had integrated his disability into his total self concept and was continuing to enjoy a successful career.

Characteristic feelings commonly communicated about the disabled person in this situation include:

- 'If it happened to me, I'd fall apart'
- 'It's such a pity'
- 'I could never handle that'.

I'll do it, don't worry

Alison, wheelchair-bound for the past five years because of paralysis below the waist, mentioned to her supervisor that she was finding the new word processing package difficult to grasp. The supervisor listened carefully to Alison as she explained what she found difficult and why, then expressed an understanding of the problems and stated: 'I'll see what I can do for you'.

Later that week, whilst having lunch with the departmental manager, the supervisor mentioned Alison's difficulties. They both agreed that Alison should go back to the old word processing package: 'After all, Alison has enough to contend with and she tries hard to do as much as the others'.

The 'I'll do it, don't worry' reaction, is similar to pity. The supervisor feels sorry for Alison and also sees her as being in need of help, immature, and generally incapable of managing personal affairs and their associated frustrations. The well-meaning supervisor adopts an over-protective, dependency-fostering, advocative role. As Alison's 'saviour' the supervisor extends special privileges and at times may actually perform the task for her. By extending special assistance, a degree of pressure or personal guilt that the supervisor may feel is lifted.

By encouraging the departmental manager to make special provisions for Alison, the supervisor has unwittingly fostered dependency, rather than accountability and self reliance. The supervisor has also short-circuited a process that had the potential for growth and development: instead the result may increase Alison's sense of helplessness and despair. Had Alison been encouraged to work hard and perhaps have further training, and had the outcome been successful, Alison's self image as well as the manager's and supervisor's perceptions of Alison would have been more positive.

The characteristics of this response by a manager are:

- 'Give (the employee) a break'
- 'It's too difficult for you'
- 'It's OK, I understand'.

I know what's best for you

Bob had been blind since birth, and had been employed as a switchboard operator in various companies for six years. The current employer was a firm of accountants and Bob had arranged an appointment with the personnel manager to ask about further career opportunities. At the meeting, Bob talked about a long-standing interest in mathematics and his desire eventually to become an accountant. He mentioned the advances in technology opening new horizons to blind people, and the fact that in America blind people were already doing accountancy work. The personnel manager interrupted at this stage and asked whether Bob knew that their firm required people to have a degree before entering.

Bob replied that he was aware of this and that his parents would sponsor him through an Open University course if the firm was prepared to offer him the chance at the end. The personnel manager appeared to disregard all this information and began to ask Bob if he enjoyed the switchboard work, complimenting him on his ability in this area. Bob said he did enjoy it, but wanted a new challenge. The manager then asked Bob if he had thought about taking on other duties in addition to the switchboard, such as booking flight arrangements and couriers. The discussion continued with the personnel manager emphasising the potential increase in Bob's existing work if he wanted it. The manager did most of the talking mentioning several times how valued Bob was in his existing job.

The personnel manager is often in the position to provide either encouragement and a sense of optimism or to discourage and dampen enthusiasm. In the above the personnel manager reacted negatively, and Bob's aspirations were effectively suppressed.

Having gone through the motions of soliciting Bob's ideas for the future, the personnel manager then proceeded to impose their own limitations on Bob's ambitions and on the educational and vocational opportunities that appeared to merit further exploration. The personnel manager obviously believed that a blind person could not become an accountant in their firm. Having responded negatively they have made a judgement about Bob's future success in achieving his objectives. Although they may have been well-meaning and may possibly have made a conscious effort to protect Bob from potential failure or rejection by the firm, Bob's right to autonomy and self determination was stifled.

It is important to focus on the person's ability and the way in which disability may be overcome or compensated for. People do achieve goals which were seemingly impossible. The person's goal should be respected and properly researched by both parties before a decision can be made. A decision that raises false hopes should be avoided, as should the presenting of a falsely interested, supportive image.

Responses like those of this personnel manager are typical:

- 'It doesn't make sense'
- 'Don't be unrealistsic'
- 'You'll never make it'
- 'You've got to go at your own speed'
- 'You're not ready yet'.

Discomfort

Harry had left college with four 'O' levels and had recently spent eight weeks at an Employment Rehabilitation Centre (ERC) where he had demonstrated an aptitude for clerical work. He was about to have his first interview for a part-time job. After getting along well with staff and students at the college, and people at the ERC, Harry was optimistic about his chances. Harry had cerebral palsy.

When Harry met the personnel officer, he was greeted somewhat abruptly. The personnel officer talked to Harry in a loud, harsh tone as if Harry had difficulty hearing and there was no eye contact. The personnel officer also spent less time with Harry than with other applicants. At the end of the interview the personnel officer suggested that Harry reconsider clerical work as an option and that he should take the matter up with the disablement resettlement officer (DRO).

The personnel officer had an overriding feeling of revulsion and wanted, consciously or unconsciously, to reject Harry. Harry's physical appearance was unpleasant, unco-ordinated and may have invoked feelings of disgust, anger, resentment, or frustration in the personnel officer. Trying to interview Harry became a burdensome, draining experience, and these feelings were transmitted by impatience and avoidance. People in these situations may be kept waiting and interviews may be cut short, or the usual warm greeting or extended handshake may be absent.

Another person may try to over compensate for feelings of pity, guilt or discomfort: the result is a failure to empathise with the person and the communicated message is: 'I don't feel the least bit concerned about you, your disability makes no difference'. The person like Harry who may be most in need of the manager's support and assistance is viewed with contempt by the manager, who seems intolerant of his needs and demands and resents any additional time and attention required. The comments about people like Harry are typically communicated by the counsellor or manager to other colleagues, families and friends and may include phrases like:

– 'I wish I didn't have to see (the person)'
– 'I'm stuck with (the person)'
– 'I'd love to get somebody else to see this person'
– 'This gives me the creeps'.

You're so brave

Patsy had been a research chemist for 15 years. For the last two years she had been working on a project that was now nearing completion and the expected outcome was better than predicted. Six months previously, Patsy developed a lump in her breast which was diagnosed as cancer. The type of cancer and its early detection meant that Patsy's prognosis was good. On leaving one evening her manager remarked how hard Patsy was working and how she never ceased to amaze him. This manager had uncharacteristically begun to lavish praise on Patsy for relatively inconsequential results. This was embarrassing for Patsy and seen as odd by her colleagues.

The manager in this situation is allocating an inferior status to Patsy because of her presumed physical and emotional difficulties. Patsy's actual achievements are over-valued and she is regarded as brave, remarkable and courageous. The manager apparently regards Patsy as less capable of accomplishing her tasks and meeting deadlines than her healthy colleagues. The manager is unable to come to terms with the reality that someone with whom he has regular contact has cancer, and is projecting his own inadequacy in this situation on to Patsy. Other responses typically seen in managers when confronted by people with illnesses like cancer are extremes of anxiety: because of limited previous contact with people who are ill or disabled, the manager naturally becomes tense and uneasy.

Anxiety may result for other reasons. Brought face-to-face with physical disability and illness, the manager may be reminded of his or her own mortality and susceptibility to injury or illness, or of that of someone closely related. The manager may become anxious because of feelings of inadequacy, helplessness, and embarrassment at not being able to understand what the person is saying or because of lack of ability to competently assist the person. Finally, anxiety may result from feeling overwhelmed and depressed at the severity of the person's disability.

Guidelines on appropriate responses

There is no one way in which a manager or work colleagues should respond to the person with disability. The following guidelines may however be useful and help to alleviate the stress that results, not just from the disease but from the conspiracy of silence that develops around the person with disability.

The manager should not:
 – be afraid to use the term describing their disability or disabling condition, eg cancer, stroke, blind etc. Avoid saying it, however, in a tone that conveys fear, distaste or sadness.
 – force the person to talk about it if they do not wish to. It is likely that the person will talk more freely and openly about the disability and treatment as time progresses. If however the person withdraws completely or shows signs of depression then

the person should be encouraged to see a counsellor or their GP.
- attempt to answer the person's questions about their condition, eg cancer, or what will happen.
- dismiss the person's attempts to talk about their circumstances. Where this is done, eg 'I'm sure everything will be OK', 'You'll adapt, wait and see', it is an avoidance tactic by the person being approached.

The manager should:
- familiarise themselves with the disabling condition and if or how it is treated; and with the types of reactions that people have to treatment. Without a basic understanding of these areas, and an effort to come to terms with what the disabling condition means to the manager, their ability to help and support someone else is diminished.
- establish the person's support mechanisms. Do they have close family and friends? How have they reacted? Let them know about various support groups. These may benefit the individual and their family.
- assure the person that their job is secure. If the person eventually becomes too ill to continue, the manager should remember this may only be a temporary condition. Most people will make decisions about their employment themselves on the basis of the medical information they are given. In some instances the person may be unable to return to work without some changes in their work situation.
- encourage the person to gather as much information as they need (and/or want). Many people will leave a doctor or hospital with many unanswered questions. The manager should encourage the person to write down the questions they want answered, prioritise them and then seek answers either from the medical resources or other information and support services.
- offer support to the person. Support will provide the person with a greater sense of control and help maintain self esteem.

Practical measures

There are a range of practical measures which an employer can take in order to retain or employ a person who has experienced a disability. The practical responses can be thought of in two stages: short term and long term.

Short term

- Establish contact as soon as possible after diagnosis or traumatic event – for instance, the manager could visit the person in hospital.
- Let the employee know that their financial position is secure during this phase through normal pay, sick pay, or through DSS benefit, if possible.
- Let the employee know that he or she need not have any concerns about future employment, as there will still be a position within the firm when he or she recovers, if at all possible.
- Reassure family also.

If a person is going to return to work following an illness or disabling event and their appearance or performance will have changed, it can ease this return if the way is prepared not only in terms of providing aids and adaptations to the premises and equipment, but also by preparing the person's colleagues by explaining to them what to expect. This also applies if employing a disabled person for the first time.

Long term

The return to work is only the first step for a person who has become disabled. An able-bodied person does not expect to stay in exactly the same job for ever, but expects to progress on to better jobs, to take on greater responsibilities, more managerial duties, and to receive a higher salary in respect of these greater responsibilities. A disabled person should similarly be considered for the same enhancements of job and salary in relation to competence and experience. All too often people with disabilities are passed over for promotion because the employer focuses on what the person cannot do, or may not be able to do in the future, rather than making an objective assessment of what he can do and what special qualities he can bring to a job.

The legal position

Under the Disabled Persons (Employment) Act 1944, amended 1958, an employer with 20 or more employees must employ at least three

per cent registered disabled people. It is not an offence to be below
quota, but if below quota an employer should recruit only registered
disabled people until at quota. It is possible, however, to get a permit
to employ able-bodied workers under these circumstances if no
suitable disabled people can be recruited. Many disabled people no
longer register because they feel that there is a stigma to having a
'green card' and do not believe that registering enhances their
chances of being employed. Therefore, it is now generally considered
to be acceptable practice to have three per cent registered and
unregistered disabled people on the workforce.

Under the Companies (Directors' Report) (Employment of
Disabled Persons) Regulations 1980, which form part of the
Companies Act 1948-1983, companies with 250 e nployees working
within the UK must include in their directors' report a statement
describing the previous year's policy with regard to: recruitment of
disabled people; and training, career development and promotion
of disabled people.

Checklist of things the manager should consider before employee's return to work

1   Is it likely that the person will be able to return to their old job?
    If uncertain, the manager should work through the job
    description with them and discuss those elements of the job
    description that they are able to carry out, those over which there
    is some doubt, and those that will be impossible. They should
    discuss the possibility of adapting or dropping those elements
    that will be impossible, trying out those over which there is doubt
    and adapting them as necessary, and introducing new elements
    compatible with the nature of the job. It is obviously easier to
    take this approach if there is an established staff development
    and appraisal system and/or accurate job description by
    negotiation with the individual rather than imposing anything
    from outside.
2   Will any special equipment be required, or adaptations to existing
    equipment?
    The Department of Employment can not only advise on how to
    carry out any necessary adaptations, but can also assist
    financially. The office to contact is the local Disablement
    Advisory Service (DAS) – formerly part of the Manpower
    Services Commission.

3   Is access to the work station likely to be a problem?
    A considerable amount can be done to adapt premises to make
    it possible for a disabled person to continue in work. Again the
    DAS team may be able to help with both advice and financial
    assistance.
4   Will there be any difficulties in the person getting to work?
    If a person has difficulty in using public transport, the
    Disablement Advisory Service may be able to assist with taxi
    fares through the 'Fares to Work' scheme. If the person cannot
    use a taxi either, there may be a local voluntary organisation
    operating a special transport system.
5   Will the person be able to continue living in their existing house,
    following adaptations by the Social Services Department if
    necessary?
    If he or she will have to move, the employer might consider
    paying removal expenses: they would consider paying relocation
    costs to someone moving into the area, so why not do the same
    to help an employee continue to work for the company.
6   If he or she cannot continue within their old position, would it
    be possible for them to continue elsewhere within the
    organisation, with retraining if necessary?
7   Will he or she be unable to reach a satisfactory level of
    productivity?
    If he or she will not be able to reach their old level of productivity,
    but could reach 30 per cent or more of that level, it may still be
    possible to retain the employee at no financial cost to the
    company. There is a scheme called the Sheltered Placement
    Scheme (SPS): contact the Disablement Resettlement Officer at
    the local Job Centre for details.
8   Would the person be able to return to work earlier if he or she
    started work part-time?
    The manager should consider letting the employee build up the
    number of hours worked gradually.

What the manager is doing with these measures is to protect the
investment made in the staff in terms of training and experience.
The organisation is not offering charity. If it is obvious that the
person will not be able to work either in their old job or anywhere
else within the company, it is not kind to carry him in an unproductive
position.

What to do now

Managers should not wait until an employee becomes disabled, but should draw up policy guidelines. In drawing up guidelines of how the manager and staff should act, the manager should think about how he or she would want to be treated should it happen to them; and consider whether the workplace is accessible to someone who is blind or deaf, or cannot walk far, or uses a wheelchair.

Emergency considerations

Before embarking on adaptations to premises for somebody whose mobility is impaired, an employer should check whether the adaptations would infringe fire regulations. This does not mean that employees using wheelchairs cannot be employed above ground floor level: it will depend on the topography of the building and emergency exits. Advice should be taken from the local fire brigade at an early stage. Fire considerations alone are seldom sufficient to make it impossible to retain an employee.

Evacuation equipment to help get disabled people out of a building should also be available – for instance evacuation chairs enable one person to evacuate a mobility impaired person.

Finally, the manager should check that they have done everything possible to prevent accidents at work:

- Are the machines safe?
- Does everyone know the evacuation procedures?
- Are all corridors, stairways, and circulation areas free from obstacles that people could bump into, trip over?
- Are there trained first-aiders, health and safety representatives and fire wardens?

Summary

It is a cliché among those trying to improve the employment prospects of disabled people that a disabled person makes a better employee through working harder and being more loyal than the typical able-bodied person. But everybody is different and there are good and bad employees among disabled people just as there are among able-bodied. However, it is harder for a disabled person to find work, and harder to find a job in which he is properly valued and receives equal treatment in relation to training and progression. If a person is treated well in employment, and for a disabled person this can be just being treated as if he were not disabled, he is likely to respond through loyalty and productivity.

Further reading

Birkett K *and* Worman D. *Getting on with disabilities – an employers' guide.* IPM, 1988.

Confederation of British Industry. *Employing disabled people.* London, CBI, 1983.

Manpower Services Commission. *Code of good practice on the employment of disabled people.* Sheffield, MSC, 1984.

Manpower Services Commission. *Employing disabled people: sources to help.* Sheffield, MSC, 1985.

TUC. *TUC guide to employment of disabled people.* London, TUC, 1985.

Resources

Access and Disabled Graduates Project, Branston Crescent, Tile Hill Lane, Coventry CV4 9SW. 0203 694302.

Association of Disabled Professionals, The Stables, 73 Pond Road, Banstead, Surrey SM7 2HJ. Tel: 0924 270335.

British Computer Society, Disability Committee, 13 Mansfield Street, London W1. 071–637 0471.

Cranfield Institute of Technology, nr Bedford, Beds. 0234–750111.

Disabled Living Foundation, 380–84 Harrow Road, London W9. 071–289 6111.

Local Disablement Resettlement Office (DRO) based at local jobcentres, or the area disablement advisor based at the Department of Employment Area Office.

National Bureau for Handicapped Students, 336 Brixton Road, London SW9 7AA. 071–274 0565.

Opportunities for the Disabled, 1 Bank Buildings, Princes Street, London EC2R 8EV. 071–726 4963.

Queen Elizabeth's Residential Training College for the Disable
    Leatherhead, Surrey. 037284–2204.
Royal Association for Disability and Rehabilitation, 25 Mortim
    Street, London W1N 8AB. 071–637 5400.
Royal National Institute for the Blind, 224 Great Portland Stre
    London W1N 6AA. 071–388 1266.
Royal National Institute for the Deaf, 105 Gower Street, Lond
    WC1E 6AH. 071–387 8033.

19 AIDS

Introduction

All available indicators suggest that the incidence of employees with the HIV virus will increase. AIDS has become a significant problem in our society, throwing into sharp focus people's feelings about sex, sexuality and drug use, and creating a real fear which arises from very deep, sometimes irrational feelings about sexuality, chastity, disfigurement and death.

Issues that disrupt the work environment need to be addressed by managers, and intelligent anticipation of these problems, adequately supported by basic training, should enable procedures to be developed for dealing with situations as they arise. AIDS is likely to evoke a very particular range of emotions and issues among employees, and therefore it is a subject which requires separate attention in this book.

One of the many repercussions of AIDS to affect the workplace has been the issue of sexual activity. Men and women, but more particularly men who travel abroad, or who are in the high risk groups, have been quick to recognise the risks associated with having more than one sexual partner. Many cases have been publicised of people contracting AIDS as a result of them or their partner having more than one relationship.

Information programmes

One example of the fear that AIDS engenders in people is vividly portrayed by a married female employee who, as a result of media attention on AIDS, became convinced that a man she'd slept with three years previously had AIDS. Every ache and pain reinforced her fear. She was unable to sleep and her work quickly suffered. With counselling she was able to see that this fear was irrational and really a manifestation of the guilt she had been carrying with her for three years. She was able to address these feelings and decided to tell her husband of her past affair. This was a risk she felt she needed to take to resolve her emotions, and happily her relationship was strong enough to withstand this.

The above case shows how an intelligent and rational person can be thrown into turmoil as a result of the fear associated with AIDS. Imagine this fear transported into the workplace, and the repercussions are potentially enormous. For this reason line and personnel managers and supervisors should be proactive, by providing educational services and introducing non-discriminatory policies; and reactive by dealing with the issues as they arise. AIDS demands that both types of employer responses are considered: neither is sufficient alone.

Many companies have held talks and seminars to inform employees of the disease and how it is contracted and how it is *not* contracted. However the range of emotions that are associated with AIDS often make effective communication difficult. One way of bringing the range of feelings and reactions towards AIDS out into the open, and to enable employees to gain a more accurate perspective of their emotions towards it, is to ask groups of managers and employees how they would deal with an employee who was upset about a co-worker with HIV. It is most likely that there will be considerable disagreement, charged emotions, fear and anger and very little understanding of the medical data or the employee's legal rights. Whilst it is easy to state that the HIV virus cannot be passed on in every day work activities, managers and supervisors may feel unable to cope with the fear and conflict that may emerge among employees, perhaps mirroring their own anxieties and values.

The workplace presents an opportunity to give reliable information and education which, if not taken, may potentially result in confusion, anger and discord. AIDS is a topic about which everyone will have an opinion; how far the facts will influence these opinions is debatable. Despite a considerable flow of information, facts about the disease are often neglected, ignored or distorted.

HIV: the sufferer's response

People who have AIDS are likely to be sensitive to rejection and prejudice. It is also likely that they will fear or anticipate a negative response. These and other reasons lead people to prefer to make use of the many specialist agencies which have been established for health care, counselling and support. Line and personnel managers should refer people to these specialist agencies whilst adopting a supportive role within the company policy or procedural guidelines.

This negative expectation is likely to be increased in the workplace and may have been verified by either personal experience or vicariously, through the experience of others in their social circle. The diagnosis of HIV or AIDS may reveal aspects of their lives to friends, family and work colleagues which have previously been hidden, reinforcing the fear of rejection and isolation. They may also feel guilty about their sexual orientation and the possibility of having passed the disease to their partners.

People in long term relationships are likely to experience emotional distress where their partner is diagnosed as HIV positive. Thoughts and emotions may be confused. Anger may be directed to the partner with questions concerning fidelity, lack of honesty, being put at risk of the disease, impending or actual isolation.

Considerable support and understanding will be needed to help the partner and family come to terms with the combined revelations of HIV diagnosis and the potential death of a loved one. Families of haemophiliacs will need special help. They will have already cared for the person through one life-threatening illness, to be confronted with an additional set of health problems. Anger and hopelessness are likely.

Lastly, the partner may have caught the virus, which will compound existing emotions and distress. This will obviously have consequences for his or her own health and well-being; in the case of women it will also have consequences for any future plans for pregnancy, since it would be likely that the virus would be passed to the baby.

For drug abusers there is the additional problem of coping with their drive to satisfy their addiction, which does not abate due to AIDS. They may continue to share needles and have sex without precautions. They are also likely to experience guilt for having the addiction, for failing to restrain from activities likely to pass on AIDS, and particularly in the event of passing it on.

The person's pre-existing disposition and personality will play an important mitigating role in determining how the person will respond to a diagnosis of HIV positive. It should be possible for a manager to identify changes in an individual's behaviour following the guidelines described in earlier chapters, (eg chapter 1 on stress) and distinguish both unusual (and potentially harmful) reactions and psychiatric complications. Referral to specialist resources would be needed at this time.

As with other life-threatening diseases, a reactive stage theory has
been developed as a framework to help identify the reactions that
people may pass through following diagnosis of HIV/AIDS. The
model proposed by Nichols (1985) is described here. Like other
models of this type it needs to be remembered that all people are
different and are unlikely to fit into a neat pattern of response.

Initial crisis

There is often vacillation between anxiety and denial. These emotions
are typically very strong and may interfere with the person's ability
to understand and respond to medical advice, possibly leading to
distortions of what they are told. The person needs time to absorb
and to come to terms with the facts. In the workplace the person
may fail to carry out instructions accurately. This is often due to
problems of retaining information and poor concentration.

Transition

This is a time when emotions become jumbled with thoughts of
anger, guilt, self pity and anxiety. Depression may occur. The person
may obsessively review their past in an attempt to understand what
they have done to 'deserve' AIDS. It is possible that some people
will displace their anger onto others, with extreme irritability and
feelings of persecution. The person's own self concept is under threat
at this time. High risk groups such as homosexuals and intravenous
drug users may already have self concept difficulties relating to the
general lack of acceptability from society as a whole. Diagnosis often
exacerbates this social isolation and reinforces feelings of rejection.
They may want to withdraw from other people, including friends
and family.

Accepting limitations

There is a continuum of illness related to HIV infection. People can
range from being HIV positive with no symptoms, through to those
with physical symptoms who are suffering from AIDS Related
Complex (ARC – at least two well defined symptoms of immunodeficiency combined with at least two laboratory abnormalities),
and to those with full blown AIDS, which describes people with
life-threatening complications developed as a result of their low

resistance to infection. People with either of the first two diagnoses may find it easier to accept a later diagnosis of AIDS than someone who was not previously diagnosed as being HIV positive or having ARC. The progression from one state to another is not automatic and may not occur.

This period is perhaps the most difficult and involves the person attempting to come to terms with the limitations which the disease can impose. There may be fluctuations between this stage and the transitional stage. The person will benefit from help in coming to terms with the limitations and from the realisation that they can still manage their lives by reacting to the disease with reason not emotion. It is at this time that spiritual concepts may be embraced to contribute to hope and relief.

Attitudes towards health and the health care system are likely to vary widely. What is a health problem for one person may not be for another. Some will trust the support and care offered by doctors, counsellors, friends and work colleagues, while others will distrust the motives and potential outcome of the help offered, particularly in the workplace.

Situational distress

This takes place when crises occur and acceptance of the situation is temporarily lost. New crises may lead to a renegotiation of previous stages in order to reach acceptance again. A crisis may be the rejection by a loved one, or family, work colleagues or the cumulative effects of stress from the circumstances facing the person. Insomnia, anxiety, depression and other symptoms can all contribute to situational distress. The person may also fluctuate between fatalism (everyone has to die sometime) to complete denial (it can't happen to me).

The manager's reactions

Managers are likely to be faced with having to take direct action should a problem related to AIDS occur. This could range from people refusing to work with a colleague they consider homosexual to interpersonal problems and harassment of the employee.

Managers may doubt their ability to make rational and responsible decisions. As a consequence there is a particular need for managers to be well informed, to discuss the issue openly with colleagues and determine what their options are in the light of rapidly changing circumstances. To deal effectively with AIDS in the workplace managers must face their own fears about the disease. Those managers and employees who hold negative attitudes towards AIDS and its association with different groups of people, eg homosexuals, will need support to come to terms with feelings and issues surrounding AIDS.

Where personnel or line managers recognise that they hold extreme attitudes and are unable to reconcile them, they should refer the employee with HIV (or work colleagues concerned about the disease) to another person, eg the company doctor, who may be better placed to help and support the individual. Alternatively the manager should themselves seek close support from colleagues in order to avoid his or her personal attitudes affecting professional behaviour.

What can be done?

Where an employee has been diagnosed as HIV positive and where management are aware of this fact, an assessment of that person's ability to perform their job may eventually be required. This assessment should be focused on any physical and behavioural manifestations of the disease that begin to impair work performance. An interview should take place with the objective of determining the nature of any impairment, its severity, the person's coping skills and personal supports, eg friends and relatives.

Line and personnel managers should seek to acquire this information in conjunction with either a medical specialist, eg the company doctor, or a trained counsellor. Information gained should be treated as totally confidential.

Gathering information of this type will be complicated by the potential range of physical problems that may emerge and change as the disease progresses. Many people diagnosed as HIV positive will feel healthy. However an infection may develop suddenly or gradually and require periods of absence whilst treatment or recovery takes place.

From the outset, the employee with HIV/AIDS is likely to see the situation as awkward, perhaps absolutely impossible. Developing a climate which is open and supportive will require a lead by the organisation itself. This can only be done by acknowledging that employees with HIV/AIDS may be distrustful, evasive or uninformative, and establishing the best ways to overcome this.

Attempts at reassurances, clear statements of the managers' professional attitude about AIDS and observation of the legal position may facilitate constructive discussions between relevant parties. Formation of a specific and non-discriminatory policy should set out to deal with AIDS in substantially the same way as other disabilities. Consequently, an employer may need to intervene where an employee with AIDS has become so severely debilitated by the disease that they cannot perform the job's essential tasks (likely to be the case at advanced stages of the disease). Arrangements for absences should also be considered. A case by case approach will be needed within a policy framework.

Considerations also need to be given to specific emotions that may emerge (eg depression, anxiety) as a result of the individual's personal circumstances, both for people with HIV or AIDS and those in close proximity to them. Practical needs such as shopping, housework, cooking, housing etc will also be of concern as the person becomes more susceptible to illness. Information relating to social and welfare rights would be valuable if the person needs to stop working.

The quality of support that a person is likely to receive is another crucial factor and will vary considerably between and within friends, family, work colleagues etc. Men and women who have been diagnosed HIV positive should have been given counselling support and this is available on a long-term basis from counsellors at the various clinics, and from specialist voluntary groups such as the Terrence Higgins Trust. Disclosure of diagnosis can strengthen bonds or sever them: the person will need help to determine who should know and how to tell them. These are aspects which should be dealt with by the specialist support groups.

Summary

It is likely that an employee diagnosed as having the HIV virus will find it difficult to trust his or her employer unless there is a climate of trust engendered by clear non-discriminatory policy statements, evidence of fair treatment for previous sufferers, or a good relationship between the individual and his or her peers and manager.

Trust is therefore the first hurdle that needs to be overcome. Talking openly and honestly about the illness and the likely repercussions on employment will enable the person to see that the situation is being discussed with their full involvement. This will encourage the person to express their anger and avoid the likelihood of it being displaced into other areas of work, for instance in relations with other employees.

The manager should find out about the support systems available to an employee with AIDS, including their relationships outside the workplace. Checks on whether the person has contact with a specialist support group are also important, particularly where the person has shown signs of depression.

The manager should remember that a person with HIV who is a valued employee has not become someone different: the change (if it is perceived) is in the attitude of people who have contact with him or her. One simple way of demonstrating acceptance of the person with AIDS is to touch them. In the workplace this can simply mean shaking hands, a simple act with no physical danger involved, that conveys a clear and open expression of support and caring.

Reference

Nichols S E. 'Psycholosocial reactions of the person with the Aquired Immunodeficiency Syndrome'. *Annals of Internal Medicine* 103 1985. pp765-7

Further reading

Aberth J. 'AIDS: the human element'. *Personnel Journal*, Vol 65, No 8, August 1986. pp 114–119.

Aids and employment. Department of Health and Safety Executive. London, HMSO, 1986. 12pp.

'AIDS and employment: the safety, confidentiality and discrimination issues'. *Occupational Health Review*, No 5 February/March 1987. pp 2–6.

'AIDS and the personnel manager'. *IPM Digest*, No 260, March 1987. pp 16–18.

'AIDS: the employment implications'. *Industrial Relations Review and Report*, No 383, 6 January 1987. (Health and Safety information Bulletin. pp 2–4.

AIDS: the employment issues. Greater London Employers'
Secretariat. London, The Secretariat.

Bayer R *and* Oppenheimer G. 'Living with Aids in the workplace'.
The first of two articles, *Across the Board*.Vol xxiii, No 9,
September 1986. pp 57–61.

Confederation of Health Service Employees. *Guidelines for health
staffs dealing with patients suffering from Acquired Immune
Deficiency Syndrome or with AIDS virus.* Banstead, COHSE, nd
iv, 52pp (Health and Safety Bulletin).

Greasley Phil. *Gay men at work*, London, Lesbian and Gay
Employment Rights, 1986, vi, 104pp.

Letchinger R S. 'AIDS: an employer's dilemma'. *Personnel.* USA,
Vol 63, No 2 February 1986. pp 58–63.

Royal College of Nursing. *Nursing guidelines on the management
of patients in hospital and the community suffering from AIDS.*
London, RCN, 1986. 63pp (Second report of the RCN AIDS
working party).

Schachter V *and* von Seeburg S. *AIDS: a manager's guide.* Executive
Enterprises Publications Co, 1986. 71pp.

Resources

Department of Employment and the Health and Safety Executive,
'AIDS and Employment'. Available from: The Mailing House,
Leeland Road, London, W13 9HL. Extracts of the publication
may be reproduced in an employee newsletter.

Department of Health and Social Security AIDS unit: a general
enquiry point where referrals will be made to appropriate staff.
The service is especially for those in the medical services. Contact:
Aids Unit, Department of Health and Social Security, Alexander
Fleming House, Elephant and Castle, London SE1 6BY. 071–972
2000.

Department of Occupational Health: advice on company AIDS
policies is available. For further information contact: Mike Bailey,
Department of Occupational Health, London School of Hygiene
and Tropical Medicine, Keppel Street, London WC1E 7HT. 071–
636 8636.

Employment Medical Advisory Service (EMAS), The Triod, Stanley
Precinct, Bootle, Merseyside, L20 3PG. 051–922 7211.

Health Education Authority: advice is available from the AIDS consultant: Health Education Authority, 78 New Oxford Street, London WC1A 1AH. 071–631 0930.

Medical Advisory Services for Travellers Abroad: provides sterile medical equipment packs for those travelling abroad, cost £9.80 (including VAT) available from IPS Ltd, 8 Stafford Estate, Hillman Close, Ardleigh Green, Hornchurch, Essex, RM11 2SJ.

Terence Higgins Trust. This organisation offers help and counselling to AIDS sufferers and their friends and relatives. A series of pamphlets is produced including: AIDS – the Facts, Women and AIDS. All pamphlets are available from: BM AIDS, London WC1N 3XX.

Helpline Service Lines open 3–10 pm daily. Telephone 01–242 1010 Vistel Service Lines open 7–10 pm daily. Telephone 01–405 2463.

20   Mental Health

Introduction

It has been estimated that at some stage in their lives between 10 per cent and 15 per cent of the working population of the UK will undergo treatment for mental illness. It is likely that many more would benefit from treatment. Usually the illness is temporary and recovery will be complete, the person returning to work with no adverse effects.

Orlans and Shipley (1983) observed that the annual certified lost time from work in the UK is typically in excess of 300 million days. At least 10 per cent of these are lost through what is officially referred to as 'psychoneurosis'. While problems of classification make this category somewhat difficult to interpret, it does provide an indication of the scale of the problem. To this figure of 30 million working days lost through 'psychoneurosis' must be added time lost through 'psychosomatic' complaints – that is, physical illnesses which either originated in, or have been exacerbated by, psychological and stress-related problems – and all uncertified absence. This would bring the figure to well over 40 million days.

Costing this absence is a complex matter although in 1982 Walter Goldsmith, Director General of the Institute of Directors, suggested the cost to the UK of stress-related absence to be in the region of £3,000 million per annum. Such estimates do not include the less measurable 'costs' of such suffering to the people directly affected, to their families and close associates, to their local community and to society as a whole.

There is no clear and precise definition of mental illness, since it is difficult to determine what constitutes 'normal' behaviour. Most people have periods in their lives when they feel anxious or a little depressed: this does not mean that they are mentally ill. Behaviour may become erratic or unusual for a period, eg showing increased irritability, or long periods of quiet. Periods like this are likely to occur when the person is less able to cope with particular stresses.

Mental illness may be usefully thought of as a continuum from well-being to mental ill-health. Every person will be somewhere along this continuum, although few will ever have perfect well-being or total mental illness (where medical help is of little or no benefit). The majority of people will experience some form of emotional problem. If people can be helped to deal with emotional problems they are less likely to become mentally ill.

Seeing mental illness as a continuum also illustrates that, for the most part, people are able to move out of the area of mental illness into greater well-being. It should never be viewed as a one-way slide downhill. Where this opinion exists it tends to be more as a result of the on-lookers' lack of understanding rather than the person's behaviour being unusual.

The most typical workplace mental illness is the 'nervous breakdown'. The hardworking employee is suddenly 'tipped over the edge' and ends up in hospital. Colleagues often see the beginnings of this type of experience but seldom recognise the likely consequences of what is happening, and far less know what to do about it.

Other mental illness will result from emotional problems after certain definable events, eg bereavement, having a baby, moving house, divorce and so on. Or a previously 'normal' person may experience a period of acute mental illness for no visible reason, which may however be attributed to suppressed past events and experiences suddenly emerging and becoming overwelming. This chapter looks at some of the more common types of mental illness and offers some constructive guidelines for the manager to help and support employees.

Depression

Depression is a state of psychological debility often accompanied by varying degrees of anxiety and despair. It is most common after loss, eg bereavement, divorce, redundancy etc, and is an understandable reaction to events of this kind but should not be confused with sadness. Feelings of guilt and unworthiness pervade the person's thoughts, the future looks hopeless, life seems to have no purpose and on occasions death by suicide is seen as the only solution.

If someone finds that they cannot cope with the demands facing them they can become downhearted, feel sorry for themselves and may cry often and lack energy, which makes them even less able to cope than before thus adding to their depression. Even talking to another person can become too demanding, and the ability to concentrate and remember things is often reduced. The person feels lonely despite having people close by and this sense of isolation can become real as the person appears to reject those who try to comfort and help them.

Loss of appetite is common, so also is constipation, sleeplessness and reduced libido. People who are depressed can also turn to alcohol in an effort to relieve the symptoms, only to find the opposite occurs.

Depression is subdivided into different categories, eg manic depression. This categorisation is medical and discussion of it is mainly outside the scope of this book.

In the case of manic depression, patterns have emerged in some families (there is up to a 24 per cent chance that children of manic depressive parents, and up to 22 per cent of people with a manic depressive child, will also develop the illness), suggesting that there is a genetic basis for the illness.

The most common signs and symptoms of mania and depression have been summarised by the National Association for Mental Health (MIND) to be the following:

Area affected	Depression	Mania
Mood:	low, sad, miserable	high, elated, euphoric
Energy level:	diminished, retarded, sometimes agitated	increased, restless
Behaviour:	slowed up, lethargic, indecisive	erratic, eccentric
Thought content:	pessimistic	optimistic
Thoughts:	slow, laboured	flight of ideas, pressure of thoughts
Speech:	slow, monotonous	rapid, may be incoherent
Insight:	often lacking	generally lacking. Patient may not think of himself/herself as ill.

The manager's response

When faced with someone who appears to be unhappy, it is very
tempting to offer reassurances such as: 'Everything will work out,
you'll see'. Saying this to someone who is depressed will have a
negligible effect. This inability to respond is itself a clear indicator
that the person is experiencing something more serious than simply
feeling down. The manager needs to be alert to this type of numb
response. The responses of colleagues around the depressed person
may also provide a useful indicator of a need for help and support.
The person who is depressed may begin to lose their contact with
other people as he or she finds themselves alienated from their usual
circle of peers. The conversation of colleagues should further reinforce
the realisation that the person needs to be approached. The manager
may hear people say things like: 'Mike's not been himself lately.'
'Jo's never been the same since her mother died.' 'Fred's been so
miserable these last couple of weeks. Nothing seems to shake him
out of it'.

The manager or the person's colleagues may continually offer
well-intentioned advice and reassurance and grow increasingly
frustrated and angry that they are getting no response.

Once the manager is reasonably confident that the person is
experiencing difficulties, a sensitive interview should be held. It is
important to avoid attempts at jokes or other banter to establish a
rapport. The interview needs to be very supportive; the purpose is
to encourage the person to seek help, not to delve into the causes of
the depression. Such activity ought to be avoided as this is the
domain of the professional counsellor, psychologist or psychiatrist
and it serves no purpose to attempt to replicate what they may do
in therapy using their resources of time, training and experience.
The manager should make it clear that it is not a disciplinary
interview (remember the person will be aware that job performance
is suffering and feel very guilty as a result) and that their job is
secure. The purpose is to help the person find appropriate help in
order to restore their well-being and effectiveness.

The manager may be the important first step in encouraging the
person to seek help. The person may lack insight to their illness and
may repeatedly say, 'I don't know what's wrong with me'. The
interview should be held at the person's own pace, which is likely
to be slow. Adequate time and privacy without interruptions are
essential; any remoteness or absence of response should be tolerated

and the interview should have a clear and systematic purpose to it, so that the person being interviewed is not left with feelings of confusion. The manager needs to be prepared for emotional expressions, typically crying (although this may not occur if the person is very depressed).

Depending on the severity of the depression the person may not need to take time off from work or receive any medication. This assessment will be made by a doctor. Mild forms of depression may be helped through professional counselling; more severe forms can often be helped by prescribing antidepressant drugs. The drugs lift many of the symptoms of depression to the stage where therapy or counselling may be useful for some people. Other people may feel that drug therapy suppresses feelings and counselling may in these circumstances be inappropriate. For some people drug therapy may itself be sufficient to resolve a period of depression. If the person is prescribed drugs and returns to work it is helpful for the manager to be aware of the effects that the drugs have on the person's ability to carry out their job fully and safely. Drowsiness is a common side effect, particularly at the beginning of treatment. Proximity to moving machinery, for instance, should be avoided. More serious periods of depression require hospitalisation. The hospital will also often provide follow-up care through out-patient treatment, and monitor the person's progress.

A number of support groups exist for people suffering from depression, and names and addresses are given at the end of this chapter.

Anxiety

Anxiety can be very useful for short periods of time and is normal. Anxiety can increase the adrenalin level in the body to help a person through a specific time of stress. Some people live 'on their nerves' or deliberately get 'keyed up' before important events, eg an approaching deadline can push the person to work harder or longer hours in order to complete the task on time.

If however the person is experiencing ongoing stress or a series of stressful events then the constant high levels of adrenalin will act against the body. Anxiety in these circumstances can become crippling, effectively stopping the person from doing anything constructive.

The cause of anxiety is generally a result of stress with which the person is unable to cope. Different people will reach this stage sooner than others, depending on their personality. Anxiety can also occur without any identifiable source of stress.

Continued anxiety will affect the way in which the person sees and responds to things. At this stage it is often difficult for the person to identify the exact cause of the anxiety and vague explanations are put forward to satisfy any enquiry. Every little change or event is perceived as a serious threat by the person. Past incidents cannot be forgotten and are constantly relived in order to establish whether the right thing has been done or said. The outcome is always seen as negative. All this self examination leads to an ongoing level of stress which makes mental ill health in the form of anxiety more likely.

The employee experiencing anxiety will find it difficult to switch off and get to sleep until the events of the day have subsided. This may take until late into the night. Lack of sleep leads to a reduced concentration and efficiency at work and increases the anxiety. The person will become irritable and their 'normal' personality may disappear. The person may begin to find fault in everything and everyone except themselves, become apprehensive about previously simple tasks and instigate petty arguments which waste more time. The person then becomes angry with themselves for allowing these incidents to occur, even apologising profusely, but also unable to prevent it happening again. In addition, negative aspects of events may dominate the person's thoughts. Where the person has experienced extreme anxiety in a specific situation (a panic attack) the person may as a consequence develop a fear of the fear itself, as opposed to a fear of the actual event. Believing that if it has happened once it will happen again, will prevent the person attempting to enter into the same situation again.

The physical manifestations of anxiety can be seen in problems of sleep, constant tension, aches, pains (particularly in the stomach), sweating, dizziness, a pounding heart and sexual problems.

The manager's response

Where the anxiety is related to a current and specific stressful situation, it may be possible to help the sufferer address it by encouraging him or her to divide the situation into smaller parts and look at each individually. It may also be useful to challenge assumptions by asking them questions like:

– What is the worst thing that could happen if you did (or did not) do that?
– In what way would that be so bad?

Questions like these can help the person to think more rationally about their situation and therefore deal with the anxiety more realistically.

If the employee's anxiety has reached the point where the above steps fail to alleviate it, he or she is likely to benefit from counselling or supportive psychotherapy. Therapy will help them to understand the nature of their anxiety and alleviate the fear that arises from the symptoms. Therapy can also help their self-image and their ability to cope. Eventually a more positive and self sufficient disposition can be achieved.

Other therapies that may be beneficial are learning relaxation, hypnotherapy and on occasions anti-anxiety drugs.

Schizophrenia

Schizophrenia is a common problem. Every year in Britain about 35,000 people are admitted to hospital with schizophrenia, making up one sixth of all people at present in hospital, and a half of all people having hospital treatment for psychiatric problems. Schizophrenia is a term for those who have serious problems with very disturbed thoughts, feelings and behaviour.

Most people with schizophrenia improve with treatment, and it is not often, these days, that people remain in hospital for long. Recovery is not always complete, and some people are left with symptoms and residual difficulties. A third of people with schizophrenia have just one attack and then return to their normal lives. The remainder are liable to further attacks, each perhaps successively more debilitating. However, overall the results of treatment are good and this is even better with a supportive home and work environment and early intervention.

There are many possible symptoms. Often the individual imagines that he or she sees or hears hallucinations; the voices can be funny (the person can be seen laughing to himself), or sometimes these voices may say unpleasant things or command the individual to do things. It is surprising how much the voices can control everyday behaviour. Sometimes the voices make sense: often they do not. The voices may talk to or about the person and may be enjoyable, upsetting or frightening. Sometimes the person has delusions that people are against him or her, or that he or she has special powers. This means a loss of touch with what is really happening. Odd behaviour might include doing or saying unusual things (eg not answering the phone or drawing the curtains and not leaving the house or room). Also the individual may have difficulty thinking clearly, and may say things that don't make sense, may ramble and use mixed speech.

Muddled thinking makes the person very difficult to talk to, and is very frightening for the sufferer. They may not be able to listen, or interpret what you say. Sometimes there is a feeling that the mind is being controlled by alien thoughts or radio waves. At other times the belief could be that their own thoughts are being spoken out loud so that everyone can hear them. The individual may lose interest generally, lose emotions, prefer to be alone and need to sleep more (withdrawal). He or she may become careless in dress and hygiene, or slow and clumsy with everyday jobs. These are some of the ways that people are affected, but every person will be affected differently. None will have all these symptoms together, some may be mild, others serious.

The manager's response

Schizophrenia will always require professional care and attention. The manager should refer the person to their GP, or seek help from other medical resources. Hospital treatment is only required if the doctor feels that the patient has a severe problem requiring close attention and treatment, or that he is a danger to himself and others. The usual length of short term admissions is three to six weeks. Most are treated out of hospital, but are likely to be very upset and frightened and their behaviour quite odd and worrying. Medication may help reduce symptoms and prevent relapse in about 75 per cent of the cases. Medication is prescribed to reduce symptoms, anxiety and restlessness and allow the person to think more clearly. There are at least 20 different types of neuroleptic drug that might be given. Some people will have depot (long lasting) injections which more easily ensure regular doses. One of the first questions that should be explored, if there are signs of a relapse, is whether the person has stopped taking the medication, whether tablets or injections. Unfortunately, if a person feels allright, they can be tempted to discontinue their medication.

Mental illness – an overview of the manager's response

The other chapters in this book identify the steps that the person in the role of counsellor can take in order to help and support an employee who is experiencing a specific problem. Mental ill-health is one example of the problems that people will encouter in their lives. It is, however, an area which is riddled with misconceptions, fear and feelings of helplessness. Mental illness is still something which is 'best dealt with behind closed doors', 'left to the shrinks', 'kept away from normal people'. Such views stop people facing the fact that mental illness, of one degree or another, is relatively common.

The manager is well placed to provide help and support that can reduce these misconceptions and the isolation that the individual (and his or her family) will experience. Often the family will be experiencing isolation as well as a sense of shame and confusion that prevents them from seeking help; and often people do not know where to get help.

If a manager suspects that an employee has a mental health problem he or she should:

1 Investigate sensitively. Gather as much information as possible and discuss worries with the company doctor or mental health specialist. Do not pretend that nothing is wrong and that the problem will go away. Talking to the specialist can reduce fears and provide support and the confidence to talk to the employee.

2 Encourage the employee to seek help from their doctor or a professional counsellor. If they are resistant to this suggestion, use the basis of any changes in behaviour or job performance to refer the person to the company doctor.

3 Discuss with the employee those aspects of the job which may have become particularly stressful and which may have contributed to the illness. This is an area which the manager may be able to adjust (at least in the short term). Where changes are not possible, explain why whilst being firm and maintaining support. The manager should not let sympathy make him or her give in to unreasonable demands.

4 Decide with the employee what should be said to the employee's colleagues. Encourage but do not press the person to be open, honest and to talk about their illness and the treatment. This will help the person come to terms with what has happened and demonstrate that they are overcoming the illness.

5 Be supportive. It will be important in the early stages of returning to work not to be too critical of poor work performance. It is likely that the employee will set themselves high standards which may initially be unrealistic. Agreeing achievable objectives will give everyone a visible gauge of progress. Attempts to do too much too soon will lead to disappointment and feelings of failure.

6 Involve (with the employee's permission) the various helping agencies that may have been included in their recovery. They should be able to provide support for the employee as well as the manager and work colleagues.

Many of the above points are related to enhancing an employee's feeling of worth, and their self confidence, making them less susceptible to doubts as to whether they are performing well. The importance of timely feedback cannot be over-emphasised. A lack of confidence and sense of inadequacy characterises most people with a psychiatric history. Verbal assurances of satisfaction rarely seem sufficient, and proper feedback about whether a job has been done well and properly could play a key role in reducing stress resulting from anxiety about performance. (This need not come from the supervisor: it could be intrinsic to the job, particularly if it relates to quality). Quantity can be gauged by comparing one's output to a fellow worker, or to a set standard.

Summary

With statistics of 1 in 7 people seeking psychiatric help before the age of 45, it is highly likely that a manager will have an employee who breaks down at work and requires help. The best way of sensing problems at an early stage is through a regular review system that lets people know how they stand at work, explores their skills, potential and their problems. This approach cannot guarantee to reduce the likelihood of a breakdown but it is the most specific approach to reducing stress at work. It gives the opportunity to make contact with those who can provide professional help and support.

Reference

Orlans V *and* Shipley P. *A survey of stress management and prevention facilities in a sample of UK organisations.* London, Stress Research and Control Centre, Birkbeck College. 1983.

Further reading

Payne R L *and* Arroba T. 'Managing illness at work'. *Personnel Review*, Vol 8, No 1, Winter 1979.

Books

Arietti S. *Understanding and helping the schizophrenic.* London, Penguin Books, 1981.
Edwards Hilary. *Psychological problems: who can help.* London, BPS and Methuen, 1987.
Gibbs Angelina. *Understanding mental health.* London, Which Books, the Consumer Association, 1986.

Articles

Floyd M J. 'The employment problems of people disabled by schizophrenia'. *Society of Occupational Medicine* 34, 1978. pp 93–5.

Resources

Alzheimer's Disease Society, 158/160 Balham High Road, London SW12 9BN. 081–675 6557/8/9/0.
Anorexia Anonymous, 24 Westmoreland Road, London SW13 9RY. 081–748 3994.

British Association for Counselling, 37a Sheep Street, Rugby, Warwickshire CV21 3BX. 0788–78328.

British Association of Psychotherapists, 121 Hendon Lane, London N3 3PR. 081–346 1747

Depressives Anonymous, Fellowship of, 36 Chestnut Avenue, Beverley, North Humberside HU17 9QU. 0482–860619

Depressives Associated, PO Box 5, Castletown, Portland, Dorset DT5 1BQ.

Ex-Services Mental Welfare Society, Broadway House, The Broadway, London SW19 1RL. 081–543 6333.

Gamblers Anonymous, 17/23 Blantyre Street, Cheyne Walk, London SW10 0DT. 071–352 3060.

London Centre for Psychotherapy, 19 Fitzjohns Avenue, London NW3 5JY. 071–435 0873.

Manic Depression Fellowship, 51 Sheen Road, Richmond Surrey. 081–892 2811.

Mental Health Act Commission: Room 22, Hepburn House, Marsham Street, London SW1P 4HW, *or* Cressington House, 249 St Marys Road, Garston, Liverpool L19 ONF, *or* Spur A Block 5, Government Buildings, Chalfont Drive, Western Boulevard, Nottingham NG8 3RZ.

MIND: National Association for Mental Health, 22 Harley Street, London W1N 2ED. 071–637 0741.

National Schizophrenia Fellowship, 79 Victoria Road, Surbiton, Surrey KT6 4NS. 081–390 3651/3.

Phobics Society, 4 Cheltenham Road, Chorlton-cum-Hardy, Manchester M21 1QN. 061–881 1937.

Pre-Menstrual Tension Advisory Service, PO Box 268, Hove, East Sussex BN3 1RW. 0273–771366.

Richmond Fellowship, 8 Addison Road, London W14 8DL. 071–603 6373/4/5.

Tavistock Clinic, 120 Belsize Lane, London NW3 5BA. 071–435 7111 ext 327.

SECTION THREE

Introducing a counselling service.

21 Introducing Counselling Services

Introduction

Counselling services in Britain have developed on an ad hoc basis with isolated examples existing in different organisations. As a consequence there is only limited information available concerning the reasons why an organisation has introduced a counselling service and the way in which the counselling service is introduced and maintained.

This general lack of information makes it difficult for an organisation which is considering the introduction of counselling services to make an objective and valid assessment of:

1 The extent of existing counselling services in organisations
2 The issues involved in introducing a counselling service
3 The nature and scope of the commercial counselling services and resources available.

Before progressing with a counselling service, however, an organisation should be clear about its objectives for introducing a service of this kind and there should also be support from senior management for the concept of counselling in the workplace. Counselling is something that most managers do on an everyday basis, though they do not always think of it as such, and it is not known whether the role is performed well and whether counselling is effective in providing assistance.

In order to increase the likelihood of an effective interaction an increasing number of organisations have started to put a greater emphasis on training staff in counselling skills. In addition to these initiatives some organisations have introduced specialised counselling services. The reasons for these decisions are varied but include the following:

To enhance an individual's coping skills

Counselling skills enable line and personnel managers to deal more effectively with wide ranging problems that involve complex and varied issues of work performance, personality and mixed emotions. Since management is about utilising the abilities and capacities of people in order to get things done, counselling skills – if used appropriately – can support and enhance the managing process. Counselling, as stated in the introduction to this book, is a means of providing growth and development for people. Effective use of counselling skills will enable people to cope better and achieve greater control over their environment.

To improve morale

Counselling provides benefits both to the organisation and to individuals within it who have particular problems.

Counselling provides the opportunity for expressing the personal frustrations that are an inevitable part of human interaction in an organisation, and it also provides a way of defusing and managing them. A work situation without the means for expressing and dissipating problems can result in declining morale for the individual and consequently the organisation.

To increase employee commitment

Increased and improved communications through the effective use of counselling skills can also increase employee identification with the organisation that employs them. They can reduce feelings of estrangement from senior management that are especially prevalent in many large organisations.

To improve organisational feedback

Conflicts in the workplace often exist in an uneasy truce. The resultant frustrations may continue unchecked and unconscious conspiracies develop with the effect of stifling innovation, increasing employee insecurity and contributing to greater absenteeism and staff turnover. Evidence from existing counselling services, eg the Employee Advisory Resource (EAR) service of Control Data, and the counselling service in the Post Office, suggests that these issues are more likely to be detected and acted upon proactively to (a) alert and (b) encourage the organisation not to allow specific problems to continue without proper investigation and action. Such feedback is based on recognising themes in specific problems raised by people using the counselling service. The information provided to the organisation does not allow individuals to be identified.

With the appropriate use of counselling skills, the manager can discuss constructively and with greater confidence a person's fears, expectations, anxieties, anger and frustrations surrounding job insecurity, promotional aspirations, career choices and other general work place stresses.

To reduce absenteeism and turnover

Earlier chapters have indicated the extent to which personal problems can contribute to absenteeism in a company, with consequent losses in productivity. Counselling can help reduce the incidence of absenteeism through the early identification of employees with problems and the provision of help and support in order to ensure that the employee is able to manage or resolve the problem before it becomes a crisis.

To help improve quality and reduce accident rates

Employees who have problems are unlikely to leave them at home. The employee will be preoccupied at work – a concept sometimes called 'presenteeism'. Where this occurs there will be a diminution of decision making ability and responsiveness. The misuse of alcohol and other drugs is likely to have the same outcome. All will result in poor quality work and an increase in accident rates.

To address a specific need

A need for counselling may be perceived as a result of several incidents that are attributable to a single factor such as alcohol misuse, or a generalised factor such as stress, or to address a specific once-only factor, such as redundancies.

To enhance the employee's benefit package

The provision of a company-wide counselling service to which

everyone has ready access is one way of enhancing the employee's
benefit package. A service of this kind will complement all other
existing resources within the organisation that are available to
employees.

Existing counselling resources in organisations

Ashridge Management College conducted a survey in 1987 of a
number of major organisations who had introduced a counselling
service. Members of their counselling consultancy group,
(Counselling for Change), interviewed people involved in setting up
and/or running the service. Five main models emerged from this
survey and these are summarised below.

The welfare model

The welfare model typically developed as part of the personnel or
occupational health departments. The counsellor would not
necessarily have any specific counsellor training or specialism.
Contact with employees would usually be initiated by the counsellor
with sickness reports used as the main criteria.

The purpose of the welfare model is to reduce absenteeism by
monitoring absences and sickness records. The model tends explicitly
to serve the interests of the employer and for this reason
confidentiality is not regarded as an issue. Employees see the
counsellor as part of the personnel department and the counsellor
is very open in contact with the employee.

The medical model

The counselling activity is located in the occupational health
department. Training is principally medically orientated, eg nurses
or doctors with supplementary counselling skills training. Emphasis
is placed on confidentiality, ethics and professionalism, the initiative
for contact with employees coming from either the medical specialist
or a member of management. People are regarded as 'patients'.
Information about absentees is also available and used in a similar
way to the welfare model.

Another similarity to the welfare model is the focus on reducing
absentee lists. The mesdical model was regarded as demonstrative
of corporate care for employees. Where a medical officer was

employed, the department also enjoyed a high status within the company.

Personal counselling model

This involves the establishment of a separate counselling function, either as a new department or resourced from an external agency. People using the service were perceived as 'clients' with the initiative for contact arising from an employee or management suggestion. The counsellors were professionally trained with wide ranging counselling knowledge and organisational experience.

The objective of this model was to help the employee to resolve their problems by increasing their ability to cope. Impact on absenteeism, turnover etc is believed to be improved as a consequence of counselling after self referral. Confidentiality was considered crucial together with the perceived neutrality of the service.

The status of the service was ambiguous. Reporting relationship for in-house services tended to be to the chief executive, external services accountable to the personnel director. Employees using the service were not always aware of the counsellor accountability.

Career counselling model

Located in the personnel department, the counselling within this model focuses specifically on issues of career change, eg retirement, promotion, redundancy, relocation, training. The objective of the service is to help employees manage their own career. The counsellors are usually personnel or management professionals with counselling skills training.

Confidentiality was considered important, together with the need to balance the individual's needs against those of the organisation. As a consequence of the latter attempts are made to influence aspects of the organisational functioning.

Organisation stress monitor model

Again staffed by trained professional counsellors who are considered to have a dual role of personal counselling and organisational problem diagnosis. Resourced by in-house staff they reported to the occupational health department at a senior level. This structure was believed to preserve independence of operation and confidentiality.

The organisational diagnostic process was a specific feature of this model in order to enable the organisation to respond to various aspects of occupational stress.

In addition to the above models of counselling services there are a number of external counsellors who provide their services on an ad hoc basis. Self referral is difficult and referral will generally be made by the company to the counsellor. Services of this kind can be less responsive and tend to become involved when the problem reaches a crisis.

Introducing a counselling service – what to consider

The following identifies some of the key questions and outlines why each of the areas is important.

A   Will the counselling service have credibility?

A1   Will employees believe that the counselling service is a helping programme?

Employees are naturally suspicious of new measures that do not appear visibly to profit the company. A counselling service is overtly a helping service which needs to be seen as an employee benefit. The benefits to the organisation and line management should also be openly stated. Only open and clear communications will engender the trust needed for a service to develop and work.

A2   Will the trade unions believe it is a help to their members rather than just a management programme?

The suspicions of trade unions will be similar to employees. A trade union may however regard a counselling service as an attempt by management to circumvent their natural role of 'protector and mentor'. They may further regard the service as an attempt to manipulate employees or to spy on their weaknesses. Concerns of this kind should be addressed quickly and openly and reassurances given.

A3   Will line managers believe that the programme will help them manage rather than coddle marginal performers?

A counselling service should adopt a neutral position within the organisation and this must be reflected in their organisational reporting relationship. It will not therefore interfere with normal disciplinary procedures where an employee's job performance fails to meet expected standards. The service provides managers with an additional resource which enables them to support employees through difficult periods until they return to their normal level of ability and productivity.

B   How will the service be structured and where should it be located?

B1   Can the counsellor's office be located so as to ensure confidential use?

This question always raises difficulties. An office is an essential tool of the counsellor's trade but if it is positioned in the personnel department people are less likely to visit the counsellor. Positioning the office in an area where access can be made from different directions, thereby reducing the feeling of having a spotlight on anyone using the service, is a distinct advantage.

B2   Will services be offered both on site and away from the facility?

If a service is to be introduced, it should be available to all employees and not just be a head office or senior management perk. This can present many logistical problems over whether the counsellor visits different sites, has people visit the base location, uses telephones and answerphones or contracts with local counsellors. People tend to feel more confident in using the service where it is externally provided off-site and provides immediate direct contact with the counsellor.

B3   Is emergency help important and needed?

Some counselling services provide 24 hour emergency access. Others operate between office hours only. Questions of this kind should be examined before introducing any service in order to avoid any later misunderstanding or misconceptions.

C   How much will it cost?

C1   What are the costs of the programme?

Crucial to any decisions to introduce a counselling service will
be the cost incurred. Various types of counselling models have
been discussed. These all have varying costs and benefits.
Decisions will therefore need to be made about the
organisation's needs and subsequently the extent of the
counselling services to be introduced and associated benefits
before comparing the costs involved.

There are no standard workplace counselling services
available in Britain, which makes comparing costs and benefits
difficult.

C2   What steps can be taken to ensure the quality of the service?

The company needs to identify clearly what it requires from
a counselling service in order to be in a position to assess the
quality and success of the service. A number of practical steps
can be taken that will contribute to the success and quality of
an in-company service, such as providing the counsellor with
an office, answerphone, administration support, counselling
supervision and on-going training.

Assessment of the prospective counselling service before it
is in use is often difficult although a number of agencies can
assist in this process, eg British Association for Counselling,
and several well established work counselling services which
can provide references from existing users.

C3   How will the service be evaluated?

Achieving an objective measure of the effectiveness of a
counselling service, eg recording absenteeism, is an extremely
complex task due to the many variables that are involved.
Research in America has shown that considerable financial
savings are achieved by organisations using counselling
services, particularly employee assistance programmes. The
extent to which the service is used is generally regarded as one
measure of effectiveness. The Employee Advisory Resource
(EAR) of Control Data Limited reports usage rates in

companies using the service as high as 25 per cent in the first year of operation. A British study being conducted in the Post Office, examining objective indicators such as absenteeism, has indicated that counselling services do significantly reduce this (and other) factors. A full report will be published in 1989.

C4.   What will start-up and subsequent costs be?

Start-up costs will vary according to the service selected and should include publicising the counselling service, communicating it to employees, and training supervisors and managers. Costs should reduce once this has been achieved, although on-going promotions and communications about the service will still be needed.

D   What type of control should exist over the programme?

D1   Will the company be able to know how their money is spent?

There is no reason why a company should not know how money is spent within a counselling service. If the counsellor is to be in-house then a budget should be submitted for approval. External counselling services should be able to demonstrate how the money will be spent and answer any queries, eg whether face-to-face counselling is available, whether this is limited to a pre-stated number of sessions, etc.

D2   Should there be control regarding who uses the programme?

Controlling who has access to a counsellor, eg by job grade, will detract from the effectiveness of a counselling service. Employees are less likely to use it if they need to 'qualify' to have access. There should be a commitment to the service by the company for all employees at the outset. Confidentiality will also be reduced if free access is not available.

D3   Should the counselling service be part of another function? If not, who will have responsibility for the service?

This aspect needs careful consideration. If the counselling role is to have a wide remit, will it be more beneficial for the service to be totally independent? The in-house service should report to the chief executive. If it is to be part of the personnel function then again this should be at the senior level. However, employees are generally very reluctant to use a service that is associated with the personnel department (see section F3). An alternative might be the chief medical officer. Whichever course is selected, the reporting structure should include clear, open and public guidelines on what is expected in order to maintain confidentiality.

E. Confidentiality

E1   How confidential will counselling really be?

This issue is the basis of any counselling service. If employees suspect that discussions are being reported back to the company or entered on personal files, they are not likely to use the service (for a discussion of confidentiality see chapter 24).

E2   What kinds of records will be kept and how will they be protected?

Confidential records will be needed by the counsellor for a number of reasons and should be secure and separate from personnel or personal files.

Examples of why records are useful and beneficial include:

a) Ongoing counselling: where a person is seen for more than one interview the counsellor may need records to act as an *aide memoir* and map the person's progress. Records of this type can be destroyed once counselling is over (but see b below).

b) Follow-up purposes with an employee: it is often useful to contact a person a short while after counselling has concluded to check progress.

c) Follow-up purposes with a referral resource; if a person is referred to a specialist service, eg alcohol treatment centre, the counsellor should contact both the person and resource in order to ascertain the quality of the referral.

d) Statistical report purposes: counselling services should keep statistical records of the extent to which their service is being used, for feedback to the organisation. Reports should not contain any information that would enable individuals to be identified.

Any records kept by the counselling services should take into account the requirements of the Data Protection Act 1984.

F   Who should staff the counselling service?

F1   Different skills, knowledge and experience will be needed according to the type of counselling service being considered. If the company is to introduce a counsellor he or she will require a range of skills over and above counselling ability. The following should be considered when employing a counsellor or contracting with a counselling agency:

Ability to:
Conduct short term counselling (six interviews or less)
Conduct crisis counselling
Assess mental health or coping skills
Assess drug/alcohol dependency and make appropriate interventions
Carry out promotion of counselling within the organisation
Develop company and programme policies
Conduct programme evaluation.

Familiarity with:
Organisational structure, job descriptions, job performance
   expectations and the disciplinary process
Industrial relations and union representation
The benefits package for the employees
Social service agencies and health care systems.

Additional skills including:
Knowledge of professional ethics and legal liabilities
Financial counselling skills
Knowledge of legal and illegal drugs
Training and public speaking ability
Writing skills
Consultative skills
Personal time management and organisational skills.

F2   Will the counsellor understand the consultation needs of
       management and of the union?

       Whilst an independent counsellor will not have any authority
       to change work practices, introduce new policies or direct
       management, he is ideally placed to identify and observe all
       of these aspects at work. Feedback into the organisation should
       be   conducted   selectively   (and   with   due   regard   to
       confidentiality) in order to influence changes that will benefit
       the employees and organisation. For instance, a new pay deal
       may outwardly be seen to be accepted and implemented. The
       counsellor may be aware however that the deal has damaged
       morale and that people are thinking of leaving as a result.
       Without feedback of this kind the organisation will not have
       an opportunity to respond.

F3   Will the counsellor be full time and in a specific role? If not,
       will there be conflicts of interest from people with two roles,
       ie personnel manager/counsellor or occupational health nurse/
       counsellor?

       This issue is often difficult to resolve and can detract from an
       effective counselling service. If the person in the counselling
       role has other duties to perform, will employees have confidence
       in the counselling role? Will there always be concern that the
       subjects discussed may be used against them or influence their
       future job prospects and security, even if unconsciously? Even
       where a manager is willing to provide help and support to an
       employee, if the culture of the organisation prevents or restricts
       the manager from fulfilling a counselling role, the result will
       be frustration and a sense of helplessness.
           In addition, any conflict between responsibility to the
       organisation and the employee is likely to come into sharp
       focus, if for instance, the employee reveals that they have been
       stealing from the company. This aspect is discussed more fully
       in chapter 24 on confidentiality.

G   What should be the scope of the counselling service?

G1   Will the programme provide assistance for all personal or behavioural problems?

Some counselling services have been introduced to deal with specific types of concerns, eg alcohol misuse. Services of this type often have considerable stigmas attached to them and are therefore used less.

If a counselling service is there to deal with the whole range of personal problems then care must be taken in the design or selection of the service in order to ensure that it can cope with the scope and breadth of potential demand.

G2   Should assistance be extended to work problems?

Extending the service to encompass work-related problems will usually take place automatically since employees will ignore restrictions of this type. Restrictions are not realistically possible since a clear distinction between work and personal-related problems is not possible. Consequently the scope and breadth of issues raised will create further demands on the counsellor and should influence the selection of people to this role (see F1).

G3   If assistance will be limited to specific problems, such as alcoholism, how will this affect acceptance of the programme by employees?

As mentioned, where counselling services are limited to specific problems people are less likely to seek help due to the stigma attached to it. Attempts to camouflage the service with different names does not work and simply adds to any suspicion and scepticism about the service.

G4   If all problems will be dealt with, are local resources available to assist with identified problems?

One of the key responsibilities of any counselling service is to develop local resources for referral purposes. (See chapter 23 on Referral). An effective service is dependent on good, professional referral support.

H   What kind of information would be fed back to the organisation, in what form and through what channels?

H1   Will information be fed back into the organisation?

This needs to be clarified and established before the start of a counselling service, and fit within the agreed abounds of confidentiality. It is possible to give information back to a company in a way that does not break the confidentiality given to the individual.

Counselling feedback should be part of the counselling function but it needs to be conducted carefully and with full regard to individual confidentiality. Employees using the service should also be informed of how, why, what and to whom the feedback takes place.

A counselling service that seeks to operate without feedback to the company is not fulfilling its role in assisting employees. Feedback should enable an organisation to address specific work practices wherever they are found to affect employees and the organisation adversely.

H2   What forms will the information being fed back to the compar take?

The company needs to know that the counselling service is being used. If the service is designed to enable employee self referral there may be no visible way of gauging how the service is being used (apart from word of mouth recommendations). Most counselling services should be able to provide statistical usage reports with a general breakdown of the types of problems being discussed by employees. Reports of this kind would not break confidentiality.

Feedback from the service may include confirmation that an employee is using the service after a company referral. No further information concerning the problem should be discussed without the employee's permission.

H3   Through what channels will the information be fed back?

There should be a single focal point for co-ordinating the counselling service within a company and feedback should be channelled through this point. This should be at a senior level.

The above provides a framework for discussion to enable the organisation to identify its needs and consider many of the key issues important to introducing a counselling service.

Selecting external counselling services

If an external counselling service is being considered, the following checklist can be used for assessment purposes. Answers to these questions should be evaluated and incorporated into the final choice of counselling service selected.

1   What does the fee for the service include?

Are there any hidden costs? Does the fee include all elements of the service as it has been described or do important elements of it have an additional cost? Does the cost include an amount for promoting the service? Is the amount of counselling available limited to the initial fee paid, is it an hourly fee, who pays for any referrals, and so on? A fixed fee at the beginning of the service stating clearly who and what it includes will provide a firm basis for the counselling service, the organisation and employees.

2   What steps will be taken to ensure confidentiality?

This aspect is crucial to a counselling service and is an issue that needs to be clarified at the start in order to avoid later misunderstanding and misconception. If this area causes conflict then a counselling service should not be introduced.

3   In what way are the counselling staff qualified to provide the service?

This aspect has been discussed earlier but should be one that an organisation considers carefully. There is no definitive answer to this question but certainly professional training and experience is essential and should be combined with an understanding of organisational culture and behaviour.

The British Association for Counselling (BAC) has drawn up standards for accrediting counsellors, and The British Psychological Society (BPS) introduced a scheme to Charter its members in 1988. Minimum standards *vis-à-vis* professional bodies and codes of ethics and practice do exist and are constantly developing but credentials should be carefully vetted and assessed against the organisation's needs.

4   Is the service able adequately to cater for employees based outside the head office location and to maintain consistency of service?

For organisations with more than one office this is an important issue since focusing a counselling service on one area of operation or a specific location can give rise to various problems that can affect the effectiveness of the service.

For instance, if the service is made available to head office, will staff at other locations resent this or will the head office staff believe that they have been singled out for 'special treatment' and question why.

The potential counselling service should alert an organisation to these issues and demonstrate how all employees and locations can be effectively served without adversely affecting the quality of the service available.

5   Can the service demonstrate its effectiveness?

The service provider should be able to introduce measures that can be used by the organisation to gauge the effectiveness of the service. This area is, however, difficult to demonstrate in tangible terms although specific indicators do exist and can be drawn upon.

6   What processes exist to inform employees of the service a) at its introduction and b) on an on-going basis?

This aspect is crucial to the success of a company-wide counselling service. The counsellors selected should have knowledge of how to introduce a service of this kind together with the appropriate materials. Experience should also extend to on-going promotion of the service since it is very easy for employees to forget about the counselling facility.

7 Is the counsellor (or counselling organisation) financially stable and capable of following through on all contract commitments?

For external services this clearly needs to be looked at in order to ensure that the service will be able to fulfil its obligations to the organisation and employees.

8 Are there any past or existing customers to which reference can be made to check the claims made by the counselling service?

In relation to external services, it should be possible to contact the counsellor's existing client organisations in order to ascertain what quality and level of service has been provided and with what results. These results should be specific to the culture it is proposing to work with. Results showing the efficiency of a service in America are less likely to be relevant to a British workforce.

New counselling services should be assessed against other criteria and certainly not be disregarded simply because no track record exists.

9 If the counselling service is to be in-house, should a consultant be hired to help develop and implement various elements?

Decisions concerning this area should be considered carefully and after checking areas such as 3 and 8 above. Consultancy services are very useful once the organisation has identified its needs, in order to assist in the development of the structure, overcoming difficulties and ensuring good quality counselling resources.

10 In what way will the counselling service be tailored to the organisation's needs?

An organisation will want to look at various counselling services and structures before ariving at a short list. Each provider should then be invited to demonstrate how its services can best meet the organisation's needs.

11 Does the counselling service or counsellors have any liability insurance?

This is an important protection for both the counsellor and the people using counselling resources.

12 Is the service or counsellor affiliated to a private treatment centre or other specialist service?

It is important that the counselling service is an independent broker for specialist services. This is to ensure that the employee and the help they would most benefit from can be matched in an unbiased way.

13 Does the counsellor or counselling service adhere to a code of ethics?

Different professional bodies each have a code of ethics. The company should ask to see what code the counsellors adhere to. If they do not work within such a code they should be asked why this is.

Summary

Implicit to the success of any counselling service is a commitment to it by senior and executive staff. Support is also needed from management and trade unions. Without these aspects even a well designed and resourced counselling service can flounder.

Introducing a counselling service is not simply a matter of recruiting a counsellor or training someone in-house. A great many issues need to be considered, discussed and decided upon, not least of which is why the organisation is thinking of doing it.

Without sufficient forethought and planning, introducing a counselling service can potentially lead to an increase in problems. The areas listed in this chapter provide a framework for organisations to evaluate their needs and expectations as well as being the key areas to check when considering who shall provide the counselling service.

SECTION FOUR

This section covers some practical issues that need to be considered when running a counselling service.

22 Training

Introduction

The previous chapters establish the relevance and value of 'counselling at work' and identify a wide range of situations and circumstances where counselling skills can be used with advantage.

Should the manager now train to become a counsellor? Almost certainly NOT!

Counsellors are still a rare breed and it is unlikely that anyone would be recruited to such a specialist post without relevant counselling experience and qualifications.

The vast majority of people who use helping skills at work are not employed as counsellors and it is misleading to think they are. If autocratic managers, for example, suddenly change and start counselling subordinates instead of directing them, staff will be suspicious of their motives. People become confused when their expectations of others are not met, particularly when the other person has a vested interest in the outcome of any transaction. Most relationships at work fall into this category. For most staff, counselling skills are only an adjunct to their main responsibilities. Successful helpers at work incorporate such skills into their formal role and relationships rather than attempting to don the distinct role of counsellor for special occasions.

How can a manager learn to use counselling skills at work?

Although employers usually train staff for their operational responsibilities, communication and relationship skills are often seen as innate qualities which cannot be taught, or are assumed to exist and consequently overlooked. This is typified by the sales representative who is excellent in his role, promoted on this basis but subsequently fails to manage the sales team, or the manager who treats appraisal interviews as an opportunity to discipline employees. By failing to establish a framework for evaluating interpersonal effectiveness or enabling people to learn good practice, such organisations forfeit a major opportunity to improve all round performance.

Counselling skills can be learnt and a systematic approach will help to avoid wasted effort and disappointment.

What training is needed?

All decisions about training start with the learner's needs. The manager should go through the following check list, seeking feedback from others, at work or outside, where appropriate:

a) Why do I want to learn counselling skills?
b) What will they enable me to achieve at work – for myself, for others, for the organisation?
c) How can they be used in the context of my work, role, other people's expectations and the organisation's culture?
d) Does the requirement arise from involvement in certain organisational procedures or tasks?
e) What are my existing personal resources – knowledge, skills, values, attitudes, awareness, relationships, etc and weaknesses?
f) Are there constraints – money, time, priorities, willingness – to change myself or my relationships with others, or the organisation?
g) Are there any other implications, eg the effect on family, social life, voluntary activities, etc?
h) What do I want to be able to do at the end of it?

How can the manager learn new skills?

Once he or she is clear about their motives for learning and their willingness to make the changes involved, how can they acquire new skills and what are the options open?

Training is the most efficient and effective way of learning new skills in a planned, systematic way, but the market is wide and growing and it is essential to establish adequate criteria to guide the learner's choice of courses.

General principles

Training should be matched to the specific needs of the individual concerned and the circumstances in which the learning is to be applied. There is no merit in absorbing theoretical concepts or complicated jargon which cannot be used in the practical situations faced at work. Indeed such specialisation can mitigate against the effective application of what is learnt by over complicating the issues involved and introducing additional elements into the process. This is not to argue for a narrow interpretation of needs or a too highly focused syllabus but rather for objectives which are specifically related to the needs of the learner rather than some academic definition of the subject.

The BAC is tackling this issue by emphasising that the differing objectives for training should carry equal status. Training options are seen as branches leading to alternative but equally important learning rather than as a hierarchical ladder of expertise.

The three main branches at work can be described as follows:

1   Counselling skills linked to formal work procedures

Where the need to use particular skills arises from specific work procedures, eg job appraisal reviews, career development interviews etc, the organisation's vocational training programme should offer adequate preparation for practitioners. It makes sense to press for 'in house' arrangements in these circumstances so that the courses can be 'tailor made', but if this is not possible external courses run by organisations like the Industrial Society offer the chance to learn about the counselling skills involved in particular processes like appraisal.

2   'Barefoot' counsellors helping through informal relationships

Even when specific formal procedures are not involved it is still important to understand the organisation's training policy and arrangements, in order to identify any opportunities that exist within the scope of the general training programme; and to spot the gaps. Some employers now recognise the importance of concepts like human resource development which incorporate personal problem solving and staff development. If counselling or the use of counselling skills are not included in such programmes then they should be.

3   Counsellors and specialist helpers

Existing counsellors and others with a substantial element of counselling written into their formal responsibilities should already have recognised and sought appropriate training. Such staff should receive regular supervision on their counselling and this covers training needs. Anyone aware of gaps in their competence will find the new BAC scheme for recognising counsellor training a valuable aid to finding a suitable course.

What to look for in a course

If there are several courses available which appear to match the desired learning goals, how can a choice be made between them? If there is only one available, is it worth attending?

If the learner is fortunate enough to find an appropriate course 'in house', it is still essential to evaluate the arrangements to ensure that they meet the person's needs. Unfortunately, British management is still notoriously reluctant to invest in its most valuable asset, people. This means that the majority of employees who recognise the need to improve their helping and interpersonal skills will be forced to look outside their organisations to find suitable training.

Practical factors such as cost and timing often influence choice but, despite that, the overriding priority is to ensure that the course meets his or her needs, as mentioned earlier. This means not only matching training objectives to his or her own but also ascertaining that the course offers an effective learning environment.

Most people have suffered from courses that look good on paper but fail to deliver practical learning of use in the 'real' world. The learning environment comprises all the factors that affect learning but the training methods employed and the experience, attitudes and values of the tutors are crucial elements, particularly in courses concerned with personal effectiveness like counselling training.

The following guidelines will help readers to recognise effective programmes.

Methods

Skills cannot be learned solely from a book or a lecture, no matter how informative and entertaining each might be. An essential part of the process is 'learning by doing'; the learner must be able to try out new behaviour and then modify it as a result of this experience in order to improve. Obviously the final test of any learning rests on its effectiveness in the field, but a skills course must include sufficient practice in order to give a basic level of competence for members to build on later. Equally, members will need to know how to learn from future experience if their training is to amount to much in the long term.

A person's ability to help others depends to a large extent on how well they know themselves, their beliefs, values and the aspects of their life that concern them. Is the person aware of how such factors affect their relationships and ability to work with others? For instance, the supervisor who believes that women are naturally submissive will label ambitious assertive women as trouble makers, and managers who suppress their own feelings will find it difficult to help people who need to express theirs. Any course that fails to address such issues will fail to offer sufficient grounding for the skills being developed.

Finally, people need to make sense of their learning. Why do new ways of communicating and relating to others facilitate change, and how do these ideas fit in with wider theories about problem solving, empowerment and personal development? Sufficient theory is therefore necessary in order to satisfy this need for intellectual understanding, order and completeness.

It is important that there is an appropriate balance of these elements within the overall training package in order to meet the demands of the subject together with enough flexibility of approach to cater for the unique learning style of each participant. Counselling skills should be moulded into the person's own style of interaction, and not imposed on a person. If this does not happen it is likely that the skills will not be applied consistently, which may result in suspicion from the person being approached.

Experience, attitudes and values

The course publicity will indicate a great deal about the course and the attitudes and values of those involved in running it. Are the objectives of the training clear and precise? Is the information about the syllabus and methods employed sufficient to give the learner confidence that it has been thoroughly prepared and will meet his or her needs? Is there an opportunity to discuss requirements and to influence the programme in due course? Does the organisation and its staff seem efficient and reliable?

Few course brochures provide all the background needed to judge adequately the service offered, however, and most people will need to contact and possibly meet the organisers at some stage in order to clarify various points of detail.

The following brief will help in covering the main areas of importance in ascertaining the nature of training courses.

a) What are the objectives of the training and how will the outcome be evaluated? How much attention is given to the practical application of learning and is this tailored to the learner's situation? Does the course draw on examples from work, and are real cases used to develop skills and understanding and is there any opportunity to apply learning back at work as part of the course? If so, is on-going support or supervision offered? Is there provision to continue learning and development after the course? Can past course members be asked how they are using the skills acquired?

b) Is the timetable planned in advance and what provision is there to respond to individual needs? How many students are catered for and what is the staff/student ratio? Is all the learning directed by tutors or do participants work on their own at times? Does the class stay together throughout or are different structures used and if so how?

c) Are courses held in purpose-built training accommodation with a full range of equipment? How are audio-visual aids used, eg are commercial films shown or sessions recorded for feedback to students? What is the balance between various teaching methods like lectures, discussion, group work, role-play, awareness exercise, feedback and written work, and what is their relative importance in the programme? Is there a book list and library available? Are handouts provided? How important is theory in relation to experience on the course?

d) Will participants be expected to look at and talk about their emotions and feelings or divulge personal details either to staff or other course members? How are issues of trust and confidentiality handled?

e) Who are the staff/tutors and what are their qualifications and background? What is their experience of (a) counselling within the environment where students will apply their learning; (b) training which has these objectives; and (c) supporting participants with personal concerns that emerge during the course?

f)   Any other aspects that concern the learner should be discussed.

The aim in asking such questions is not of course to get perfect answers. No such course exists, and what are the right answers anyway? The process will however help the learner to assess the values, priorities and capabilities of those involved. Whatever the factual answers to the questions, even greater insight into the motives and abilities of those running the training should be gained by the way they handle these enquiries and their willingness to listen and respond to the individual's concerns. Unless they demonstrate respect for the individual – acceptance of differences, responsiveness to needs – the individual should keep looking.

If the individual is unable to satisfy him or herself that the course organisers have given sufficient thought to the design of the training programme then it may be useful to approach an organisation like the British Association for Counselling for impartial expert advice. At present BAC is developing guidelines for different kinds of counselling training together with advice on the accreditation or recognition of trainers. Other sources of information include local educational establishments and voluntary organisations like the Westminster Pastoral Foundation and RELATE (previously National Marriage Guidance Council) although some of the training offered by such bodies may be focused on their activities and only be available to people who intend to work in those areas.

Summary

Most people who use helping skills at work are not counsellors. Indeed, any attempt to fulfil the role could well cause confusion and suspicion by undermining the formal work roles and expectations of others at work. The task is to learn appropriate helping skills which can be integrated into the full range of work responsibilities and relationships. The learner should be clear about his or her needs and how to evaluate learning before embarking on a course. They should look for a practical course run by people who understand the situation and are committed to the value of counselling. Finally, they should choose training that looks beyond the course itself back to the workplace in order to validate learning and provide a sound basis for further development.

23　Referral

Introduction

The BAC Code of Ethics and Practice states that a counsellor has a responsibility to 'take account of the limitations of their competence, and make an appropriate referral when necessary. It is their responsibility, as far as possible, to verify the competence and integrity of the person to whom they refer a client'. The important and crucial process of referral is often taken for granted.

The following notes should help to clarify what referral is, why it is necessary, how it is done and the potential outcome.

What is referral?

Referral is the term given to the process whereby a person who has sought help and assistance from another person, eg doctor, manager or counsellor, is encouraged to take up an alternative source of help and assistance, once the nature of the problem has been identified and assessed.

Why does it take place?

The alternative source of help will have more specialist skills and experience and is therefore likely to be more beneficial to the person in helping them to resolve or manage their problem. The specialised resource will also have more time to spend with the person, without the distractions and demands of the workplace. The conflicts that exist for managers between time spent with an employee who is very much in need and ensuring the smooth operation of the department or business can be difficult to resolve and should be avoided. The manager should also be aware of conflicts of personality, or dislikes. In these situations the motive for referral may be to get rid of the individual, and the referral should be handled with the same care and sensitivity as in any other circumstances.

By encouraging the employee to seek an alternative source of help, the manager is providing valuable support and assistance. They are not relinquishing their responsibilities: these will continue to be the employee's job performance, behaviour and well being in the workplace.

The manager should also have a clear understanding of their own emotional needs and an awareness of any areas of personal sensitivity that may reduce his or her effectiveness whilst helping other people, eg death, AIDS, alcohol. The manager would be unwise, for instance, to talk to someone who has been made redundant on the day that he or she knows they are also likely to be dismissed. It would be difficult for the manager to try to comfort someone who has been the victim of violence the night after his or her own house has been broken into. Recognising and accepting emotional needs does not happen enough and some people constantly subjugate their own needs in preference to others. Doing this reduces that person's effectiveness in helping others.

When should referral take place?

Referral is a sensitive task that should be timed carefully. Taking account of the above reasons as to why referral is necessary, it is important to assess the nature and complexity of the problem, and the circumstances surrounding the counselling.

Too little time spent with someone can leave them feeling unimportant, rejected and unprepared for the referral. Too much time can result in the person opening up to the point where they will feel cheated and vulnerable if nothing happens (apart from referral). A careful balance needs to be maintained between these two extremes.

How is referral carried out?

Having reached the stage where an assessment has been made of both the counsellor's and individual's circumstances and a decision made that referral would be beneficial, it is crucial that the person is involved in the decision and understands why referral is being proposed. If the counsellor feels before the end of the first interview that referral would be beneficial, the suggestion only should be made at this time. This gives the person time to think about the idea and the counsellor time to check that suitable resources are available.

The counsellor should not, the next time the employee is seen, immediately start to discuss referral, but should allow the employee time to talk about the developments that have occurred between meetings. It is important to maintain a balance between this and allowing the interview to assume the depth that is best left to the referral resource. The interview should be structured to allow sufficient time to discuss referral; perhaps by introducing the subject with a direct question: 'Have you thought about talking to someone outside work about (the problem)?' The reply yes or no will enable the counsellor to investigate the person's thoughts and feelings about referral. The counsellor should be aware that as the person has spoken openly, they may feel that they are simply being passed on, and feel let-down and weary of going through the whole process again.

Provided the first interview was handled with care, the employee will trust the counsellor and value their opinion about the next move. The counsellor should resist recommending or stating that the employee should see a specialist resource; the decision must come from the person who is seeking help. Information about the specialist and what is involved will facilitate the decision.

Although the motive for referral is to enable the employee to manage or resolve their problem, if the interview has been initiated due to poor work performance, behaviour or relationships at work, then it would be beneficial to remind them of the purpose of the interview and the benefits of referral. Ultimately however, the decision as to whether or not to take up referral is the employee's alone.

What information does the employee need?

The employee needs as much information as the counsellor can give them. The counsellor can expect to be questioned about the resource or resources being suggested. Any lack of knowledge or confidence in the resource will quickly be detected. Over enthusiasm will arouse suspicions about the motives for referral and may undermine confidence in it. Information should include the name of the resource or contact person and whether or not there is the need for an initial interview before actual counselling or treatment starts. This is sometimes called the reception interview and is commonplace in counselling centres where there may be more than one counsellor (for instance RELATE). The purpose of the reception interview is further to ensure that the person is matched to the most suitable counsellor available. Information concerning any costs that might be incurred and how these will be paid should also be discussed, as well as whether or not the person is eligible to claim them back through private medical care, whether the company will pay, or whether it will be the individual's responsibility. If it is likely that the company will pay, then the individual may need reassurance about the confidentiality of the referral and reasons for it. Concern about confidentiality will be heightened if the counselling (or treatment) requires significant periods away from the workplace. These issues should be considered and discussed with the person before referral is made.

Checking the referral resource

A number of national agencies exist which are well recognised and which usually have a central office which can advise on local counselling resources and the procedures involved in referral to them. Examples of these include:

- British Association for Counselling (BAC)
- RELATE (formerly the National Marriage Guidance Council)
- CRUSE (The National Organisation for the Bereaved).

Checking individual counsellors is far more difficult unless they belong to nationally recognised bodies that require a minimum level of training and qualifications or require members to maintain agreed standards and work within a code of ethics. At the moment anyone can set themselves up as a counsellor, and therefore caution is necessary.

Some counselling or specialised agencies are available via GPs and it would be worth encouraging the employee to check this route. Consideration should be given, when making referral, to the person's sex, culture and sexual orientation.

What feedback should the manager receive after referral?

Any feedback that may be forthcoming will come directly from the person who has been referred. As soon as they make contact with the referral agency or counsellor all further information exchanged between these two parties will be confidential. Only with their permission will the counsellor divulge any information. The confidentiality that is maintained between the individual and the counsellor may be crucial to making an effective referral and should be respected.

Should the manager follow up with the employee?

Follow-up is important in order to provide on-going support. Support in this context means maintaining contact with the employee to show that the manager is interested in their circumstances and progress. It does not involve duplicating the counselling that is taking place with the referral resource. Follow-up will also provide an important source of feedback concerning the referral itself, for any future need.

If, however, the person has not taken up the referral the manager should not be disappointed. In many situations it is sufficient for the person simply to know that an additional source of help is available to which they have access. It may be that the person was not yet ready to go on and talk in greater depth about their situation, and indeed the counselling that they received with the manager or counsellor before referral may have actually enabled them to cope or manage their circumstances better.

Where referral has been recommended as a result of declining job performance, the manager, when making the referral, should make it clear to the employee that if job performance continues to suffer as a result of their problem and referral is not taken up then the company has recourse to the usual disciplinary procedures (see chapter 14).

Resource

Counselling and psychotherapy resources directory. British Association for Counselling. Updated annually. Provides names of individual counsellors and organisations in different geographical areas.

24 Confidentiality

Confidentiality is the single biggest concern a person seeking help from another in the workplace will have. This is due to a number of factors beyond simply not wanting anyone else to know about personal features of one's life. Concern in the workplace is greater since it is widely believed that any sign of weakness or inability to cope will damage career prospects and/or job security.

Some people may believe that 'confidential' interviews are subsequently entered on personal files, and that the counsellor is a management spy. Doubts like these are difficult to dispel and they should be acknowledged.

The person seeking help may either directly ask the questions: 'How do I know what I say will be confidential?', 'What guarantees do I have?', or assume that the conversation is confidential. It is essential therefore that the limits (if there are to be any) governing confidentiality are unambiguous, predefined and agreed with the employing organistion as well as communicated at the beginning of any counselling interview to every person seeking help. The extent of the confidentiality should be public knowledge for every person who has access to the counselling facility and be in writing, eg in an employee handbook.

Each person in the counselling role should exhibit consistent adherence to the predefined guidelines, since a breach by one person will damage the credibility of all others working to the same principles. This will include the manager using counselling skills as well as the professional counsellor or counselling function.

Where, in exceptional circumstances, a third party needs to be informed about the nature, content or consequences of the person's problem, the need to tell should initially be discussed with the individual concerned. This may occur where the counsellor is put in a compromising position. In the workplace this may be where an employee seeks help after committing a criminal offence which would make it impossible for the employee to continue work, eg a bank clerk stealing cash.

The BAC Code of Ethics and Practice for Counsellors proposes in Section B. 1.4, the following guidelines: 'Counsellors who become aware of a conflict between their obligation to a client and their obligation to an agency or organisation employing them will make explicit the nature of the loyalties and responsibilities involved.' Where conflicts occur, therefore, the individual should be made aware of this as soon as possible. If the person has committed a serious criminal offence, for instance, the manager or counsellor may be obliged to inform the employer or police. The individual should be advised that if they continue to tell the counsellor about the offence that third party notification will take place. The counsellor should encourage the individual to go to the third party himself. If, however, the individual refuses, the manager or counsellor should explain why they are going to inform the third party and consider with the individual the likely consequences of doing so. Wherever possible permission should be sought from the individual before breaching confidentiality.

Other relevant sections of the BAC Code of Ethics and Practice are as follows:

BAC Code of Ethics and Practice – Section 2 – Confidentiality

2.1 Counsellors treat with confidence personal information about clients, whether obtained directly or by inference. Such information includes name, address, biographical details, and other descriptions of the client's life and circumstances which might result in identification of the client.

2.2 'Treating with confidence' means not revealing any of the information noted above to any other person or through any public medium, except to those to whom counsellors owe accountability for counselling work (in the case of those working within an agency or organizational setting) or on whom counsellors rely for support and supervision.

2.3 Notwithstanding the above sections 2.1 and 2.2, if counsellors believe that a client could cause danger to others, they will advise the client that they may break confidentiality and take appropriate action to warn individuals or the authorities.

2.4 Information about specific clients is only used for publication in appropriate journals or meetings with the client's permission and with anonymity preserved when the client specifies.

2.5 Counsellors' discussion of the clients with professional colleagues
should be purposeful and not trivialising.

A number of counselling services provide statistical feedback to the
employing organisation which shows usage but does not identify
individuals. That this feedback occurs should be made known to all
employees. In situations where a person needs to be referred for
treatment or therapy and will consequently be required to spend
time away from the workplace, the employee will need to inform the
employer. Where there is support and trust in the counselling service
it is likely that permission will be given without the need to divulge
the reasons.

The person seeking counselling has a right to expect and receive
confidentiality. Counselling is a relationship based on trust.
Observation of the agreed limits of confidentiality should be
maintained at all times.

Resource

The BAC Code of Ethics and Practice for Counsellors is available
from The Administrative Officer, BAC, 37a, Sheep Street, Rugby
CV21 3BX.

25   Cross Cultural Issues

Many workplaces employ people with varying cultural backgrounds. Culture can mean people with the same nationality but a differing social class, status, age and so on, but in the context of this chapter it will be taken to mean people of different nationalities or cultural origin. The situations described in the preceding chapters may require the use of different skills and language when talking to a person with a different cultural background. Some people may be very suspicious of the use of counselling and misunderstand the goals and objectives which apply to counselling, eg helping the person to help themselves, confidentiality. It is important therefore to restate and reinforce the use of counselling in the workplace in order to ensure that, at the very least, every employee appreciates what is involved, what it means, and what the potential outcome will be.

Where a counsellor is likely to be working with people of multi-cultural background they should supplement their counselling skills with additional areas of knowledge and self-awareness. This increased sensitivity will assist in the process of counselling and in the ability to relate to cultural variations in communication, attitudes and values. If possible, these areas should be requested when on a training course or should be added by means of additional training courses. Munro *et al* (1985) identified the following areas of importance for such counsellors:

The counsellor should:

a) Become aware of their own cultural values and beliefs and how these affect their perceptions of other cultural groups, and how they may conflict with an employee's values and beliefs.
b) Develop an openness and flexibility towards other cultural groups and an understanding of the political, economic and social forces affecting those groups.
c) Acquire some basic knowledge of the specific cultural groups they may be working with, eg language, customs, values and history.

As mentioned, these additional aspects should if possible be incorporated into counselling skills training courses and should include:

a) acquisition of basic information about specific cultures
b) basic language training
c) role playing, simulation exercises and case study discussions of cross-cultural counselling situations
d) contact with members of as many different cultures as possible.

Reference

Munro E, Marthei R J *and* Small J J. *Counselling and skills approach.* London, Methuen, 1985.

26   Supporting the Helper

Introduction

Counselling and helping people in the range of situations covered in this book is both a demanding and satisfying task. It is important that the person providing the counselling should understand the impact the counselling process will have on themselves. No one is able to work closely with another person without being affected by that person's circumstances, difficulties and emotions.

The ability to empathise with the other person is an essential quality in establishing a counselling relationship. Most people will be reluctant to seek help from someone who appears cool and remote. Just as important, however, is the ability of the counsellor to recognise and accept the need for support for themselves in order to provide an effective counselling resource.

Support for the counsellor in the workplace can be viewed in two ways:

1   Support for the person in the role of counsellor
2   Support from the employing organisation.

Support for the counsellor

This can be achieved through joining a counsellor's organisation and participating in its activities. Where these groups exist they should provide emotional support and embrace many of the qualities central to counselling, ie be non-judgemental, confidential, genuine etc.

Contact with other people doing similar work will enable the counsellor to continue to develop their skills and self awareness, share ideas and discuss the wider issues facing the counsellor in the workplace. In addition to these aspects it will be necessary for the counsellor to undertake on-going, critical self evaluation concerning their ability and effectiveness.

The counsellor should also regularly review why they are counselling and what rewards they gain from it. Personal growth and changes in personal circumstances (a change in work role, promotions, personal problems etc) will affect the counsellor's readiness or suitability to counsel. One forum for recognising these issues is the support group. (Individual supervision is another. This is essential and more appropriate to the professional counsellor).

John Murray, the personnel counsellor for News International, has drawn up guidelines describing how a support group should be formed, its objectives and operation. The guidelines include the following headings:

– Who are the groups for?
– What form will the group take?
– How to achieve this
– Establishing the group – drawing up guidelines
– Contact for the group
– Process of the group
– Facilitator for the group
– Establishing the group
– Maintenance of the group.

(The full guidelines are available from the Counselling At Work Division (CAWD) of the BAC).

Support from the organisation

Where an organisation is not totally committed to the concept of counselling in the workplace there is likely to be a lack of trust between those who engage in counselling and helping and those who manage the organisational resources that allow it to take place. This may result in the counselling activity taking place in an atmosphere of uncertainty about funding for resources, eg interviewing facilities, the counsellor's own training and development, and future continuance.

Potentially more undermining than the above is the situation where the person trained in counselling receives little or no support from immediate colleagues. This may take the form of direct criticism about the methods and objectives of counselling: 'What good does talking about it do?'; 'There's nothing to this counselling business – anyone can do it'; 'Why are we wasting money training people?'

Comments like these demonstrate the frequent misconceptions of the role of counselling in the workplace, and it is up to the counsellor or manager to establish and communicate the objectives and benefits of the counselling activity or service.

The consequences of a lack of support

Where neither of the types of support described above are available, the person in the role of counsellor is likely to feel unrecognised and unimportant and that what they are doing is neither appreciated nor effective. Counselling is likely to suffer as a result possibly causing harm to the person seeking help. The person will lose interest and resent having accepted the role. Ultimately the counselling role could fall into disrepute and be abandoned.

Many of the questions in chapter 21 on introducing a counselling function, if addressed honestly by the organisation, could help avoid the establishment of a counselling facility before the organisation and its management is ready to receive one. Support for the person in the role of counsellor in the workplace is the combined responsibility of the individual (who should seek personal support) and the organization (who should support and not undermine initiatives of this kind).

Conclusion

Every employee possesses skills, experience and knowledge which can be viewed as a form of 'human capital'. Investment is made by the organisation, when it recruits a new employee, in developing that employee's skills, experience and knowledge, and returns are expected on those expenditures. If an employee's performance declines, or they become ill, or are injured at work or simply leave, costs are incurred that represent a negative return on investment.

There is a considerable volume of research and statistical evidence that shows the likely incidence of specific problems affecting individuals. The impact on the individual and consequently on the organisation's investment is unpredictable.

The organisation is not able to control the stresses that are likely to affect every person at some stage and problems at work will spill over into the home. Nor is it possible for a person to package problems arising in the home and leave them there. Interaction of this kind can be cumulative and destructive, with a detrimental impact on the individual and negative repercussions in the other areas of the person's life, including the workplace.

If an employee has personal problems it is likely that less attention will be given to their job. Their mind will at best be distracted, at worst focused on their problem. Where problems begin to affect job performance adversely the employer has a legitimate right to intervene and take appropriate action. If a mechanism exists to help the employee manage or resolve his or her problems the employee is far more likely to be restored to full productivity at an early stage and the employer's investment protected.

Counselling is an effective mechanism that offers both the individual and the employer a course of action which will enable both parties to achieve a positive outcome.

The workplace is in many ways a very appropriate focal point for counselling intervention. The majority of people spend a large proportion of their life at work. If for whatever reason this segment of their life is jeopardised, motivation to seek help with a problem is likely to be greater. In many cases emotional and other problems first become apparent at work, either as a result of formal interactions within a company, eg performance appraisal, or through changes in the person's normal work and interpersonal behaviour.

The use of both counselling and counselling skills is being increasingly accepted in the workplace as a valid process which can: enhance the quality of formal interactions; provide the manager and supervisor with the confidence and skills to identify and discuss underlying issues; give the experience to know how to refer and support an employee experiencing personal problems. In this way counselling and the use of counselling skills do not undermine or circumvent existing company channels of communication or procedures, but add to them.

Many benefits can be derived from the use of counselling and counselling skills in the workplace, including the following:

a) Protection of the organisation's investment in people
b) Improvement in productivity
c) Reduction of accident, sickness and absenteeism rates
d) Improvement in decision making, group cohesiveness and co-operation
e) Improvement in the quality of communciation
f) Provision of a mechanism for individual growth and development
g) Release of management time
h) Contribution to an environment of trust and openness.

If the use of counselling and counselling skills has so many benefits, why is there not more of it?

Large sections of the business community continue to regard the use of counselling skills as an unnecessary appendage to existing management skills and practices. The professional counsellor also tends to have reservations about the efficacy of managers using these skills in the workplace.

Organisations question the cost and productive value of training in counselling skills and use of counselling as opposed to other more recognised training courses and methods visibly relevant to business. Professional counsellors question the calibre of the counselling skills training annd the individual's expectations on completion of training, and how the skills will subsequently be used.

Previous efforts to introduce counselling into the workplace through attempts to transplant its philosophy and theories, without any acknowledgement of the suspicion that has and does surround counselling, have often failed. Counselling in the context of employment is different from counselling in a therapeutic setting. These differences need to be acknowledged and understood (particularly by counselling professionals seeking to 'sell' counselling to industry) if the concept of counselling is to be introduced and used correctly in the workplace.

Suspicion may be further fuelled since the terms counselling and psychotherapy are often used interchangeably. Past examination of these terms has tended to conclude that it is not possible to agree upon the essential differences between them. However, in very simple and broad terms the goal of therapy is to help the person feel good or better. Therapy helps a person look inward to achieve increased awareness and self insight. Counselling is problem-solving or problem management with people; it adopts the perspective that people can think best when they think aloud with someone else who will question their thoughts, help them to clarify their thoughts and help to start the process of generating solutions or managing situations more effectively.

At the practical level, the introduction of counselling may not be seen to be relevant to alleviating such problems as attendance, productivity, concentration or decision making. These and other areas are traditionally the domain of motivational theories or disciplinary actions. If the outcome remains unsatisfactory after these sorts of initiatives, the option of more direct action – either moving the person sideways or out – is always available, certainly tangible and on occasions correct. Something is seen to be done, whereas the process of counselling may take longer, may be considered imprecise or less tangible, and therefore not deemed appropriate to the workplace.

The acceptance of theories and concepts derived from the social sciences into the workplace is however quite common. Psychology, for instance, is fundamentally associated with counselling and should consequently be seen to have the same positive applications in the workplace as other processes.

Whilst all employment theories strive to help the organisation or manager understand the behaviour and attitudes of employees to the betterment of the company, counselling strives to help the individual understand and help themselves. New employment policies and methods derive from a common problem viewed in a new way. Similarly, counselling can help the individual look at an existing problem from a new perspective. Both result in benefits for the company. Counselling is potentially more effective since the individual finds and reaches the decision for themselves and is therefore more likely to be committed to making changes that will enable them to manage their situation.

Scepticism of counselling and its benefits also has a lot to do with the British cultural background. In America counselling or therapy is more common-place and people speak openly abut their need for this support. The British tend to be more insular and turning to counselling for help can be regarded as a sign of weakness. One well known redundancy counselling consultancy, when describing its services, stated that they tried to avoid using the term counselling since they felt that if employees thought they were going to be 'counselled' they would stay well clear.

The application of counselling and counselling skills into the workplace is here to stay for as long as organisations recognise the value and cost effectiveness of protecting its human assets. Acceptance of these principles will always require the commitment and support of senior management. These aspects help to shape the culture of the organisation and emphasise the recogniton by the organisation of the value of its human resources in contributing to its success and profitability.